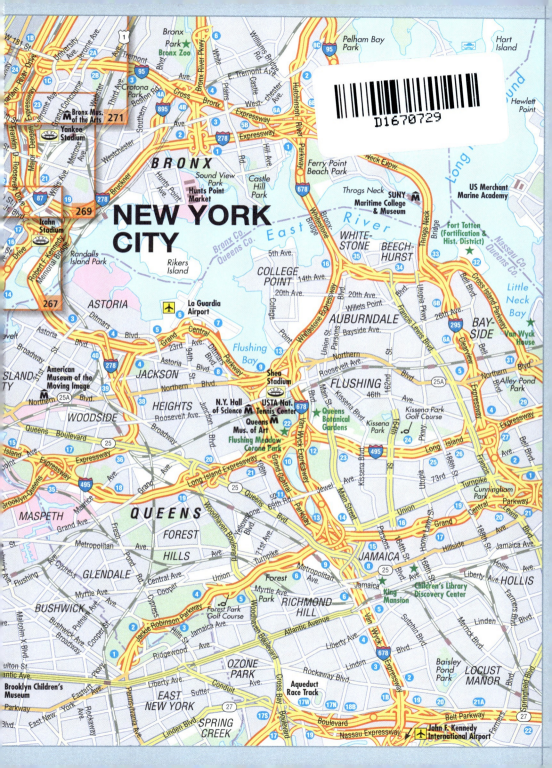

NEW YORK

Sound and Fury, the art deco installation that graces the main entrance of the GE Building (part of the Rockefeller Center) was created in 1933 by the renowned architectural sculptor Lee Lawrie.

If New York is the "city of cities", then Times Square (below) is not just at the heart of this great city, but also of the Western world.

ABOUT THIS BOOK

Tom Wolfe, who lives just outside New York City on Long Island and whose *Bonfire of the Vanities* is one of the best-known and most successful New York novels, said "there is no other city with such pride, luster, and triumphalism". Wolfe's novel captures perfectly the intoxicating excitement of the city that is like no other on earth.

At the beginning of the 17th century, long after European cities such as London and Paris had become internationally famous, New York was still an unknown Native American village. It was not until the late 18th century that what was to be called Nieuw Amsterdam developed into a prominent economic and financial hub. The city then became a collecting-place for people who had left Europe as a result of financial hardship or political pressure, wishing to start a new life in America. New York offered endless hope, infecting rich and poor alike – even if many immigrants were left to scrape a living in inhuman conditions on the Lower East Side.

New York, New York. The lights on Times Square, Broadway, the Empire State Building, giant temples to culture such as the Met and MoMA, Fifth Avenue and Christopher Street, the finest restaurants and the largest department stores, a tide of yellow taxis and the Statue of Liberty at the entrance to the bay, an unbowed symbol of freedom. The city has had to weather many storms in its history, but even in its darkest hours New York has always been able to rely on the irrepressible dynamism and pioneering spirit of its citizens.

New York is not a place for nostalgia. Looking back only confirms that each day is consigned to the past by the next, that nothing is as constant as change; and what city is more synonymous with change than New York, whose citizens had internalized the slogan "yes we can" long before it was coined by Barack Obama?

It is against such a background, that this *Photo Guide* encourages visitors to explore the city. An introduction to its history is followed by an exploration of each neighborhood, illustrated with fabulous photographs that reflect New York in all its infinite variety. The final atlas section and websites will help readers find out more about this city which offers so much.

A view across the Brooklyn Bridge of the city that never sleeps: as the lights go on in the evening life takes on the pulsing rhythm of neon advertisements; New Yorkers' energy seems inexhaustible.

TIMELINE

THE HIGHLIGHTS

CONTENTS

Lavishly illustrated, this *Photo Guide* is both inspirational and practical. The "Highlights" section will take you on a journey of discovery through the tourist must-sees of the city, while the "City Explorer" expands on this with comprehensive and invaluable information, compiled by experts, on all the hotels, restaurants, and other destinations you might wish to visit near each sight. There are also recommended city walks with maps.

CITY EXPLORER

CITY ATLAS KEY

TIMELINE

From an undistinguished village to a thriving metropolis – little did colonial official Peter Minuit realize the rapid development the settlement was to undergo when he bought Manhattan Island from the Native North Americans for a few guilders. Already a significant financial and commercial hub by the late 18th century, after the American War of Independence it grew into a city of global importance. Attracting many thousands of immigrants, the city rapidly became the much-quoted "melting-pot" of races and religions, a trend that has continued over the years. Today the population of New York City is well on its way toward 9 million and still rising.

From left: the earliest surviving view of the city was painted in 1626 by the engineer Kryn Fredericks, who faithfully reproduced the windmills and houses; the fort shown in the painting is an artistic addition that was never realized. Henry Hudson in a 19th-century print that has been tinted later. Peter Stuyvesant in an oil painting by Hendrick Couturier (17th C.). A map of New York in 1767, taken from an 18th-century engraving.

Prehistory
The Lenape Native North Americans settle in the Hudson Valley. The Iroquois live further to the north.

1524
Giovanni da Verrazzano drops anchor in what was to become New York Bay.

1609
Seafarer Henry Hudson is the first European to set foot on what was later to become Manhattan Island.

1624–1625
Dutch settlers found "Nieuw Nederland" (New Netherland). The date of the construction of Fort Amsterdam is considered the founding of New York.

1626
Peter Minuit, Director-General of Nieuw Nederland, purchases Manhattan, naming the colony "Nieuw Amsterdam".

1647
After the colony suffers financial crisis, Peter Stuyvesant is named Director-General and revives trade.

1664
During the Second Anglo-Dutch War, Stuyvesant surrenders the city to the British, who rename it "New York" after the Duke of York.

1754
The British conduct the French and Indian War.

1763
The end of the war sees the British in control of North America.

The first explorers

The first Native North Americans settled in what was to become New York over 3,000 years ago. The Lenni-Lenape, whom the new European settlers called "Delawares", belonged to the Native North American people who spoke the Algonquin language and lived from agriculture and hunting. The Iroquois tribes

Henry Hudson on his way to new discoveries (19th-C. hand-tinted engraving).

settled further north and formed a democratic league whose rules were later to

become a model for the American Constitution. Whilst the Lenape were wiped out or driven away by the European settlers, the Iroquois succeeded in retaining control of the lucrative fur trade, and through skilled diplomacy have preserved their identity to this day. Giovanni da Verrazzano was the first European to drop anchor in what was to become New York Bay.

Henry Hudson's ship, the Half Moon encounters Native North Americans settled around the Hudson River in 1609 (19th-C. engraving).

Although he was followed by several others, including the Portuguese Estevar Gomes, no one seemed interested in establishing a permanent settlement on the island of "Mannahata". In 1609 the English seafarer Henry Hudson navigated the river which was to be named after him, searching for trade routes and the fabled North-West Passage. Since he was employed by the Dutch East India Company, he claimed the land for the Dutch crown and in the course of the following years more Dutch colonists settled in what would later become New York. They included 110 men, women, and children who settled there in 1624 as part of the new West India Company.

Nieuw Amsterdam

The Dutch were principally interested in the lucrative fur trade, building two trading posts in "Nieuw Nederland" – Fort Orange (named after the Dutch House of Orange-Nassau), in what was to become Albany, the present-day capital of New York State, and Fort Amsterdam, on a site now occupied by the Alexan-

Henry Hudson on an exploratory tour, negotiates with Native North Americans in the Hudson River Valley (Severino Baraldi, 20th century, private collection).

der Hamilton US Custom House – and bartered enthusiastically with the Native North American league. In fear of hostile warriors and the British, most of the colonists settled in Nieuw Amsterdam and it rapidly grew into a town. A palisade fence was constructed to the south of the settlement, and the path along the "wall" was later to become Wall Street. Peter Minuit, the Director-General of the colony, sealed the purchase of the land in 1626 by exchanging trade goods worth 60 guilders with the Native North Americans for the island of "Mannahata".

Bad management and ongoing disputes with hostile indigenous groups eventually led to an economic crisis which drove Nieuw Nederland to the brink of ruin; trade improved only after the West India Company sent Peter Stuyvesant as the new Director-General. However, even he proved to be powerless in the face of growing pressure from the British to challenge its trading empire. The British solved this problem by allying themselves with the feared warriors of the Iroquois and moving the operational base of the fur trade to Albany. It was only after the French and Indian War however, a continuation on American soil of the larger conflict, the Seven Years' War, that British rule was cemented. Anyone thinking that more

In September 1626, Peter Minuit, a reform minister from Wesel on the Rhine, bought the island of Manhattan on behalf of the Dutch West India Company from the Native North Americans for a handful of trade goods; oil painting, 1939 (American School, Collection of the New York Historical Society, USA).

crown, which had laid claim to the land around the Hudson River for itself. On 18 August 1664, three ships carrying several hundred British troops anchored in the Bay of Nieuw Amsterdam and forced the Dutch to capitulate; Nieuw Amsterdam fell to the British without a shot being fired. They changed the name to "New York", after James, Duke of York.

French & Indian War

New York and its eponymous colony developed into an important commercial hub in the 18th century, with only the French in Canada to the north peaceful times were finally to come in the wake of the numerous battles that had been fought around New York, however, was soon to be disappointed: the spark of the coming War of Independence had been ignited in New York, too. Meanwhile New York continued to grow, with the slave trade, not to be abolished until 1827, one of the principal motors of the city's economy. Africans had been a familiar sight in the colony from as early as the beginning of the 17th century, and slave trading was the preserve of the Dutch West India Company, who ran a flourishing slave market on Wall Street.

This advertisement for Arbuckle's Coffee, printed in New York by the Donaldson Brothers in 1892, depicts the history of the city in a series of vignettes (from top, counterclockwise): a street in Nieuw Amsterdam, Peter Stuyvesant, Ethan Allen commanding at the Battle of Ticonderoga (1775), the destruction of the statue of King George III on the Bowling Green as a sign of a new-found national self-awareness after the Declaration of Independence (1776), Hudson's ship, the *Half Moon*.

From left: "Life, liberty, and the pursuit of happiness" are the core values of the Declaration of Independence, first read out to George Washington's troops (lithograph, Kurt Morton, 20th C.); a portrait of George Washington by Samuel King (1749–1819); the British Commander-in Chief, Sir William Howe in a watercolour painting by Charles MacKubin Lefferts (1873–1923); the departure of Washington's victorious troops.

1765
Representatives of the North American colonies meet in October to take measures against the British crown's tax regime.

29 June 1776
Hundreds of British warships appear in the Bay of New York.

9 July 1776
After Philadelphia, New York becomes the second city in which the Declaration of Independence is proclaimed.

26 August 1776
Beginning of the Battle of New York. Approximately 20,000 British troops attack Brooklyn (originally Breuckelen) from Staten Island.

November 1776
After losing the Battle of Long Island, General Washington cedes the city to the advancing British troops.

1778
The French side with the Americans in the American War of Independence.

1779/1780
The Spanish and the Dutch join the rebels in the fight against the British crown.

1783
The British sign the Treaty of Paris, recognizing the sovereignty of the US in America, and George Washington returns to Manhattan.

The colonies revolt

On 16 December 1773, colonial officials boarded British merchant ships in the port of Boston and dumped its cargo of tea overboard into the water, in protest at the British government's newly-passed Tea Act. It was an event that became immortalized as the Boston Tea Party. Protesting against the taxation imposed by the British

A replica of the Fraunces Tavern is to be found not far from Wall Street, in Manhattan's one remaining block of houses (54 Pearl Street) that date back to the 18th-century.

on all goods imported into America and calling for "no taxation without representation", indignant New Yorkers followed suit in April 1774 and heaved more British cargo into the sea. The British crown took a dim view of this and sent troops to the "colonies", but the colonists were determined to fight for their independence. The United States Declaration of Independence, signed on 4 July, was proclaimed on 9 July 1776 to the sound of

cheers from hundreds of soldiers and civilians. The excited crowd subsequently advanced to the Bowling Green, a small square at the southern tip of Manhattan, and tore the statue of the British king, George III, from its plinth. The New Yorkers had celebrated prematurely, however – seven long years were to pass before they achieved the independence they desired.

General George Washington used the Morris-Jumel Mansion (65 Jumel Terrace) in Washington Heights as a headquarters in September and October 1776.

Battle commences

By the summer of 1776, George Washington, the commander-in-chief of the Continental Army, was encamped with his troops in Brooklyn: New York was a likely target for the British army and an attack was expected in the near future. The first British warships duly appeared in the Bay of New York on the morning of 29 June, and the following weeks saw around 32,000 troops under the command of General William Howe, the British commander-in-chief, take up positions on Staten Island. General Washington

had approximately 6,000 men at his disposal to oppose this mighty force; when the battle started, on 26 August, they stood little chance. Within a few hours, over 2,000 Americans had fallen and Washington had little other choice but to flee to Manhattan with the remnants of his army and set up a barricade there. In November, he and his troops fled the city and so began years of deprivation for New

Yorkers. The ever-present threat of the British was compounded by two devastating fires: 493 New York homes went up in flames on 21 September 1776 in the Great Fire of New York, which was thought to have started in the Fighting Cocks Tavern. Trinity Church, the tallest building in the city, was also destroyed. A mere two years later a further 50 or so houses were lost in another fire, which broke out in the heat of August on Cruger's Wharf. Many New Yorkers died or were made homeless; sickness and poverty threatened their very existence.

NEW YORK 1765–1783
The struggle for independence

Liberty for America

Only after the French, the Spanish, and the Dutch had entered the war to fight on the side of the North American Continental Army did the situation start to change. Troops under George Washington's leadership began to force the British south and ever more loyalists to the British crown fled to Manhattan, their last stronghold. The North American troops proved unstoppable, and on 25 November 1783 Washington and his troops marched triumphantly into Manhattan, accepting the British commander's surrender on the same spot where Peter Stuyvesant and the Dutch had been obliged to lay down their arms. New York had shaken off the chains of British rule and was now free to rise as an independent city.

Washington still guards the New York Stock Exchange, the world's biggest stock market.

George Washington

George Washington, the first and one of the greatest presidents of the USA, is also one of the most significant figures in American history. Considered the father of American democracy, he laid the foundations for America's rise to its status as a world power. Born on 17 February 1732, the son of a planter in Virginia, he started

George Washington saying farewell to his officers in the Fraunces Tavern, New York, in 1783 (19th-C. hand-tinted engraving).

driving the British from Boston, but he lost the Battle of New York and retreated with his army to regroup at Valley Forge in Pennsylvania. In an unparalleled action, he and his troops crossed the icy Delaware River on 26 December 1776 and wiped out the enemy forces at the Battle of Trenton. This victory strengthened the troops' morale and their desire for

work as a surveyor before joining the army and earning his first military laurels as a young officer in 1754 during the French and Indian War. After the end of the war he cultivated his family's estate at Mount Vernon, entering into a marriage of convenience with a wealthy widow, Martha Dandridge Custis. Like most plantation owners, he suffered an increasing tax burden from the British crown and was one of the first to rise up against its rule; in May 1775 he was made commander-in-chief of the Continental Army. Washington initially succeeded in

independence of the colonialists, helping them to defeat the British on several further occasions until the latter's eventual capitulation. George Washington was instrumental in drafting the American Constitution and on 4 February 1789 he was elected the first president of the United States of America. He was sworn in on 30 April in front of the Federal Hall in New York. Washington held office until 1797 and died in 1799. He was awarded the first Congressional Gold Medal for outstanding service to his country.

Trumbull (*c.* 1804); his opponent Aaron Burr (1756–1836, oil painting by John Vanderlyn, *c.* 1802); DeWitt Clinton (1769–1828, oil painting by John Wesley Jarvis, *c.* 1820); Washington Irving (1783–1859, undated engraving), known by the pseudonym "Diedrich Knickerbocker"; George Washington being sworn in as the first president of the USA (undated chalk lithograph).

9 June 1784
Alexander Hamilton, the USA's first minister of finance, founds the Bank of New York, basing it in Walton House in Manhattan.

30 April 1789
The democratic social organization, the Tammany Society, is founded as a response to the elite officers' clubs of the upper classes.

1792
Influential stockholders meet at Wall Street and agree on strict rules governing financial transactions – the forerunner of the New York stock exchange.

1804
The foundation of the New York Historical Society. One of the Founding Fathers of the United States, Alexander Hamilton, is shot and killed in a duel with his political rival, Aaron Burr.

1807
Robert Fulton trials the first commercially successful steamboat, the *Clermont*, on the East River.

From 1820
New York becomes the largest city in the USA, with around 150,000 inhabitants.

1825
New York's seaport grows in importance with the opening of the Erie Canal, linking the city with the smallest and most southerly of America's Great Lakes.

The Erie Canal

DeWitt Clinton, Governor of the State of New York from 1817 to 1822 and again from 1825 until his death in 1828, had a revolutionary plan: in order to increase the importance of New York's port and to enable merchants and farmers in rural New York to transport their produce inland

The festivities at the opening of the Erie Canal (oil painting by Anthony Imbert, *c.* 1825).

at affordable prices, he proposed the building of a canal from Lake Erie to the Hudson River to connect the Great Lakes with the Atlantic. Most of his contemporaries considered him mad, deriding the project as "Clinton's Ditch", but he succeeded in raising seven million dollars for the undertaking, a sum almost unimaginable at the time. The project was completed, and for the opening in 1825 DeWitt Clinton was at the wheel of the *Seneca Chief*, the first ship to navigate the canal. It was a personal triumph for Clinton. The opening of the Erie Canal, and the resulting reduction in transport costs by up to ninety percent, signalled the beginning of a new era for New York, where the population boomed. It also helped open up the west to settlement.

A booming city

New York soon recovered from the aftermath of the War of Independence. Although most of the British loyalists had emigrated to Canada or returned to England, the population of the city doubled in size to 24,000 in the course of just two years. The industrialization of the American north and the city's importance as an international hub of finance had been anticipated by a close acquaintance of George Washington's, Alexander Hamilton. He passionately advocated the devolution of the burden of debt left over from the War of Independence to the federal government and brought economic momentum to the city, founding the Bank of New York and helping establish the New York stock exchange. The city soon developed into a market place of world trade.

In the (Royal) Navy

The War of 1812 once again set the Americans against the British, who had begun pressing Americans into the Royal Navy and were attempting to extend their domain through a pact with a confederation of Native North American tribes. During the course of the war, the British occupied Washington DC and set fire to many buildings, including the Presidential Mansion (the White House). The American defence of Fort McHenry in September 1814 inspired a poem by Francis Scott Key, which when set to music became the patriotic anthem "The Star-Spangled Banner".
The war lasted until 1815 and concluded with an overwhelming victory for the Americans after the Battle of New Orleans. Numerous battles also took place at sea and on the Canadian border. Although Royal Navy ships blockaded the port of New

York, the city largely escaped the war unscathed. In fact, the war rather suited the business community because it increased demand and raised prices.

"Magnus Apollo"

DeWitt Clinton was another significant figure in early 19th-century New York, who was to make his mark on the city. Serving a total of three terms as mayor between 1803 and 1815, as well as holding the office of Governor of New York in his later years, he was a career politician, known to ally and enemy alike as "Magnus Apollo" because of his imposing physique. He had a new city hall built and was instrumental in the founding of the New York Historical Society, as well as numerous other institutions. In 1807 he established a commission to develop Manhattan Island. The commission recommended a grid street plan, with avenues running north–south and streets crossing these at right angles. The only diagonal road to be accepted was Broadway. The justification for this plan was that it would make the parcels of land easier to divide and sell. Four years later, in 1811, the authorities did indeed ordain a regular grid street plan for the area north of 14th Street, creating 2,000 long narrow blocks subdivided into equal plots of land measuring 7.50 m by 30 m (25 feet by 100 feet). This arrangement drove up the price of land, but even today it makes getting around Manhattan much easier. The construction of the Erie Canal was the crowning glory of DeWitt Clinton's career.

Top: Broadway, the oldest north–south route through Manhattan, seen from the Bowling Green, New York's oldest park, in 1828 (tinted engraving by W. I. Bennett, 1830).

John Jacob Astor

The price of land in New York began to skyrocket after 1800, and real estate became a profitable business. Speculators came to the city from all over the world to get a piece of this

new wealth, and among them was a young German called John Jacob Astor, born Johann Astor, from Walldorf in Baden-Württemberg.

The son of a butcher, he had emigrated with very little money to the United States after the War of Independence. His unerring sense of business led him to invest in the fur trade, the most profitable area of commerce before the turn of the century, and this made him a fortune. His American Fur Company controlled large areas, reaching as far as the Great Lakes and Oregon. When fashions changed and beaver fur in particular was no longer in demand, he diversified, specializing in real estate, and New York became his new area of operations. Noticing how rapidly the city was expanding, he invested more than $200,000 in fallow land north of the city limits. This act of speculation proved to be a gold

mine, and when the city expanded to the north, the value of his real estate increased exponentially. He invested the profits in more land, a little further north. The income from his leases and rents in New York alone brought in an annual income of $1.2 million. When he died in 1848, he was worth $25 million. The dynasty he began included John Jacob Astor IV and William Waldorf Astor who between them founded the Waldorf-Astoria Hotel.

Top: The ballroom of the first 13-floor Waldorf Astoria Hotel; above: dressed for success; John Jacob Astor in an undated oil painting by Gilbert Stuart.

Leaving their mark on the city (from left): Frederick Law Olmsted (1822–1903) and Calvert Vaux (1824–1895), who were involved in planning the layout of Central Park in 1858; John August Roebling (1806–1869), who built the Brooklyn Bridge; and Elisha Graves Otis (1811–1861), shown far right demonstrating his elevator in 1853, whose invention made the construction of skyscrapers possible.

1835
The first edition of the *New York Herald* is published.

1851
The first edition of the *New York Times* is published.

1853
The first World's Fair in the USA is held at Crystal Palace in Bryant Park.

1857
New York's first passenger elevator is installed on 23 March, at 488 Broadway.

1861
The American Civil War begins, ending in 1865 with the collapse of the last Confederate resistance.

1868
The first elevated railway service begins between Dey Street in south Manhattan and 29th Street on 3 July.

1870
The population of New York exceeds one million.

1879
Completion of St Patrick's Cathedral on Fifth Avenue.

1886
On 28 October President Stephen Grover Cleveland unveils the new Statue of Liberty on Bedloe Island.

1892
Ellis Island's checkpoint for immigrants is set up.

1898
New York, which until this time had consisted only of Manhattan and the Bronx, is combined with Brooklyn, Queens, and Staten Island.

Gangs of New York

As more and more immigrants needing cheap accommodation moved into the area, the city fathers had the Collect Pond, a body of fresh water set in the insect-ridden marshland south of Manhattan, drained and filled in. New tenements were built, but the land remained

A riot in the slum district of "Five Points", 1827.

swampy in places. As the land value dropped, the poor gravitated towards the area and from the 1820s it began to develop into the slum district called "Five Points", named after the five roads which converged here (Mulberry, Anthony, Cross, Orange, Little Water). It had the highest rates of criminality in the city. Reputedly there was a murder every night for 15 years in the Old Brewery, a tenement block with some 1,000 immigrant residents. The intense overcrowding resulted in further misery and disease. Unemployment was high, prostitution was rife and street gangs like the Roach Guards, the Dead Rabbits, or the Bowery Boys ruled. The slums were only dissolved between 1885 and 1895, and the inhabitants resettled in New York's other suburbs.

Top: View of New York, 1870. Below: A scene from the great fire of 1835.

The rule of violence

The 19th century was marked by explosive developments and social tensions. The discord between ethnic groups in many cities, resulting in racial attacks on African Americans, Irish Catholics, and other immigrants, was echoed in New York. Hopes of achieving a better standard of living in New York led to an almost unimaginable flood of immigration as people poured into the city, principally from Ireland, Germany, and Eastern Europe. Yet New York did not welcome them with open arms; work was poorly paid and the rooms in the overfull tenements were breeding-grounds for disease. The social divide between the rich citizens of Fifth Avenue and the poor immigrants in cheap lodgings in the south-ern part of Manhattan was as wide as ever, which led to considerable tensions. There was violence in the poor quarters even during the American Civil War (1861–1865), during which the northern states fought the southern states to preserve the Union and abolish slavery. When high losses in the war led the government to introduce conscription, it was announced that wealthy men could buy themselves out for $300. The poor immigrants took to the streets, smashing windows, tearing down telegraph poles, and fighting bloody running battles with the police. Their anger was also turned on the black population, whom they blamed for the war. Only after the government had rescinded conscription in New York were tempers mollified.

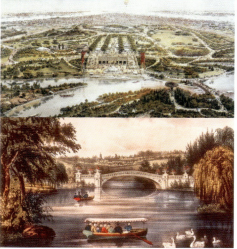

Top: Summer in Central Park, 1865. Bottom: The Bridge, Central Park, c. 1860.

The voice of America

Even war and social unrest could not hold up the city's rapid development; instead, the Civil War brought economic progress and the city's many immigrants contributed widely to its political and cultural advances. The first edition of the *New York Times* appeared in 1851, soon achieving an international distribution and reputation, and even today it is considered "the voice of America". Two years later, in 1853, Elisha Graves Otis unveiled the first fall-proof safety elevator, thus clearing the way for the skyscraper to rise.

A little miracle

Frederick Law Olmstead and Calvert Vaux were landscape gardeners with a dream; for years they had demanded a "green lung" for their giant city, and their dream was fulfilled in 1858 when work was begun on Central Park. Some ten million wagonloads of earth, 25,000 trees, and a quarter of a million shrubs later, New York had acquired a fine urban park. The stony wasteland in the north of the city was transformed into a place for relaxation and leisure. That by the 1850s there was any land left undeveloped in the center of Manhattan is astonishing enough; that it was used for a park for the people, rather than for residential or commercial building, is little less than a miracle. The park was open to the public even as it was being built, and today it is home to joggers, inline skaters, and horseback riders, as well as hosting many entertainment events.

In the name of liberty

The rapid expansion of the city continued after the Civil War. Nowhere else was there more wealth, yet nowhere more poverty. More and more immigrants arrived, doing backbreaking work in the slums of south Manhattan to build a new future. Although an economic crunch in 1873 created a flood of unemployment in the depressed suburbs, New York's progress continued, unaffected by crises and tensions. The Brooklyn Bridge was completed in 1883, a striking symbol of the city celebrated as the "eighth wonder of the world". Electricity and the telephone conquered the city, and on 28 October 1886 President Grover Cleveland unveiled the Statue of Liberty on Bedloe Island, a symbol of the country's unshakeable ideals that was visible for miles around. That the statue had been the creation of a French sculptor, born in Colmar in 1834, who had been thinking less about noble ideas of freedom than about getting a good likeness of his mistress, in no way detracts from the symbolic importance of the Statue of Liberty. It represents freedom, justice, and friendship among foreign nations. Her creator, Frédéric-Auguste Bartholdi, said of her: "I would like to praise the republic and the liberty to be found across the ocean, and hope one day to find the same here."

Inset images right: "Miss Liberty" – seen close up through the lens of Ruffin Cooper (1942–1989).

The older the skyscrapers get, the more they resemble venerable old figures, defining the city's skyline. This is especially true of four urban icons: (from left) the Flatiron Building, the Woolworth Building, the Empire State Building, and the Chrysler Building. Whilst the Empire State Building was once the tallest building in the world, many people – New Yorkers and visitors alike – consider the Chrysler Building the most beautiful.

1902
The era of the skyscrapers begins with the unveiling of the Flatiron Building.

1904
27 October: The first Metro train runs between City Hall and Times Square.

1911
The New York Public Library, one of the greatest public libraries in the USA, is opened on 23 May.

1913
Completion of the Woolworth Building, and the opening of Grand Central Station, and the Apollo Theater in Harlem.

1929
"Black Friday" (25 October) – a major crash on the New York Stock Exchange. The Museum of Modern Art (MoMA) opens.

1930, 1931
The Chrysler Building is opened on 28 May 1930 and the Empire State Building on 1 May 1931.

1940
The World's Fair in Queen's exhibits exciting technical innovations such as television sets, air-conditioning – and nylon stockings.

1941
The Japanese attack on Pearl Harbor brings America into World War II.

1945
New Yorkers celebrate the end of the war with a ticker-tape parade on Fifth Avenue. Foundation of the United Nations (UN).

The New York Subway

This underground city consists of a gigantic network of shafts and tunnels, like the blood vessels and arteries of a mighty giant (but one suffering unfortunately from stress and high blood pressure!). The network of 29 lines is exactly 842 miles long – laid end to end it would reach to Chicago. There are 468 stations, 31,180 turnstiles, 161 escalators, 11,450 signals, and 2,637 switches. Until 1940, when the City of New York took over the running of the network, three subway firms competed for passengers: IRT, BMT, and IND. The Interborough Rapid Transit (IRT) began service in 1904, with

On the Hudson River subway train, photo by Edwin Levick, c. 1901.

its first line running from City Hall to Grand Central, Times Square, and then up to 145th Street and Broadway. The Brooklyn-Manhattan Transit (BMT) built the elevated railway in Brooklyn, and the Independent Subway (IND) was established by the city in 1920, serving Eighth and Sixth Avenues in Manhattan and the other boroughs. Today, the New York City Subway is the world's only subway system to run 24 hours a day, every day of the year.

Courage, confidence, and a head for heights were the requirements for construction workers on skyscrapers (above and right on the Empire State Building, completed in 1931).

The sky's the limit

New York began the 20th century with a landmark event: in 1902 the Flatiron Building was unveiled, the first skyscraper with a clad-steel frame; this was a turning point in the history of New York, as it was now possible to build skywards, ushering in a new age of expansion. The Woolworth Building, with 57 floors, followed in 1913, a new record for the city, which led to new legislation decreeing that sky-scrapers should taper to a point at the top. Art Deco skyscrapers such as the Empire State Building and the Chrysler Building followed in the early 1930s, despite the Great Depression. One of the city's most beautiful buildings, built for the Chrysler Corporation, it looks particularly spectacular and distinctive when lit up at night.

Highs and lows

As progress overtook the city, things were coming to a

Hollywood took advantage of the public profile of the Empire State Building in classic films like *King Kong* (1933, above right). The Chrysler Building's architecture "got the point" (right, photograph by Margaret Bourke-White, 1931).

head on the Lower East Side. More and more European immigrants were flocking to New York, life in the tenements was dreadful, and the working conditions in most of the factories defied description. Harlem, once a Jewish district, had become a black quarter, and jazz and blues began to take off with performers such as Duke Ellington and Bessie Smith setting the musical tone. Further to the south, Broadway became the home of theater and entertainment. Many

venues first opened their doors in the period between the two World Wars: Radio City Music Hall was unveiled with a spectacular stage show, and Richard Rodgers, Oscar Hammerstein, Cole Porter, and George Gershwin all wrote unforgettable classics. Only the stock market crash on Black Friday and the subsequent Great Depression that it triggered made the city pause for thought, but after Fiorello LaGuardia had been sworn in as the new mayor, things began

looking up again. Here was a politician prepared to fight corruption and organized crime. His extension of the subway network and construction of numerous municipal residential building projects sowed the seeds of a boom that was to begin with the victory parade at the end of World War II. The United Nations was founded the same year, and New York was chosen as the headquarters of this organization devoted to maintaining world peace.

New York has earned the title of "capital city of the world", but many individuals have also made their mark: Andy Warhol (1928–1987), for whom success in New York was simply "a job"; Woody Allen (born 1935), creator of the most beautiful cinematic love letter to Manhattan; the late night talk show host David Letterman (born 1947); and Sarah-Jessica Parker (born 1965), who found fame with the TV series, *Sex and the City*.

1946
New York is chosen as the United Nations headquarters in east Manhattan.

1973
New York unveils the new World Trade Center. The "Twin Towers" succeed the Empire State Building as the tallest structure.

1975
Bankruptcy hovers over New York's municipal finances.

1983
Construction of Donald Trump's "Trump Tower".

1989
David Dinkins becomes the first black mayor to take office in New York's City Hall.

1993
A car bomb attack on the World Trade Center.

2001
On 11 September, terrorists steer two jets into the Twin Towers of the World Trade Center.

2008
US investment banks in crisis. Barack Obama celebrates his election victory as the first black president of the USA.

May 2009
Traffic-calming measures introduced on Broadway, Manhattan's main cross-town route.

9/11

The world held its breath on 11 September 2001. As part of a combined attack on the USA's commercial and political districts, members of the Al-Qaida terrorist organization steered two jets filled with passengers into the Twin Towers of the World Trade Center. American Airlines Flight 11 hit the North Tower of the World Trade Center at 8.46, and at 9.03 a second plane (United Airlines 175) hit the South Tower. The jets were laden with fuel and behaved like giant incendiary bombs, setting fire to several floors of each tower. More than 2,000 people were trapped. Although it was initially assumed to be an accident, the impact of the second plane and the reports of the explosions at the Pentagon in Washington DC and in Pennsylvania soon revealed these to be calculated attacks. The Federal Aviation Administration (FAA) ordered the immediate grounding of all flights and a state of emergency was declared in New York. An army of police officers and fire fighters was mustered to help free the people still trapped, but at 9.59 the South Tower collapsed, burying in rubble not only those caught inside but also many fire fighters. The North Tower followed at 10.28. More than 2,700 people died in New York alone. The catastrophe affected the city deeply, uniting its citizens in a terrible grief. Today the site is being redeveloped with new buildings, along with a museum and memorial to those who lost their lives in the attack.

The main new building to be erected on the site of the former Twin Towers – 1 World Trade Center – is intended as an important symbol for the city. Its height, 541 m (1776 feet), was not determined by accident; it is intended to commemorate the year of the US Declaration of Independence.

Until their destruction on 11 September 2001, the 415-m (1,361-foot) and 417-m (1,368-foot) high Twin Towers of the World Trade Center (WTC) were the tallest buildings in the world (top). In 2006, work on 1 World Trade Center (1 WTC for short), a new building designed by Daniel Libeskind, was begun at Ground Zero, the former site of the WTC (above and above left).

Above: The debating chamber in the United Nations headquarters. Member states of this successor to the League of Nations are dedicated to common goals: maintaining world peace, upholding international law, and protecting the human rights of all.

Yes they can!

New York in the second half of the 20th century was a dream and a nightmare at the same time. In the 1950s, writers of the Beat Generation such as Allen Ginsberg (*Howl*), William S. Burroughs (*Naked Lunch*), and Jack Kerouac (*On the Road*) put the new Beat movement firmly on the map. With a nonconformist message that rejected the mainstream values of the time, the Beat movement would ultimately give way to the counterculture of the 1960s. Andy Warhol's Factory in the same decade, and the legendary Studio 54 in the 1970s, came to represent unadulterated narcissism and hedonism. No one followed the rituals of disco nights in Brooklyn more attentively than John Travolta as Tony Manero in *Saturday Night Fever*, and no one hit a contemporary nerve more accurately than Lou Reed's *Walk On The Wild Side*. In the 1980s, Times Square became an outsize red light district, Michael Douglas's performance as the avaricious Gordon Gekko defined Wall Street's image, and Madonna's irresistible rise to pop-icon status proved the old showbiz maxim that "if you can make it there, you can make it anywhere". Bret Easton Ellis's novel *American Psycho*, a nightmarish vision of the world of a Wall Street yuppie, Patrick Bateman, was published in 1991, a year in which 2,000 murders saw the city at the height of a crime wave that was to subside only slowly in the following years. In

1993, the World Trade Center was targeted in a terrorist bomb attack for the first time, but it is the dreadful events of 9/11 which are most deeply imprinted in the collective memory. This most appalling of tragedies was perceived as an attack on the soul of America, on the identity of a nation whose Declaration of Independence of 4 July 1776 proclaimed the pursuit of happiness as an inalienable right. As dreadful as these events were, and as painful their memory, the cooperation, the perseverance, and the unbroken optimism of New Yorkers at the time was unequalled. People have since sought to return to a normality which may have never really existed in the city. Perhaps this is why the new "Freedom Tower" is now simply called "1 World Trade Center", after its location, and Times Square, long since cleaned up, is to become pedestrianized.

Above: The navel of the world: travelling in a cycle taxi in Times Square.

THE HIGHLIGHTS

DOWNTOWN MANHATTAN

New York City is divided into five boroughs – Manhattan, Brooklyn, Queens, The Bronx, and Staten Island – throughout which are hundreds of districts or neighborhoods such as Greenwich Village and SoHo. For this reason, New York has been called a "city of neighborhoods". Sandwiched between the Atlantic estuary of the East River and the Hudson River, Manhattan Island is neatly and simply divided into Downtown (stretching from the island's southern tip to 30th Street), Midtown (from 30th Street to Central Park) and Uptown (from Central Park to the far north, into Harlem and Washington Heights).

THE HIGHLIGHTS: DOWNTOWN MANHATTAN

1 Liberty Island

2 Ellis Island

3 Staten Island Ferry

4 Battery Park

5 Robert F. Wagner Jr Park

6 Museum of Jewish Heritage

7 National Museum of the American Indian

8 Fraunces Tavern

9 Trinity Church

10 Wall Street, New York Stock Exchange

11 World Financial Center

12 World Trade Center Site (Ground Zero)

13 St Paul's Chapel

14 South Street Seaport Historic District

15 Brooklyn Bridge

16 Woolworth Building

17 Civic Center

18 TriBeCa

19 Chinatown

20 SoHo

21 Little Italy

22 Lower East Side

23 East Village

24 Greenwich Village

25 Chelsea

26 Meatpacking District

27 Flatiron Building

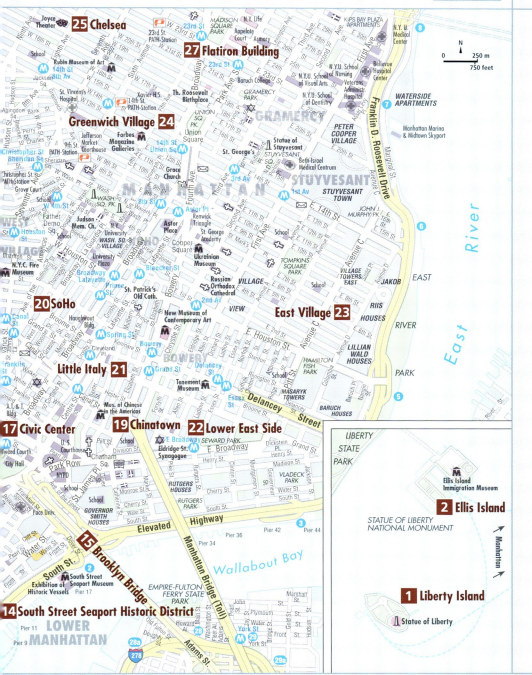

25 Chelsea

27 Flatiron Building

Greenwich Village 24

20 SoHo

Little Italy 21

17 Civic Center

19 Chinatown

22 Lower East Side

East Village 23

15 Brooklyn Bridge

14 South Street Seaport Historic District

LOWER MANHATTAN

LIBERTY STATE PARK

Ellis Island Immigration Museum

2 Ellis Island

STATUE OF LIBERTY NATIONAL MONUMENT

1 Liberty Island

Statue of Liberty

THE HIGHLIGHTS:
DOWNTOWN MANHATTAN

More than 15 million people entered the United States via Ellis Island (right). They were greeted by the Statue of Liberty on Bedloe Island, later renamed Liberty Island, at the mouth of New York Harbor (below). Below right: the Immigration Museum on Ellis Island commemorating those seeking a new life in the USA.

INFO Theater in the Museum

Several times a day in summer a 30-minute show at the Ellis Island Museum dramatically depicts the arrival of famous immigrants.

Take Statue of Liberty Line (departs from Battery Park every 35 mins.); Tel (212) 561 45 00; performances Apr–Sept, daily, every 45 mins. from 10.45–16.00; www.statueofliberty.org

New York's most iconic monument, the Statue of Liberty, is French. It was conceived as a gift to the United States by political activist Edouard René Lefebvre de Laboulaye, admirer of the American constitution and critic of Napoleon III, together with sculptor Frédéric-Auguste Bartholdi. The huge statue, said to be inspired by the Colossus of Rhodes and modeled after either the artist's mistress or mother, was constructed in France and then dismantled and transported to America in crates. It was finally unveiled on its site on Liberty Island on 28 October 1886. Now a UNESCO World Heritage Site, the statue's foundations weigh some 24,000 tons and her robes conceal a steel frame constructed by Alexandre Gustav Eiffel, who went on to build his famous tower. Every immigrant arriving between 1892 and 1954 to seek a new life in America was processed at Ellis Island at the mouth of the Hudson River.

THE HIGHLIGHTS: DOWNTOWN MANHATTAN

INFO Exotic Aquaria

The ferry service runs 24 hours daily between Manhattan and Staten Island and is used by about 20 million people annually, both commuters and visitors to New York. The ships are painted bright orange so they can be seen more clearly in fog.

Since 2008, tropical fish have found a spectacular home in two giant acrylic glass tanks in Staten Island Zoo, right next to the St George Ferry Terminal. Each tank holds more than 200 exotic species in a fascinating underwater world.
1 Bay Street, Staten Island, Tourist information: Tel (718) 816 20 00

The Staten Island Ferry connects the southern tip of Manhattan with Staten Island, which lies in the bay. About 200 million passengers a year travel between South Ferry (Whitehall Street) and St George Ferry Terminal. In the 18th century the short trip was covered by only two private sailboats, but by the 19th century the first steamships had arrived. There was a disaster in 1871, when the *Westfield*'s boiler exploded, killing 85 people. The ferries have been owned and operated by the City of New York since 1905. In 1897, the 20-minute crossing cost 5 cents, and the price was not changed until 1972, when it became 10 cents. In 1975 it was raised to 25 cents, in 1990 to 50 cents, but after 1997 the journey became free, and there isn't a better value sightseeing tour of downtown Manhattan – the ferry has absolutely magnificent views of the city's skyline and bridges.

THE HIGHLIGHTS: DOWNTOWN MANHATTAN

INFO Musical evenings

From 7 p.m. on Thursdays in July and August there are atmospheric musical performances in Clinton Castle. Free tickets are distributed on a first-come, first-served basis at the entrance.

Battery Park; Tel (212) 344 34 91; Jul–Aug Thurs19.00; www.thebattery.org

Battery Park (below) and Robert F. Wagner Jr Park merge together seamlessly. Right: The impressive skyline of Battery Park City and the World Financial Center tower above both. Below right: The Museum of Jewish Heritage.

BATTERY PARK 4 ROBERT F. WAGNER JR PARK 5
MUSEUM OF JEWISH HERITAGE 6

Battery Park lies at the southernmost tip of Manhattan and is the starting point for trips over to the Statue of Liberty and Ellis Island. Its name is derived from the Dutch artillery ("batteries") stationed on the coast here during the Colonial period in the 17th century.

Next door, Battery Park City and the office blocks of the World Financial Center stand on artificial land reclaimed during excavations for the World Trade Center. The Castle Clinton Monument, a fort constructed to defend against the British, is located in

the park. The gap between Battery Park and Battery Park City was filled in during the 1990s with the opening of Robert F. Wagner Jr Park, named after a former mayor of the city. The Museum of Jewish Heritage has the symbolic hexagonal shape of the Star of David.

THE HIGHLIGHTS: DOWNTOWN MANHATTAN

The US Custom House is decorated with groups of sculptures by Daniel Chester French, symbolizing the continents of Asia, America, Europe (below), and Africa. Above and bottom right: The Fraunces Tavern; a view of the rotunda of the National Museum of the American Indian (below, top right).

This museum complex consisting of the Fraunces Tavern and four other historic buildings gives visitors an idea of New York City's early days. You can also see selected exhibits from the famous Dunsmore Collection of portraits here.
54 Pearl Street; Tel (212) 425 17 78; Mon–Sat 12.00–17.00

Income tax was not introduced in the USA until 1913. Until then, excise duty collected by the customs authorities had been of more importance, and this was administered in New York from the US Custom House, a Beaux Arts building designed by Cass Gilbert in 1907.

The building now houses the National Museum of the American Indian, illustrating the history of the Native American cultures of North, Middle, and South America. The exhibits in the museum were curated in cooperation with representatives of the original inhabitants of America. The Fraunces Tavern, in which General George Washington said farewell to his officers in 1783, is an exact replica of the house built for Samuel Fraunces in 1719. Fraunces also served Washington as a steward.

THE HIGHLIGHTS: DOWNTOWN MANHATTAN

The sandstone building of Trinity Church (below) is hemmed in amongst the skyscrapers of the Financial District. Right: The interior of the three-nave basilica. Below right: the Biblical scenes depicted on the bronze doors by Richard Morris, near the historic cemetery.

INFO Concerts

Twice a month Trinity Church is turned into a concert hall, and famous exponents of all kinds of musical styles, from folk to classical, can be heard. The impressive Trinity Choir is one of the best in the USA.

74 Trinity Place; Tel (212) 602 08 00; www.trinitywallstreet.org

The current Trinity Church, built in 1846 to a neo-Gothic design by Richard Upjohn, was preceded by a series of Anglican churches: the first was built as early as 1698, but burnt down eight years later, in 1706. A second church constructed on the site, consecrated in 1790, was demolished in 1839 for safety reasons. The modern church's bronze doors are reminiscent of Lorenzo Ghiberti's "Gates of Paradise" for the Baptistry in Florence. A bronze by Steve Tobin was placed in front of the church in 2005 to commemorate the tragic events of 9/11. Parts of the church's historic cemetery date back to the 18th century, and it includes the graves of Alexander Hamilton, the first US Secretary of the Treasury, and Robert Fulton, the inventor of the steamship. The church has a museum that hosts special exhibitions throughout the year illustrating the history of the church and the parish.

THE HIGHLIGHTS: DOWNTOWN MANHATTAN

The neo-classical façade of the New York Stock Exchange (below and right), designed by George B. Post in 1903, is reminiscent of a Greek temple. Much photographed for its sculptures of Integrity, Agriculture, Mining, Science, Industry, and Invention, representing sources of American prosperity.

TIP Cipriani, Wall Street

This branch of Cipriani on Wall Street is the designated successor to the legendary Wall Street Club and a popular rendezvous for financiers. Have a "power breakfast" or better still, sip a cocktail on the viewing terrace.
55 Wall Street; Tel (212) 699 40 96; Mon–Fri 6.30–22.30.

WALL STREET, NEW YORK STOCK EXCHANGE (NYSE) 🔟

The heart of New York's Financial District is Wall Street, which runs along the site of a wooden defensive wall erected by the Dutch in 1653. Alexander Hamilton, the country's first Secretary of the Treasury, hit upon the idea of making New York a headquarters for stock trading and issued federal government bonds to offset the debts incurred during the War of Independence. Although Wall Street thus became synonymous with finance, it's wotrh noting that the Stock Exchange is actually located round the corner, on Broad Street, between Wall Street and Exchange Place. In 1936 a marble relief entitled *Integrity Protecting the Works of Man* was placed above the Corinthian pillars of the façade, representing the Stock Exchange as the index of the nation's wealth; this was later replaced with a lead-covered replica. It's a fascinating area to explore and worth a visit.

Traders on the New York Stock Exchange dealt face to face until 2005, when an electronic system was installed (below). Membership as a broker or trader is conditional on acceptance by the Securities and Exchange Commission (SEC) and the exchange is led by a Board of Governors. The city's financial primacy means brokers have to keep an eye on developments in the world's markets (below right). Arturo Di Modica's sculpture, *Charging Bull* (right).

THE WORLD'S FINANCIAL HEART

On 17 May 1792, 24 businessmen and bankers met under a plane tree on Wall Street and signed an agreement to regulate the purchase and sale of shares and bonds, thus laying the foundations for the New York Stock Exchange. The "New York Stock & Exchange Board" extended and formalized these revolutionary rules in 1817, and the current title of the "New York Stock Exchange" was finally adopted in 1863. Initially, two sessions were held, in which the president of the exchange would call out the stocks and members submitted their offers. Each member had their own chair, or "seat" at the exchange, and in 1817 this privilege cost $25. The NYSE is currently the largest stock exchange in the world. It has been state-regulated since 1934 and is run by a private corporation of stock brokers and traders; the oldest stock index is the Dow Jones Index. Listed on the stock market since 2006 as the NYSE Group, the concern created "NYSE Euronext, Inc", the world's first transatlantic stock exchange, in a merger in April 2007. The acquisition of the American Stock Exchange (AMEX) in October 2008 gave rise to the "NYSE Alternext US".

THE HIGHLIGHTS: DOWNTOWN MANHATTAN

TIP Devon & Blakely

There is a yawning gap between the towers of the World Financial Center (seen right with the Hudson River marina) where the Twin Towers of the World Trade Center once stood. At the heart of the complex there is a large winter garden with shops and restaurants (below).

The extensive shopping and dining area of the World Financial Center has something for everyone. The Devon & Blakely restaurant is renowned for its sandwich creations and unusual soup ingredients. *3 World Financial Center; Vesey St; Tel (212) 240 74 50; Mon–Fri 7.00–18.45.*

Excavations for the World Trade Center produced enough spoil to create a strip of shoreline on which Battery Park City was built. The hub of the complex, built in the second half of the 1980s to designs by César Palli, is the World Financial Center: four granite and glass office blocks of differing heights, with up to 51 floors and post-modern copper roofs. Each building reflects a basic architectural form: a truncated pyramid, a cupola, a pyramid, and a ziggurat (stepped pyramid). The façades of towers two and three were badly damaged during the attack on the World Trade Center in 2001, but they were soon repaired. The WFC has a total area of 27,000 sq. m (291,000 sq. feet) and is home to such financial giants as Dow Jones and American Express. The open plaza has a view of the Hudson River and North Cove Yacht Harbor. Those interested in architecture would enjoy a visit and the view is spectacular.

THE HIGHLIGHTS: DOWNTOWN MANHATTAN

"I've seen a lot of things, but the worst thing about being down there was that you couldn't see anything. No bodies, no computers, no telephones, no doors, not even a door handle. Do you know how many door handles there were in the World Trade Center?" (Sal D'Agonstino, firefighter)

INFO Tribute WTC Visitors Center

Five galleries feature information on various aspects of the devastating terrorist attacks. Survivors and victims' relatives also conduct moving tours of Ground Zero. Daily, 11.00, 12.00, 13.00, and 15.00.
120 Liberty St; Tel (212) 393 91 60; Mon, Wed-Sat 10.00–18.00, Tues 12.00–18.00, Sun 12.00–17.00.

WORLD TRADE CENTER SITE (GROUND ZERO) 12

Built on square foundations to heights of 415 m (1,361 feet) and 417 m (1,368 feet) respectively, the stainless steel Twin Towers of the World Trade Center were, for a few weeks after their completion in 1974, the tallest buildings in the world, only ceding this crown to the 443-m (1,453-foot) high Sears Tower in Chicago. The Twin Towers, each containing 110 floors, were part of a complex of seven office buildings that were connected to the World Financial Center by an underground passage and by a bridge. Known as Ground Zero since the attack of 11 September 2001, the 6.5-ha. (16-acre) site was not completely cleared of rubble from the destroyed towers until the summer of 2002. It was originally planned that five new skyscrapers were to be constructed here, although the financial crises of 2009 entailed significant revisions to these plans.

THE HIGHLIGHTS: DOWNTOWN MANHATTAN

INFO Guided tour

The World Trade Center, situated right behind the old cemetery on the west side of St Paul's Chapel, was destroyed on 11 September 2001. Reverend Stuart H. Hoke (below) was one of the survivors of the attack that turned this place of prayer into a memorial.

There are daily guided tours describing the history of the church and the Ground Zero memorial. The tours are free, but the large crowds make booking a slot in advance worthwhile.
209 Broadway;Tel (212) 233 41 64; Memorial:Mon–Sat 10.00–18.00, Sun 8.00–16.00.

ST PAUL'S CHAPEL **13**

St Paul's Chapel, in which George Washington once worshiped, was completed in 1776 and is New York's oldest church. It was created by master craftsman Andrew Gautier who probably based the design on James Gibbs's church of St Martin's in the Fields in London. Apart from the addition of a spire in 1796, the building has remained unchanged since its consecration. During the rubble clearing after the attacks of 11 September 2001, this Episcopal chapel (which belongs to the Anglican church) was used by workers to take a rest. Miraculously, the church was not destroyed during the attack: a nearby tree dissipated the effects of the shockwaves so completely that not even a window pane was broken. Only a stump and the roots of the tree survived, inspiring the sculpture which now stands in front of Trinity Church – *Trinity Root* by Steve Tobin.

THE HIGHLIGHTS: DOWNTOWN MANHATTAN

The East River (right) connects Long Island Sound with New York Bay. The pull of the tides causes the water to flow so fast that even in winter ice cannot form. This explains the importance of the bay as an anchorage in the days of tall ships (below, the four-masted *Peking*).

INFO Visitors' Center

The visitors' center has plenty of information about interesting events in the museum district, such as boat trips and open-air concerts, as well as a permanent exhibition of the history of the South Street Seaport.
12 Fulton St; Tel (212) 748 85 90; Apr–Oct Tues–Sun 10.00–18.00, Nov–Mar Fri–Sun 10.00–17.00.

SOUTH STREET SEAPORT HISTORIC DISTRICT

The old port area between Water Street and the East River is now a listed monument. In the middle of the 1960s a group of citizens calling themselves the "South Street Museum" began collecting boats and buying up dilapidated buildings in the port area. About ten years later, the notion arose of transforming the area into a living district, with restored and new buildings, museums, stores, and old sailboats, some of which could house museums themselves. Schermerhorn Row, with its warehouses and offices built in 1813, is the pride of the port. The Fulton Fish Market has become a shopping mall and a small lighthouse commemorates the sinking of the *Titanic* in 1912. Pier 17 has three floors of restaurants and stores, and a fantastic view of Brooklyn Bridge. Head to the visitors' center for information on activities in the area. It's a great place to come for shopping and dining.

THE HIGHLIGHTS: DOWNTOWN MANHATTAN

When it was unveiled, the Brooklyn Bridge was hailed as a miracle of engineering and was the longest suspension bridge in the world. The "Elevated Pleasure Walk", a wooden pedestrian path above the road, was designed for strollers – certainly the most beautiful promenade in the city.

TIP Pier 17 Pavilion

In 1985 a pier for gourmets was opened next to the fishing piers. There are stores and restaurants on Pier 17, surrounded by wooden decks with a fantastic view of Brooklyn Bridge as you drink your sundowner cocktail.

89 South St/Fulton St; Mon–Sat 10.00–21.00, Sun 11.00–20.00.

This legendary bridge, spanning the East River between Manhattan and Brooklyn, was opened in May 1883 after some 16 years of construction. Not including the approach roads, it is 1,052 m (3,451 feet) in length; including the approach roads 1,825 m (5,987 feet). Its first day of service saw 150,000 people cross the bridge. To convince contemporary sceptics of the structure's stability, Barnum's Circus sent a herd of elephants over the bridge. Designing the Brooklyn Bridge was originally the responsibility of the German architect, John Augustus Roebling, but he died shortly after construction began. His son Washington took on the challenge with his wife, Emily, and supervized the subsequent work. The Brooklyn Bridge was the first suspension bridge to incorporate steel wires: the monumental construction eventually incorporated 24,000 km (15,000 miles) of wire. It's a truly spectacular feat of engineering.

THE HIGHLIGHTS: DOWNTOWN MANHATTAN

TIP Carnegie Deli

The Woolworth Building (below, the view from City Hall and the roof; right, the lobby) was soon described as the "Cathedral of Commerce", but according to the architect, Cass Gilbert, it was based on Gothic town halls rather than sacred architecture.

Even though the legendary King of Corned Beef and Pastrami, Milton Parker, has left his famous delicatessen bar for ever, it still serves the best New York-style kosher sandwiches.

854 Seventh Ave/55th St; Tel. (212) 757 22 45; daily 6.30–16.00.

On its unveiling in April 1913, the Woolworth Building was hailed as the "eighth wonder of the world". At 241 m (790 feet) in height it was the world's tallest building (until 1930) and the man who commissioned it, Franklin Winfield Woolworth, never omitted to mention that he had paid for it – all $13.5 million's worth – in cash. His rise to department store king had begun with a "five cent store" in Utica, New York. When this went bust he tried his luck in Lancaster, Pennsylvania, extending his range to include goods that also cost a dime. He opened his first store in New York in 1896 and at the time of his death, in 1916, he owned an empire of more than a thousand keenly priced stores around the world and had also amassed a personal fortune of $65 million. A relief of him – counting his money – can be found in the lobby of the Woolworth Building, the so-called "Cathedral of Commerce".

More than 200 newspapers are produced in New York City: "Let's be clear about one thing – we're not in the paper business, we're in the news business; and as long we define ourselves with the word 'news', we've got a bright future". (Arthur Ochs Sulzberger, *New York Times*)

NEWSPAPER ROW: "ALL THE NEWS THAT'S FIT TO PRINT"

Running east of City Hall Park, Park Row was known as "Newspaper Row" in the 19th century. Among the 15 papers that had settled in the Financial District, due to its proximity to City Hall, was the *New York Evening Post*, founded by Alexander Hamilton in 1801 (although since 1906 it has been situated in Vesey Street and since 1934 it has appeared under the title "New York Post"). Even the *New York Times*, whose 1889 motto "All The News That's Fit To Print" still appears on every masthead, was originally based here. Now listed as a national monument, the original New York Times Building (41 Park Row) was designed by George B. Post in 1889. It is currently part of the campus of Pace University, which coincidentally offers courses in publishing and computer studies. The offices of the various media companies have long since been scattered across the city, and Newspaper Row's publishing past is commemorated by just one public space: Printing House Square, between Park Row, Nassau, and Spruce Street. It features a statue, designed in 1872 by Ernst Plassmann, of American founding father Benjamin Franklin, clutching a copy of the *Pennsylvania Gazette* – of which he was the editor.

THE HIGHLIGHTS: DOWNTOWN MANHATTAN

INFO Civic Center Walking Tour

The Municipal Building towers over the Civic Center (below). Its dome is an architectural reference to the comparatively much smaller City Hall (right, to the left of the picture). Opposite City Hall there is a monument dedicated to Nathan Hale, who was hanged by the British as "America's first spy".

This three to four-hour sightseeing tour starts at South Street Seaport and leads past the Brooklyn Bridge to the historic Criminal Courts Building, the County Courthouse, the Hall of Records, and City Hall, then past the Woolworth Building and on to St Paul's Chapel. Recommended.

South of Chinatown, bounded to the west by Broadway and to the east by the East River, lies New York's legal and administrative district – the Civic Center. Its many public buildings include City Hall, the oldest in the United States, which is still the headquarters of the city's administration. It was constructed between 1803 and 1812 by Joseph François Mangin and John McComb Jr in the "Federal Style" that developed out of the British Colonial Style after the War of Independence. The City Hall Park alongside the building had been open ground in the 18th century, used for grazing cattle, as an assembly point, and for military exercises. The Municipal Building, an office block completed in 1914 to accommodate increased space needed for city administrators, provides an architectural contrast to City Hall. A visit to City Hall as part of a sight-seeing tour is highly recommended.

THE HIGHLIGHTS: DOWNTOWN MANHATTAN

TIP TriBeCa Grill

The actor Robert de Niro is co-owner of the TriBeCa Grill (below), a destination restaurant for gourmets, and after 9/11 was a driving force behind the "TriBeCa Film Festival" (right, from left: de Niro, festival organizer Tahir Muhammad, Meryl Streep, and Martin Scorsese).

Owned by film star Robert de Niro since 1990, this restaurant is noted for its robust cuisine and fresh ingredients. The excellent wine list has won a Wine Spectator award.

375 Greenwich St/Franklin St; Tel (212) 941 39 00; Mon-Sat 11.30–15.00 and 17.30–23.00, Sun 17.30–22.00

TriBeCa (the "Triangle Below Canal Street") is another example of how New York continually reinvents itself. In the mid-1970s this was a run-down industrial area known as the "Lower West Side", until a property developer recognized the potential of its many empty factories and warehouses and invented the new abbreviation. His gamble paid off: TriBeCa was suddenly "cool" and many artists from nearby SoHo relocated their ateliers, studios, and rehearsal rooms here, as the rents were relatively cheap. TriBeCa has remained chic and trendy but is now also expensive, and the in-crowd has long since moved on. The triangle of streets between West Broadway, Canal West, and Chambers Street now encloses more restaurants than galleries – including some of the best in the city, and they make a great place for relaxing and recuperating after a day spent exploring the city.

THE HIGHLIGHTS: DOWNTOWN MANHATTAN

Manhattan's Chinatown grew up in the 1870s. It is now a "city within a city", and the large Asian community here is the biggest outside Asia: glazed ducks in a street kitchen (below); the view down Pell Street (below right); a market stall in Catherine Street (right).

INFO Chinese New Year

Chinatown celebrates the Chinese New Year between January and February in spectacular style: there are firework displays and daily processions with traditional costumes and fire-breathing dragons, and the area's many restaurants join in the festivities.

The Chinese enclave south of Canal Street is now home to around 200,000 Chinese people, the largest Asian community outside Asia. All the signs are written in Chinese characters and the smell of Peking duck and exotic sauces wafts from the open doorways. Thanks to its 200-plus restaurants, more than 300 flourishing textile and clothing firms, numerous shops and grocery stores, and seven daily Chinese newspapers, Chinatown can consider itself an independent metropolis within Manhattan. The Buddhist Temple of America is located on Mott Street and the Church of the Transfiguration, built in 1801 and Catholic since 1850 (once an important focus for Irish and Italian immigrants) has had a Chinese priest since 1970. The infamous "Bloody Angle", the scene of past violent skirmishes between opposing Chinese street gangs (known as the "Tong Wars"), can be found on Doyers Street.

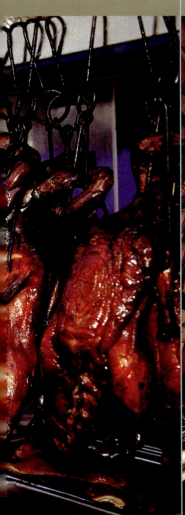

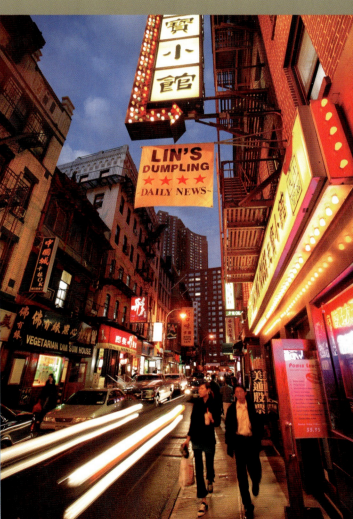

THE HIGHLIGHTS: DOWNTOWN MANHATTAN

Visitors to SoHo will probably meet up under a fire escape before going to the galleries and quirky antiques stores. The most interesting stores are to be found on Prince Street, West Broadway (right, Stefano Gabbano and Domenico Dolce in their store), and Spring Street.

TIP Apple Store, SoHo

The Apple Store in SoHo's old post office is a real New York institution, with all the Apple creations you could want in a completely relaxed atmosphere. The daily workshops with insider tips are free.

103 Prince St; Tel (212) 226 31 26; Mon–Sat 9.30–20.00, Sun 9.30–19.00.

According to former mayor, Ed Koch, an artist's role in New York is "to make a district so attractive that the artists can't afford to live there any more". And the real estate broker's job, one might add, is to package it attractively: just like TriBeCa, the abbreviation SoHo ("South of Houston") has commercial roots, referring to an industrial area south of Houston Street once known as the "South Village". In the 1960s the area, which had largely been left to become dilapidated, started to attract artists and bohemian types. They quickly moved into the empty loft spaces and deserted factory buildings – at least until Ed Koch's prediction was truely fulfilled. Soho has now become a trendy locale famous for its destination shopping. It's a great place for exploring antique stores and unusual galleries and for admiring a wonderful, unique collection of cast-iron architecture.

Appearances can be deceptive: in SoHo, what looks like marble, brick, or sandstone is usually cast iron. Although this material is slow to burn, changes in the building codes in 1911 meant that buildings like this also had to fit fire escapes (below). SoHo's architectural highlights include the cast-iron Haughwout Building (detail, right middle), built in 1857, and the Singer Building (details right, left, and far right) with its delicate ironwork.

ART AND ARCHITECTURE IN A CAST-IRON FRAME

SoHo's streets also have a long tradition of combining art and architecture. However, it is one that was long neglected until the 1960s, and would have dwindled to nothing had conservationists not realized the rarity value of the cast-iron houses which are common here. Many have now been restored. Cast iron became a popular building material in the 19th century because it was lighter and cheaper to work than stone or brick, and it permitted the architect to prefabricate decorations and façades in the foundry and then have them bolted together on site like plates. Cast iron was also prized for its fire resistance. The era of cast-iron buildings only really ended with the construction of steel-framed skyscrapers in the 1890s, and New York retains the world's greatest concentration of façades wholly or partly constructed of cast iron. The most beautiful houses are, unsurprisingly, in the Cast Iron District, between West Broadway, West Houston Street, Canal Street, and Crosby Street. Green Street, at the heart of the district, has over 50 buildings spread across five blocks, all built between 1869 and 1895. This is certainly the area to come for students of architecture.

THE HIGHLIGHTS:
DOWNTOWN MANHATTAN

INFO San Gennaro Festival

The myth lives on, even if Little Italy is gradually being squeezed out by Chinatown into Mulberry, Mott, Grand, and Broome Streets. The charm of the trattorias has remained, and the smell of maccheroni and pizza still drifts down the streets (below). Lombardi's (right) is the oldest pizzeria in America (1905).

Little Italy is turned on its head in the middle of September. During the ten-day festival in honour of St Gennaro, the patron saint of Naples, Mulberry Street becomes Via San Gennaro. Relics of the saint are carried through the streets and delicacies are handed out at every street corner.
www.sangennaro.org

"I grew up in a world which was more European than American", the director Martin Scorsese once said; like his acting alter ego, Robert de Niro, he grew up in Little Italy. Scorsese's grandparents, who partly brought him up, were illiterate Sicilian peasants who spoke no English and who, like many southern Italians, had left conditions of poverty to emigrate to New York, where some 40,000 Italians lived in a district stretching from Canal Street to Houston Street. A world of its own, it now exists only in films. Modern-day Little Italy is amongst Manhattan's smallest ethnic quarters, with some 5,000 Italians living in about four blocks; the rest have moved on, to Brooklyn or the Bronx. If you visit the area in the middle of September during the local festival, you may think you have been transported to Italy itself. This is the area to come for authentic Italian food.

THE HIGHLIGHTS: DOWNTOWN MANHATTAN

Eldridge Street synagogue is a reminder of the Lower East Side's Jewish roots, although the area is now largely inhabited by Latino and Asian immigrants. There is also a guided tour of the synagogue. Right: The Lower East Side Tenement Museum.

TIP Historic Orchard Street

The old Jewish business district has since developed a multicultural mixture of interesting stores. The boutiques and market stalls have something for everyone, from exotic foodstuffs and utensils to designer fashion. Visitors' information: 261 Broome Street.

At the beginning of the 20th century, Manhattan's Lower East Side, the district between the Bowery and Clinton Street, East Houston, and Canal Street, had the world's largest Jewish community. These immigrants lived in generally appalling conditions in six or seven-floor tenements. Often they were squashed into tiny, windowless rooms, sharing dilapidated cupboards and rusty washbasins, with a single toilet in the hall. It was so unbearably hot in summer that many residents slept on the roof. The Tenement Museum in Orchard Street commemorates the difficult conditions experienced by the immigrants on the Lower East Side. The district still has some 300 synagogues and a few Jewish stores, but most of New York's Jewish population now lives outside Manhattan. This multicultural area now boasts a fascinating range of fashion and food stores, as well as interesting market stalls.

THE HIGHLIGHTS: DOWNTOWN MANHATTAN

TIP Indian Food

The eastern part of the East Village contains "Alphabet City", consisting of Avenues A, B, and C, one of the most fashionable areas of the city (inset, below left, the intersection at 3rd and 13th Streets and, right, a 24-hour supermarket; below, four snapshots from the area).

East Sixth Street's many Indian eateries have gained it the nickname "Little Bombay". Angon on the Sixth (320 East 6th St), Banjara (97 First Ave/6th St), the Brick Lane Curry House (306–308 East 6th St), Calcutta (324 East 6th St), and Mitali East (334 East 6th St) are particularly recommended.

The north part of the Lower East Side was already known as the "East Village" by the 1950s, and nowadays the whole area east of Broadway between 14th and Houston Street bears the name. The area where Peter Stuyvesant had once owned land was first inhabited by an elite – the Astors and the Vanderbilts of 19th-century New York high society. Immigrants of various nationalities later moved into the area, which became a place for beatniks and would-be beatniks in the middle of the 20th century. Allen Ginsberg, Jack Kerouac, and other such literary giants gave readings wherever a podium could be found, and John Coltrane played his heart out in smoky jazz clubs. The hippies followed, to be succeeded by the punks, and even today the East Village, where artists such as Keith Haring and Jeff Koons first came to prominence, is a home for the authentically avant-garde.

THE HIGHLIGHTS: DOWNTOWN MANHATTAN

A stroll through Greenwich Village reveals a range of attractive terraced houses (below). Washington Square (right) is the spiritual, if not the geographical heart of the district, with a lively and bustling scene (below right).

TIP St Mark's Place

A charming mixture of junk, second-hand stores, and cafés: bars and restaurants make this street well worth a visit. The punk store, Trash & Vaudeville, at 4 St Mark's Place should not be missed, nor the Holiday Cocktail Lounge at 75 St Mark's Place, where Frank Sinatra used to perform (18.00–2.00, daily).

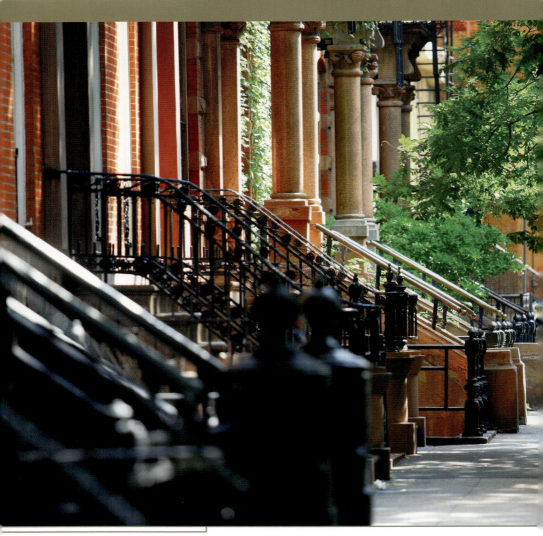

New Yorkers call the area between 14th Street and Houston Street, Hudson River and Broadway Greenwich Village – "the Village" for short – and the area's winding, tree-lined streets and alleys do still give the impression of the village it was at its foundation in 1696. In 1822 the area expanded when many New Yorkers fleeing a yellow fever epidemic settled downtown, further to the south. However, 13 years later, in 1835, it could still claim to be "the ideal of peaceful and respectable living", if Henry James's description in his novel *Washington Square* is to be believed. In 1913 the journalist John Reed, who was to go on to found the first Communist party in the United States, clambered up the triumphal arch in Washington Square to declare the "Independent Republic of Greenwich Village". No visit is complete without some time spent in this lively and unique corner of New York.

THE HIGHLIGHTS: DOWNTOWN MANHATTAN

TIP The Bitter End

Night cruising in the Village (below, inset left); Christopher Street (below); 7th Avenue/corner of Bleecker Street (below right). If you need sustenance, there are Arturo's pizzas in Houston Street. The fortune teller (right) might know your chances of winning the lottery.

When film producer Fred Weintraub opened this club in 1961 it became a stage for thousands of star performances and live recordings. New York's oldest rock club is still the place to hear top-class live music performed in front of the famous "brick wall". *147 Bleecker St; Tel (212) 673 70 30; 20.00–4.00, daily.*

Greenwich Village only became the hub of the sub-culture in the 20th century. *The Village Voice*, the city's first alternative weekly newspaper, was founded by Dan Wolf, Ed Fancher, and Norman Mailer in a two-room apartment in the fall of 1955. Six years later, in July 1961, one Robert Allen Zimmerman first came to the area; calling himself Bob Dylan, he found in the intellectual climate of New York University, for whose students Washington Square is almost an annexe campus, the same sympathetic hearing it had afforded the poets of the "Beat Generation". A lively nightlife developed around Bleecker Street, the first gay movement began on Christopher Street, and modern actresses like Gwyneth Paltrow and Sarah Jessica Parker have found homes in the still independent district. For a night with the stars, astrological and possibly A-list, head here for a pizza, a stroll and a spot of rock 'n' roll.

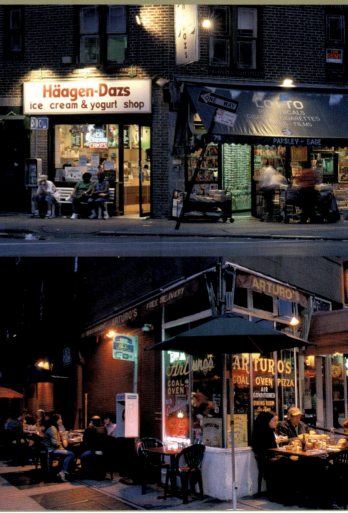

The pagan festival of All Hallows' Eve has turned into Halloween, and the whole town seems to dress up for the occasion. Even the cops put on a good face for the sometimes decidedly adult entertainment (right). This might be connected with the Celtic belief that the souls who have died in the last year are allowed to return home for a brief period only, so the celebrations will soon be over...

FUN AND GAMES: THE VILLAGE HALLOWEEN PARAD

Rosy-cheeked women with giant busts, flashing skeletons and scary ghosts, fabulous animals and dragons, garish drag queens and dancing princes, screaming witches and grinning devils: the Village Halloween Parade has become to Manhattan what Carnival is to Rio. Every year on 31 October more than 50,000 masked New Yorkers and an estimated two million visitors celebrate the spirits' return; according to Celtic legend, they are allowed to pass among the living only on Halloween. And they do! The first parade in October 1973 was just a small procession organized by a company making masks in Greenwich Village. Only the following year, after the Theater for the New City had got involved, several thousand masked people were singing and dancing on Sixth Avenue, and since 1975 the Village Halloween Parade has been a spectacular event. Merry New Yorkers in the oddest costumes follow giant "puppets" made of plastic and papier-mâché, dancing to cheerful rhythms supplied by a wide variety of bands. Furthermore, even after the terrorist attacks of 9/11, New Yorkers refused to miss out on the parade. Rudolf Giuliani, the mayor at the time, called the parade an "opportunity for healing" for the city, and the theme that year was the phoenix, rising from the ashes.

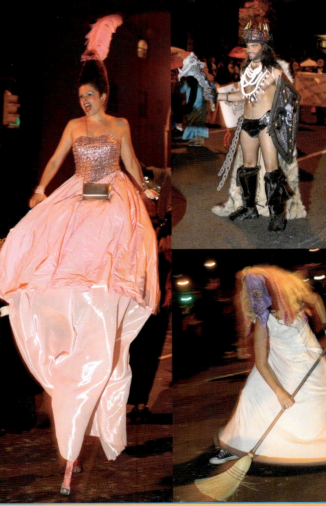

"Strip him, bathe him, and bring him to my tent", as Cher is reported to have said in her wilder days, when she liked someone. It's certainly possible that her double in "Lips" on Bank Street – the "ultimate in drag dining"according to their own advertising – was thinking of this when preparing her act (below); "Cindy Lauper" and "Whitney Houston" (below inset); George Segal's "Gay Liberation Monument" of two same-sex couples in Christopher Park, a tiny spot of green surrounded by a fence which is over 100 years old (right).

GAY PRIDE: NEW YORK OVER THE RAINBOW

Before 28 June 1969, gays and lesbians had to hide their sexuality; in most bars and cafés they were even less welcome than non-whites (even Greenwich Village, the last redoubt of the counter-culture, was more tolerant in terms of race). Of all people, it was the Mafia that improved things, buying the Stonewall Inn in Christopher Street and turning it into a gay and lesbian bar. Everything was done very discreetly, of course: a bouncer inspected new arrivals through a peephole, to buy alcohol you had to become a "club member", and no resistance was offered to the monthly police raids – at least not until 28 June 1969. During the raid, gays and lesbians took to the streets and openly resisted the police for the first time. They sang "We Shall Overcome", the anthem of the black civil rights movement, and found a new self-image: gay pride. The first gay and lesbian parade to Central Park took place in the summer of 1970, and "Christopher Street Day" is now celebrated round the world. The former Stonewall Inn at 51 Christopher Street, is now a listed monument. The parade is now a huge and exciting event and vistors come from around the world to take part.

THE HIGHLIGHTS:
DOWNTOWN MANHATTAN

The lovingly restored, listed buildings of the terraced houses in the Chelsea Historic District are particularly worth seeing (right). Below: the view across the district's roofs. Below, inset: the charming and alternative Chelsea Hotel: a legendary place to stay for artists.

INFO Rubin Museum of Art

A unique art collection from the Himalayas housed in an old department store, with paintings, sculptures, fabrics, and religious pictures from the 12th century onwards.

150 West 17th St; Tel (212) 620 50 00; Mon, Thurs 11.00–17.00, Wed 11.00–19.00, Fri 11.00–22.00, Sat, Sun 11.00–18.00.

In the middle of the 18th century, Chelsea was a farm belonging to a retired English marine officer, Thomas Clark, who had named it after the famous Royal Military Hospital in London. Nowadays this area, bounded by 14th and 34th Streets, and Sixth Avenue and the Hudson River, is one of the most attractive and desirable addresses in New York. Chelsea's historic charm, some of which is still apparent today, is due in part to the writer Clement Clarke Moore. The grandson of Thomas Clarke, he inherited the land and sold it on according to a largely not-for-profit, family-friendly building policy. The results were, and indeed still are, unmistakeable: the pretty terraces in Chelsea's Historic District have regularly been acclaimed as the nicest in New York. This is a very pleasant area for a leisurely stroll. Try guessing which stars live in which houses.

THE HIGHLIGHTS: DOWNTOWN MANHATTAN

TIP Jazz Record Center

Chelsea's cosy feel is only enhanced by the many little stores "just round the corner" (right), from antique stores to bookstores and hairdressers. The shiny chrome of the Empire Diner on 10th Avenue (below), apparently much beloved of Bette Davis, is an art deco gem.

Jazz experts have been augmenting larger or smaller private collections of the best sounds with vinyl, CDs, and specialist literature bought here. The selection of Blue Note classics is particularly excellent. *236 West 26th St, Room 804; Tel (212) 675 44 80; Mon–Sat 10.00–18.00.*

Chelsea also has a musical past: at the beginning of the 20th century, most of the music publishing houses in the USA had their offices on 28th Street, all working industriously on the "Great American Songbook". The *New York Herald* journalist Monroe Rosenfeld likened the tinkling of the practice pianos, which could be heard out on the street, to tin pans being knocked together, naming the street "Tin Pan Alley". The Chelsea Piers – four landing stages between 17th and 23rd Streets – stretch out into the Hudson River like fingers. On the 16 April 1912 an "unsinkable" ship – the *Titanic* – making its maiden voyage had been due to arrive, but it was never to reach its destination. Nowadays the spot is one of New York's largest sport and leisure complexes, with a health club, a day spa, training center for gymnastics, two basketball courts, a rock climbing wall, ice rinks, a golf club, and dance studios.

The best art galleries are to be found in Chelsea, which styles itself the "Gallery Capital of the World". The art guide in the *New York Times* weekend supplement and the Chelsea pages in the New York edition of *Time Out* magazine are a good place to look for more details. There are many artists working around the galleries, such as the critically acclaimed Charline von Heyl. She was born in Mainz in Germany in 1960, but has been based in New York for the last 10 years (below, her studio; right, a photo gallery on West 25th Street).

ART AND LIFE: THE (HE)ART OF NEW YORK

New York is a vibrant city, continually changing and always exciting, as can be witnessed in its art. New York affords its artists more freedom and offers more inspiration than most other cities in the world. However, "art needs patrons" as the Viennese composer Otto M. Zykan once said, and that was long before the latest financial crisis. It is little wonder, perhaps, that it was in New York that pop artists such as Andy Warhol blurred the lines between art and artisan, and former graffiti artists such as Keith Haring turned their hand to both art and merchandizing. Art in New York has to be affordable, and so many artists have had to adapt. This is especially true of female artists like Charline von Heyl, who was Jörg Immendorf's assistant and a member of Martin Kippenberger's circle; since 1996 she has been part of the New York scene, described by the *Village Voice* as revolutionary and exceptional in that she is firstly a woman, secondly a painter, thirdly an abstract painter, and fourthly over 35 years old. However, while she may have an atypical career, her paintings typically reflect New York in their vibrancy and dynamism. Visit some galleries and seek out the latest developments in New York's endlessly energetic and constantly evolving art scene during your stay.

THE HIGHLIGHTS: DOWNTOWN MANHATTAN

The bold and the beautiful now flock to clubs such as the PM lounge (below) in the Meatpacking District, whose dark streets (right) they would have avoided a few years ago. With luck you might even see Sarah Jessica Parker shopping or the model Claudia Jordan window-shopping (below right).

TIP Spice Market

Jean-Georges Vongerichten's restaurant is a world-renowned hotspot with an East Asian feel. Sophisticated and exotic dishes are served in an authentically Oriental setting. Book early!

403 West 13th St; Tel (212) 675 23 22; Sun–Thurs 12.00–00.00, Fri, Sat 12.00–1.00.

The Meatpacking District is on Manhattan's West Side and consists of around 20 blocks between Chelsea Market to the north and Gansevoort Street to the south. Traditionally this was where butchers worked, and so the district was named; in around 1900 there were as many as 250 abattoirs and warehouses in the district. In the 1980s drug dealers and prostitutes moved into the dark alleys and the area's reputation plummeted, a situation which only changed in the 1990s when designers, artists, and writers discovered the area. Famous fashion designers such as Diane von Fürsten-berg and Christian Louboutin, as well as "hip" firms such as Apple, opened branches here. They were followed by restaurants, such as Pastis and the Buddha Bar, as well as night clubs like Tenjune, One, and Cielo. Put the Meatpacking District on the itinerary for atmosphere and (window-)shopping.

THE HIGHLIGHTS:
DOWNTOWN MANHATTAN

TIP 230 Fifth

The Flatiron Building achieved its iconic status without any superlatives; it was never the highest building in the city. Its fascination lay in its external shape (below, at twilight). Right: Two photographs of the Flatiron taken during the construction phase.

The literal highpoint of New York clubbing is to be found above the 230 Fifth nightclub: enjoy champagne amongst the palm trees in the Rooftop Garden: a roof terrace on the 20th floor with a fantastic view of the skyscrapers.
230 Fifth Ave; Tel (212) 725 43 00; 16.00–4.00, daily.

The Flatiron Building was originally called the Fuller Building and caused a sensation even as it was being completed in 1902. The architects Daniel Burnham and John Wellborn Root had used the wedge-shaped parcel of land at the intersection of 23rd Street, Fifth Avenue, and Broadway to the full, erecting a similarly wedge-shaped skyscraper with a steel frame whose design was revolutionary for the time. Clad in light limestone and terracotta, and only 2 m (6.5 feet) wide at its front, the building resembled a giant smoothing iron and was known as the "Flatiron Building" ever after. Its shape, cause by Broadway's diagonal course through an otherwise grid-shaped city plan, has meant that this 86-m (282-foot) high building of 22 floors has remained one of the best-known and most photographed skyscrapers in New York, and one of its iconic landmarks.

MIDTOWN
MANHATTAN

New York's heartbeat beats loudest and fastest in central Manhattan, and you can really feel the pulse of time here. Gigantic towering skyscrapers such as the Empire State, the Chrysler Building, and the Trump Tower make deep canyons of the streets. Historic buildings like Grand Central Terminal and the New York Public Library are ever present reminders of the city's eventful history. Fifth Avenue revels in luxury, a mecca for chic shoppers and footsore tourists alike, and the bright neon lights of Times Square and Broadway sparkle with life even during the day in the "city that never sleeps".

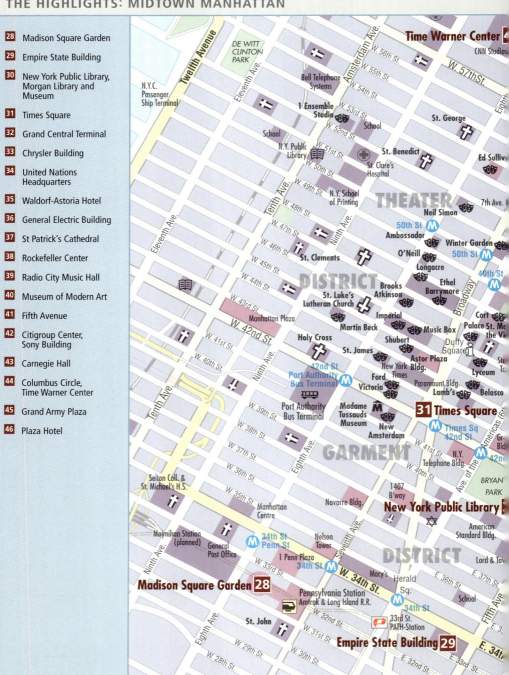

THE HIGHLIGHTS: MIDTOWN MANHATTAN

TIP Eleven Madison Park Restaurant

Playing Madison Square Garden one day is every rock and pop musician's dream; Elton John has fulfilled this no less than 60 times and holds the record (right). The beautiful Pennsylvania Station building was demolished to make way for the complex, to the outrage of architectural conservationists.

Enjoy the finest French cuisine served in a sparkling art deco setting with high ceilings; you will need to be wearing the right clothes to get into this elegant restaurant.

11 Madison Ave; Tel (212) 889 09 05; Lunch: Mon–Fri 12.00–14.00, Dinner: Mon–Thurs 17.30–21.30, Fri, Sat 17.30–22.00.

"The World's Most Famous Arena" is how Madison Square Garden now advertises itself. This multi-function venue, built on Pennsylvania Plaza in 1968, is home to the New York Rangers ice hockey team and the New York Knicks basketball players; even the world-famous "Ringling Brothers and Barnum and Bailey Circus" has made a guest appearance here. Among some of the most famous events to be held at Madison Square Garden were the legendary boxing matches between Joe Frazier and Muhammad Ali, the Concert for New York City following the September 11 attacks, George Harrison's epic Concert for Bangladesh, and John Lennon's last concert before his murder in 1980. The plain building complex contains a stadium seating 20,000 people and a function room seating 1,000. There are also exhibition rooms, restaurants, malls, and even a cinema on the site.

THE HIGHLIGHTS:
MIDTOWN MANHATTAN

The Empire State Building has been atmospherically illuminated almost every night since 1975; the lights are turned off only during the bird migration season, so the flocks do not fly into the side of the building. On public holidays the building is lit up in red, white, and blue, the colors of the Stars and Stripes.

The 86th floor has a spectacular view for 80 km (50 miles). There are binoculars for hire and an instructive audio guide. If you want to go higher still, you can buy a ticket for the view from the 102nd floor.
350 Fifth Ave/34th St; 8.00–14.00, daily; tickets online: www.esbnyc.com

Since the destruction of the twin towers of the World Trade Center, the Empire State Building is once again New York's tallest building, at 381 m (1,250 feet) in height or 449 m (1,473 feet) including the radio mast. As many as 34,000 workers, including many Mohawk Native North Americans, were employed at peak times during the skyscraper's construction. Designed by the architects Schreve, Lamb & Harmon, it was opened on 1 May 1931 when President Herbert Hoover pressed a button in the White House in Washington, turning on the lights in the building in Manhattan. Officially there are 102 floors, but only 85 of these contain office space that can be rented. On the 86th floor of the building there is a viewing platform and at the top is a dome originally intended as a mooring-place for airships; this plan had to be abandoned, however, due to the dangerous updraughts.

From the roof of a skyscraper you can see the "humus of old buildings on which this fantastic model world is constructed" (Henry Miller): the view from the Hotel Le Parker Meridien, looking towards the Upper West Side (near right); from the Empire State Building down into the canyons of the streets (far right). Below, clockwise: the Citicorps, Lipstick, Met Life, Crown, General Electric, and New York Life Insurance Company Buildings.

SKYLINE: SKY WALKERS AND SKYSCRAPERS

New York's skyscrapers are neither the oldest (those were built in Chicago in 1880) nor the tallest (nowadays these are all in Asia), but amongst them there are probably the most beautiful (the Chrysler Building) and certainly the most famous (the Empire State Building). Their construction became possible with the development of resilient types of steel and safe elevators. Their load-bearing structure invariably consisted of a frame, which was generally one of two types: either a "skeleton frame" or a cantilevered frame. In the first instance, a frame mostly constructed from stable steel columns and beams supports all the walls and floors, and in the second, the main support is a central concrete column, housing the elevator and utility shafts, from which the floors are suspended. The Empire State Building was one of the last steel-framed building projects to be built with riveted steel beams before more reliable welded joints replaced this technique. The construction of New York's skyscrapers is impossible to imagine without the the aid of the Mohawk iron workers – Native North American construction workers who were known as "skywalkers" for their agility and their ability to balance on vertiginous steel beams which were sometimes only 15 cm (6 inches) across.

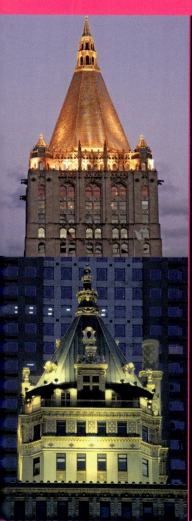

THE HIGHLIGHTS: MIDTOWN MANHATTAN

The main reading room (below) of the New York Public Library seats 500. Anyone living, working or studying in New York can apply for a reader's card. Amongst its treasures are manuscripts and incunabula once belonging to John Pierpont Morgan. Below inset: a Bible illustration.

INFO Bryant Park

The green hub of Midtown lies behind the Public Library. There is lots of entertainment on offer in Bryant Park, the "witchcraft" kiosks sell snacks, and the Open Air Film Festival is held from the middle of June to the middle of August.
59th–110th St/Fifth Ave; Festival info: Tel (212) 512 57 00.

New York Public Library is one of the world's greatest libraries, housing some 49.5 million documents, including more than 18 million books. It occupies a monumental Beaux Arts building located on Fifth Avenue which was designed by the architects Carrère & Hastings in 1911. Bryant Park, which adjoins the western end of the library, is also worth a visit. John Pierpont Morgan (1837–1913) was not only a successful financier, but also one of the greatest collectors of rare books and original manuscripts of his time. In 1906 he had the architectural practice of McKim, Mead & White design a magnificent building for the garden behind his house on Park Avenue and Madison Avenue, where his collection of treasures, including rare manuscripts, books and prints, can still be seen today.

THE HIGHLIGHTS: MIDTOWN MANHATTAN

The New York building code prescribes that all new builds on Times Square are to be fitted with brightly-lit advertising hoardings, to maintain its current appearance. Some landlords earn more from the advertising signs than they do in rent.

TIP Hard Rock Cafe

This gigantic café-restaurant on Times Square is an institution, with mementos on the walls of big stars and all kinds of rock music from Jimi Hendrix to Bruce Springsteen.

1501 Broadway; Tel (212) 343 33 55; Sun–Thurs 11.00–0.30, Fri, Sat 11.00– 1.30, Fri, Sat, Sun breakfast: 8.00–10.00.

You can hear New York's heartbeat on Times Square. The city fleshpots have become a sterile consumer arena *à la* Disneyworld. Mighty shopping malls and themed restaurants now set the tone in a place which once was notorious for its seamy side: the pickpockets, drug dealers, and hookers have moved on and the XXX-rated posters, porn stores, and peepshows are now all but forgotten. In 1900 the Square was still a rural area; it was then called Longacre Square and was a storage area of stables and barns. It was not named Times Square until 1904, in honor of the long-respected newspaper the *New York Times* which was building a giant office block there. Events from all over the world have flashed across the famous newscrawler on the façade since 1928; nowadays it is edited from Eighth Avenue. Each year crowds of people congregate in the square, the focus of the city's New Year celebrations.

A lifestyle is a terrible thing to waste.

Advertising is such an integral part of New York life that sometimes reality and fiction seem to undergo a curious fusion. The neon lights and huge billboards give the city an almost surreal air, as witnessed by the series of images by German photographer Erich Dapunt pictured below.

ADVERTISING IS – HALF? – THE BATTLE: ADVERTISE ME

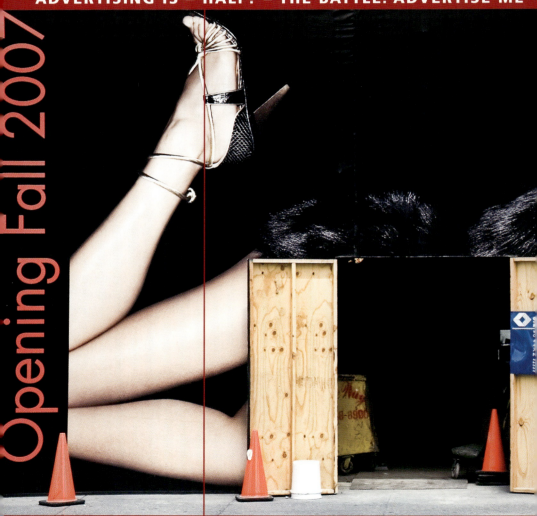

Opening Fall 2007

Strangely enough, it all began with a waste product. At the beginning of the 20th century a Frenchman, George Claude, was trying to extract pure oxygen from the air. So many noble gases were being captured in the process that he and his partner Jacques Fonseque tried to think of a commercial application, and the neon sign was born. The entrance to the Paris Opera was neon-lit in 1919 and the New World became so enthusiastic for this kind of advertising that today you could easily believe it was an American invention. It's little wonder that these giant illuminated screens have become such a common sight in Manhattan given that even in 1861 the city already had some 20 advertising agencies and that it is now home to the Omnicom Group Inc., one of the largest advertising concerns in the world. The group has 1,000 agencies in more than 100 countries, and produces campaigns costing billions of dollars. Advertising has long been part of New York's life blood, and giant neon billboards are not limited to Times Square. For 50 years the New York Festivals have awarded prizes for the best advertising campaigns. Advertising and New York are inextricably linked. Think Manhattan, think neon. It will be interesting to see how speedily online advertising develops in the city in the next few years.

"If you walked a block along Broadway and opened all the doors, you would discover a hundred different worlds" (Nick Cohn). Called the "Great White Way" for its many lights (also once the name of the Algonquin Native North American warpath), Broadway is a microcosm and the most famous street in the world. Although Broadway crosses the whole of Manhattan, the stretch in question is the so-called "Theater District" between 41st and 53rd Streets and between Sixth and Ninth Avenues.

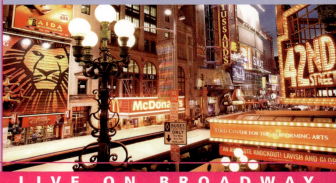

SHOWTIME: LIVE ON BROADWAY

JULIE HALSTON   HEATHER LEE   KATE BUDDEKE

If showbusiness has a birthplace, it is to be found in New York. Even in the initial waves of immigration, theater performances were considered a very welcome escape from the trials of the immigrants' daily lives. The theatre was almost a second home for them, not least as many of the plays were performed in their original languages. Initially there were only amateur performances; the first professional production was of Shakespeare's *Richard III* at the New Theater in Nassau Street in 1750. The 19th century was the great era of vaudeville shows, which combined drama, music, comedy, and circus acts. The start of the 20th century saw the dawning of the real age of Broadway, as more and more theaters moved into the area around Times Square, the center of New York night life at the time. The Empire Theater moved from Herald Square to Broadway in 1893, and from then until 1930 many more theaters opened, such as the New Lyceum. After a short crisis in the 1980s, spectacular musicals such as *Cats*, *The Phantom of the Opera*, and *The Lion King* continued the earlier successes. Nowadays there are about 40 large theaters active on Broadway and a multitude of smaller ones and catching a Broadway show during a trip to New York is a memorable experience.

TAMMY BLANCHARD

THE HIGHLIGHTS: MIDTOWN MANHATTAN

The main entrance on 42nd Street is topped with three sculptures representing Mercury, Hercules, and Minerva (below); the Grand Central Oyster Bar in the station is legendary (right); the majestic roof, fretted with golden fire (below right); inside the station (below, inset).

TIP Oyster Bar

You may need deep pockets to eat in Manhattan's legendary temple to seafood, but the quality of the oysters, fish, and seafood, and the atmosphere under the arched roof, makes the cost worth it.

89 East 42nd St/Vanderbilt Ave; Tel (212) 490 66 50; Mon–Fri 11.30–21.30, Sat 12.00–21.30.

Built in the Beaux Arts style, and decorated with baroque and Renaissance elements, Grand Central Terminal opened in its current form in 1913 after several years of construction. It remains the largest and busiest rail station in the world. A Roman triumphal arch provides an orientation point at the entrance on East 42nd Street. Corinthian columns support the giant arched windows and in the middle a bronze statue commemorates Cornelius Vanderbilt, the railroad magnate. Known as the "Commodore", Vanderbilt combined the dozen or so railroad services he owned into the "New York Central System" and it was his grandson who built the station. A roof decorated with stars arches over a flagstone floor in the magnificent main hall, which is 12 floors high and intended to resemble Roman baths. It is popularly referred to as Grand Central Station by New Yorkers and is used by more than 125,000 commuters daily, while millions of people visit or travel through it each year.

THE HIGHLIGHTS: MIDTOWN MANHATTAN

The Chrysler Building on Lexington Avenue is a masterpiece of art deco architecture, reminiscent of the bars of a car radiator. Every trick was used in the race to be the tallest building in the world: the crowning spire, some 55.5 m (182 feet) long, was manufactured in secret and only installed at the very end of the project.

INFO Helicopter tour

A helicopter trip over Manhattan is not exactly cheap (about $150 for 15 minutes) but is unforgettable: look the Statue of Liberty in the eye, slip between skyscrapers across Central Park and fly on to George Washington Bridge.
Tel (702) 648 58 73;
www.viator.com

Built in 1930, the Chrysler Building was not just intended as office space for the car firm of the same name, but also as a memorial for its owner, Walter P. Chrysler, whose career had begun on the shop floor of the Union Pacific Railroad. "His" skyscraper was to rise as steeply into the New York sky as his career had risen when he moved into the car industry, and it was also to be the most beautiful and the tallest building. Most New Yorkers would agree that his architect, William Van Alen, succeeded aesthetically, and in the matter of height Van Alen found himself in a running battle with his former partner, H. Craig Severance, who was planning the tallest building in the world for the Bank of Manhattan Company. At 319 m (1,046 feet), the Chrysler Building was the victor – but its victory only lasted a year, after which it was overtaken by the Empire State Building.

Among New York's art deco gems are the incomparable Chrysler Building (below, the entrance area and an elevator door in the interior) and the monumental Rockefeller Center, where works by 30 artists can be admired in the foyers and gardens and on the façades (right).

ART DECO: ART AND ARCHITECTURE

405

Art deco is a term describing one of the most imaginative, whimsical, and indeed artistic movements of the 1920s and 1930s. The name originally came from a crafts exhibition (the "Exposition Internationale des Arts Decoratifs et Industriels Modernes") which was held in Paris in 1925 and soon attracted interest across the Atlantic. Developed as a counter to what were regarded as the excesses of art nouveau, the style influenced every branch of art and design, as well as fashion, furniture, and architecture. The designs were typified by sleek, streamlined forms and geometric patterns, created by artists who plundered a rich diversity of historic sources for their work. This fusion of modernity and history produced opulent and lavish designs created from both valuable and new materials, such as marble, granite, steel, chrome, and bakelite, with bold tonal schemes. In the explosive boom years of early high-rise construction, art deco offered New York's architects all kinds of new possibilities: artistic decoration outshone mere functionality, streamlining the skyscrapers' block-like appearance and bringing a playful element to the city's otherwise rather sober building styles. Art deco buildings are today considered some of the city's most stunning constructions.

THE HIGHLIGHTS:
MIDTOWN MANHATTAN

The picture below shows the 166-m (544-foot) high UN Secretariat Building to the right of the Chrysler Building. The flags are arranged alphabetically according to the names of the member countries represented in the General Assembly (right).

TIP Delegates' Dining Room

Head chef Daryl Shembeck cooks for UN ambassadors, heads of state, and (if you book 24 hours in advance) visitors to the United Nations Building. There is a fantastic view of the East River to go with the lunch buffet.
1st Ave between 42nd and 48th Sts, 4th floor; Tel (212) 963 76 25; Mon–Fri 11.30–14.30.

The Headquarters of the United Nations (UN) is located on what is considered to be international soil on the banks of the East River, on the site of a former slaughterhouse district. John D. Rockefeller Jr bought the land and donated it to the United Nations. The USA provided an interest-free loan of $67 million, and between 1947 and 1950 the simple tower in which the UN Secretary-General's office is based was constructed to a design by an international committee of renowned architects that included Le Corbusier, Oscar Niemeyer, and Sven Markelius, to name but a few. Later the General Assembly Building, which is used as an auditorium, was added, along with the Conference Building and the Dag Hamarskjöld Library. The gardens and the lobby of the General Assembly Building are open to the public and the other buildings are accessible on guided tours.

THE HIGHLIGHTS: MIDTOWN MANHATTAN

When the Waldorf-Astoria was opened on 1 October 1931 it was the biggest hotel in the world. The lobby (below); cocktails in the Bull and Bear Bar (below right); there is a large clock in the lobby (right) which was originally made for the World's Fair in Chicago in 1893.

TIP Breakfast and Brunch

Each Sunday 14 chefs prepare over 100 dishes for the famous Waldorf-Astoria brunch, which is spectacularly presented on 12 themed tables. During the week a superb breakfast can also be found in the Peacock Alley hotel restaurant.
301 Park Ave; Tel (212) 872 12 75; Mon–Fri 7.00–10.30, Sun 10.00–14.15.

Designed by Schultze & Weaver, this legendary hotel on Park Avenue opened for business in 1931 and is one of the city's most fascinating art deco buildings. You can still play Cole Porter's piano, which stands in the lobby. Now officially marketed under the name "Waldorf=Astoria", with two dashes, it originally had one hyphen as it had been two hotels with a connecting corridor. "Meet me at The Hyphen" became a popular song and expression at the time, with the word "hyphen" used to refer to the hotel, but the name did not stick. William Waldorf Astor built the original 13-floor Waldorf Hotel in 1893, and four years later his cousin, John Jacob Astor, built the Astoria, which was four floors higher, right next door. Construction work on the Empire State Building meant that the building had to close. When the new hotel was built, the name was changed to Waldorf-Astoria.

The General Electric Building is particularly beautiful; its art deco crown (large image) suggests radio waves, after the broadcasting company which commissioned the building. The lobby (below right) has art deco features and the clock (right) boasts a GE monogram for "General Electric".

TIP Ava Lounge

There's a chic party scene on the 15th floor of this dream hotel. The outdoor lounge has a beach look, inside there are cool sofas. The view across Manhattan at night is amazing.

210 West 55th St/Broadway; Tel (212) 956 70 20; Sun–Tues 17.00–2.00, Wed 17.00–3.00, Fri–Sat 17.00–4.00.

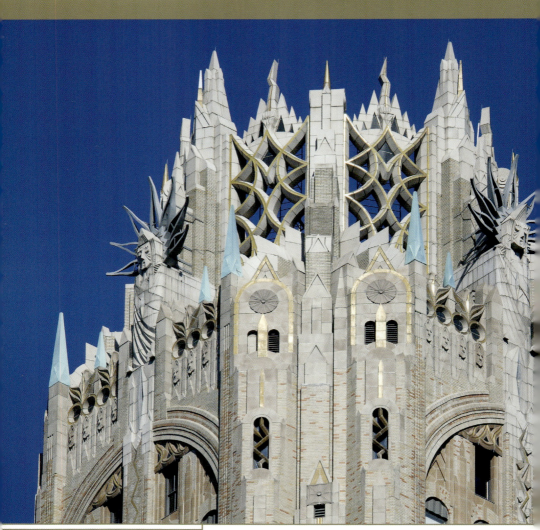

THE GENERAL ELECTRIC BUILDING 36

One of New York's most complete art deco creations is this strikingly beautiful building on Lexington Avenue, originally built to a design by the Cross & Cross practice for the broadcasters RCA ("Radio Corporation of America") and later the headquarters of the General Electric power company. The historic building – not to be confused with the GE (General Electric) Building which is in the Rockefeller Center – makes interesting architectural references to St Bartholomew's Church, which stands beside it. When the office block was constructed, the materials used – brick, aluminium, and stone – were chosen to harmonize with the church, while the rear elevation of the General Electric building was styled partly to form a backdrop to it. The architectural harmony is visually stunning and the building certainly ranks amongst New York's finest examples of art deco design.

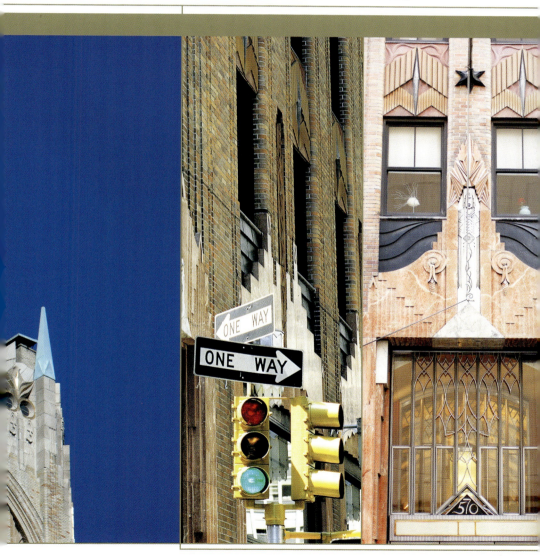

THE HIGHLIGHTS:
MIDTOWN MANHATTAN

INFO Organ masses

Symbols and symbology: Atlas may carry the world, but the clergy provide the spiritual leadership. The two 101-meter (331-foot) high towers were added only nine years after the completion of the church, which was constructed to last – the massive bronze doors alone weigh nine tons (below right).

The sacred architecture is all the more impressive when the two majestic Kilgen organs are played. Organ masses are held Monday to Friday at 8.00, 12.00, 12.30, 13.00 and 17.30, and on Sundays at 9.00, 10.15 (with a choir), 12.00, 16.00 and 17.30.
460 Madison Ave; Tel (212) 753 22 61.

In 1828 the Roman Catholic Church in New York bought a parcel of land outside the city limits for use as a cemetery. In 1850, after the undersoil had proved too stony for such a purpose, Archbishop John Hughes decided to commission a cathedral along European lines for this spot on Fifth Avenue. Eight years later, work on a neo-Gothic cathedral designed by the architect James Renwick started; it was completed in 1879. In 1910 it was dedicated to St Patrick, the patron saint of Ireland. A statue within its walls commemorates Elizabeth Ann Seton (1774–1821), the founder of the order of the Sisters of Charity and the first American citizen to be canonized. St Patrick's Cathedral, which can seat 2,500, is the see of the archbishop of New York. Over 5 million people per year come to the cathedral to visit or pray. If you have time, try to attend an organ mass here.

THE HIGHLIGHTS: MIDTOWN MANHATTAN

Paul Manship's statue of Prometheus (below middle) guards the Rockefeller Plaza (right), the heart of the Rockefeller Center. The central building of the Rockefeller complex is the GE (General Electric) Building (below left), whose main entrance is graced by Lee Lawrie's relief entitled Wisdom (below right).

INFO Rockefeller Art Tour

An art and architecture expert will guide you through the highlights and important works in the Rockefeller Center and tell you about John D. Rockefeller's ambitious vision.

30 Rockefeller Plaza; Tel (212) 664 71 74; Mon–Sat 11.00, 12.00, 13.00, 15.00, 16.00 and 17.00, Sun 11.00, 12.00, 13.00, 15.00 and 16.00.

This gigantic complex of skyscrapers located between 47th and 50th Streets was built in the 1930s for John D. Rockefeller Jr by a crack team of architects led by Raymond Hood. The complex has since been extended several times and houses offices, television studios, restaurants, and stores. Built in 1933 to a height of 260 m (853 feet), the GE (General Electric) Building is at the heart of the complex. From its viewing platform, "Top of the Rocks", there is a magnificent view of the city's skyline. The GE Building is also home to the broadcaster NBC, whose legendary Today show – the oldest factual television show, first screened on 14 January 1952 – is broadcast every morning from 7.00 till 9.00 from a glass studio in the GE Building. Less well-known but equally fascinating is the underground concourse, home to retail stores, fast food outlets and other venues. It's New York's largest underground city.

Like father, like son: the company founder's sole male heir, John Davison Rockefeller Jr (1874–1960), also showed entrepreneurial spirit. Disregarding the global financial crisis of the 1930s he built the Rockefeller Center (below, the Rockefeller Plaza), thereby assuring 40,000 people of wages and food. He can be seen as a "construction worker" on the site of the Rockefeller Center in 1939 (near right), with his father in 1915 (far right) and at the opening of Radio City Music Hall 1932 (below left).

ROCKEFELLER: OIL MAGNATE AND PHILANTHROPIST

Descended from a family that emigrated from a small German hamlet to the New World in the 18th century, John Davison Rockefeller Sr (1839–1937) worked himself up from his humble beginnings to be head of an oil dynasty whose influence can still be felt to this day. His father, William, had traveled door to door as a quack doctor to feed his family of eight, and at 16 John began an apprenticeship with a haulage company where he was soon to be found helping to keep the books in order. At the age of 19 he moved into the oil business, founding the "Standard Oil Company" (a direct forerunner of today's Exxon Mobil Corporation) in 1870 and the "Standard Oil Trust" in 1882. Soon they controlled more than ninety percent of the refinery capacity of the entire United States. Determined to secure his monopoly with every means at his disposal, Rockefeller's occasionally rough-shod business tactics provoked legislation in 1890 (the Sherman Antitrust Act) which in 1911 was eventually to see his business broken up into separate companies. To improve his somewhat dubious reputation, Rockefeller endowed many charitable trusts, such as the internationally famous and New York-based Rockefeller Foundation, to which he donated more than $500 million.

THE HIGHLIGHTS: MIDTOWN MANHATTAN

INFO Backstage Tour

Just before the millennium, Radio City Music Hall, which is a listed national monument, underwent the most extensive renovation in its history: over $70 million were spent in providing it with the most up-to-date technology whilst retaining its historic ambience.

The tour takes you behind the scenes into a laboriously renovated 1930s world, giving away the secrets of the great stage and other interesting information; you even get to meet one of the world-famous Rockettes from the ballet company.
1260 Ave of the Americas; Tel (212) 307 71 71; Mon–Sun 11.00–15.00

Radio City Music Hall, which is also part of the Rockefeller Center, has gone down in history as the "showplace of the nation". Designed by the architect Edward Durell for the impresario Samuel "Roxy" Rothafel, who had found fame and fortune during the silent film era, the entertainment complex was opened on 27 December 1932 and has since received more than 300 million visitors from around the world. Originally intended as a variety hall, the 6,200-seat auditorium was soon refurbished as a cinema that could also host stage productions. The dance troupe, the Rockettes, became legendary, and in various formations also took part in the traditional annual Christmas shows that began in 1933. Nowadays Radio City Music Hall is best known as a live venue for rock and pop stars. The two remaining Beatles, Paul McCartney and Ringo Starr, performed here at a charity concert on April 4, 2009.

THE HIGHLIGHTS: MIDTOWN MANHATTAN

For Yoshio Taniguchi, the architect of the "new" MoMA (below and right), the museum embodies a "microcosm of Manhattan": "The sculpture garden represents Central Park, around which is grouped a city comprising the most varied buildings, used for the widest range of purposes".

TIP The Modern

The MoMa restaurant won a prize for its design, and the chef, Gabriel Kreuther, was awarded a Michelin star for his cooking. The dining room offers French-American cuisine and a view of the sculpture garden.
Tel (212) 333 12 20; Mon–Fri 12.00–14.00, Mon–Thurs 17.30–22.30, Fri, Sat 17.30–23.30.

All it took was three friends. In a clear case of girl power, the Museum of Modern Art (MoMA) was founded in 1929 by Mary Quinn Sullivan, Abby Aldrich Rockefeller, and Lillie P. Bliss, although the museum's official history still doggedly refers to the first two as Mrs Cornelius J. Sullivan and Mrs John D. Rockefeller, Jr – only Lillie, who never married, is credited under her own first name. Known as "the Ladies", "the daring ladies", or "the adamantine ladies", all three were proven patrons of the arts (and artists) and decided to find a common home for their passion and for their collec-tions. The museum opened to the pub-lic on November 7, 1929, and the ladies enlisted art historian Alfred H. Barr as its director. The museum was to move location several times before it finally ended up at its current site, built to a design by the architects Philip Goodwin and Edward Durell in 1939.

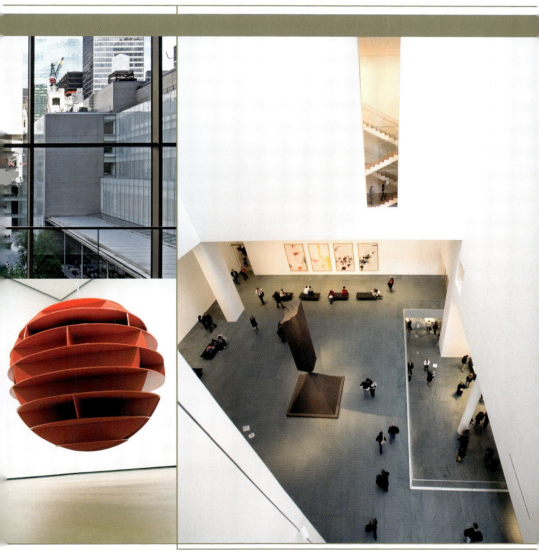

THE HIGHLIGHTS:
MIDTOWN MANHATTAN

Right from the start the MoMA was laid out as "the greatest museum of modern art in the world" (Alfred H. Barr Jr). The collection includes industrial design (below), Warhol's pop art classic *Campbell Soup* (1962, above), and Monet's Impressionist masterpiece *Waterlilies* (*c.* 1920, below, inset).

INFO MoMA Design Store

Shop for designer objects, furnishings, accessories, lamps, and much much more in a real treasure trove of beautiful designs, including pieces derived from the museum's own collections.
44 West 53rd St; Tel (212) 767 10 50; Sat–Thurs 9.30–18.30, Fri 9.30–21.00.

The Leonard Dobbs

The architect charged with the refurbishment and extension of the museum, Yoshio Taniguchi, supposedly said that for a good fee he would provide good architecture, and for a really good fee he would make the architecture disappear; on the evidence of the "new" MoMA at its historic site on 53rd Street in Midtown Manhattan, he would seem to be as good as his word. As the writer John Updike has said of the renovations, which doubled the floor space available for exhibitions and other museum functions to about 58,000 sq. m (624,000 square feet), the building seems "in no way intrusive, and in no way cheap". During the construction work, from 2002 to 2004 (the new Cullman Building did not open its doors until 2006), the MoMA was relocated to Long Island City in the furthest northern reaches of Queens, and some of the museum's holdings are still stored there.

THE HIGHLIGHTS:
MIDTOWN MANHATTAN

You'll find upmarket goods on Fifth Avenue, which runs north-south through Manhattan (below): the best addresses lie between 48th and 59th Streets. Particular pomp and luxury: Trump Tower, built for the property tycoon, Donald Trump (right and below right).

INFO The Forbes Galleries

Malcolm Forbes's collection has resulted in a varied museum, where you can see an exquisite toy collection, a host of tin soldiers, Fabergé eggs, an armada of toy ships, and changing special exhibitions.
62 Fifth Ave/12th St; Tel (212) 206 55 48; Tues, Wed, Fri, Sat 10.00–16.00.

Dividing Manhattan's Streets into East and West, Fifth Avenue begins at Washington Square in Greenwich Village, crosses Midtown, passes Central Park, and runs along the Upper East Side to the Harlem River. In the second half of the 19th century, well-off families – the Astors, Forbes, Fricks, Rocke-fellers, Vanderbilts, and others – were seeking to escape cramped southern Manhattan. They built their villas along Fifth Avenue's first few miles, bringing it the agreeable nickname of "Million-aires' Row". By the beginning of the 20th century more and more busi-nesses were moving in, causing the rich – who today mostly live around Central Park – to move further uptown. There are now flagship stores belonging to famous brands, such as Armani, Cartier, Chanel, Escada, Prada, Tiffany, and Ver-sace, to draw the crowds. It doesn't get much better than this for those who enjoy a little retail therapy.

Sisley's striking store windows stick out and draw you in (below), Macy's (below right) on Fifth Avenue. You'll mind exciting entertainment stores on Union Square (right). Faced with such a wide choice, it's no wonder so many visitors to New York succumb to shopping fever, but it's also worth bearing in mind that goods of a value of no more than 430 Euros can be imported tax free into the European Union.

ALL THAT MONEY CAN BUY: SHOPPING IN NEW YORK

New York is shopping heaven. Numerous stores and outlets offer everything the heart could desire, from sinfully expensive designer clothes to cheap jeans. Macy's, for example, the biggest department store in the world, is split between two buildings and has a sales floor of no less than 200,000 sq. m (2.1 million square feet), spread over ten floors. Bloomingdale's sells smart designer fashion at — sometimes — affordable prices, while Lord & Taylor's in the Empire State Building has classic upmarket styles. Diamond Row, between 40th and 50th Streets, is so called for the glittering jewels on display. Amongst the most popular stores on Fifth Avenue are Tiffany & Co., Prada, and Versace, and FAO Schwarz, toy heaven, is not just for children. Antiques, art, and fashion are to be found in the "scene" districts of SoHo and TriBeCa, and Greenwich Village is famous for its weird and alternative stores, which are ideal for books, records, CDs, and esoteric odds and ends; there are also specialist shops for gays and lesbians. Discount stores have congregated on Herald Square, in the shadow of Macy's, and you can buy reasonably priced fashion, bags, and shoes on Historic Orchard Street in the East Village. You really can shop till you drop; there is something new round every corner.

THE HIGHLIGHTS:
MIDTOWN MANHATTAN

Clad in aluminium and 279 m (915 feet) high, the Citigroup Center dominates the Midtown Manhattan skyline like a white giant (below, seen from Queens). The Sony Building (right) is also called "Chippendale", because the block's gable end is reminiscent of furniture of that name.

This four-floor museum boasts a uniquely exciting, informative, and entertaining array of the most up-to-date technologies, explained in highly creative ways with a strong interactive element.
550 Madison Ave/56th St; Tel (212) 833 81 00; Tues–Sat 10.00–17.00, Sun 12.00–17.00.

The Citigroup Center (formerly Citicorp Center) was designed by Hugh Stubbins & Associates – now called KlingStubbins – and built in 1977 on four nine-floor stilts. Interestingly, the stilts were not placed at the corners of the rectangular building, but were instead situated in the middle of each side. This was because trustees of St Peter's Church would only sell part of their land and property rights on the sole condition that they would be allowed to construct a new church "under" the skyscraper, This now stands beneath the extended north-west corner of the Citigroup Center. The "Sony Building" located on Madison Avenue was built in 1984 for the communications company AT&T, and is now called the Sony Building after a change of ownership. Designed by Philip Johnson, his unusual and individual design for the "world's first post-modern skyscraper" continues to cause controversy and split opinion.

THE HIGHLIGHTS: MIDTOWN MANHATTAN

Carnegie Hall was the home of the New York Philharmonic for many years: below, the entrance lobby; right, the Isaac Stern Auditorium. When the Philharmonic moved to the Lincoln Center, the hall was faced with demolition, eliciting world-wide protests, which fortunately saved the venue.

INFO Backstage Tour

The guided tour through the concert hall gives an impression of life in the limelight and is very informative about the musical legends who have performed here.

57th St/Seventh Ave; Tel (212) 903 97 65; Mon–Fri 11.30, 14.00 and 15.00, Sat 11.30 and 12.30, Sun 12.30.

Perhaps it was a good omen that the architect William B. Tuthill not only had a passion for music, but also played the cello, since Carnegie Hall, built to his design between 1890 and 1891 for the millionaire steel magnate Andrew Carnegie, remains one of the world's most renowned concert halls. As well as its magnificent architecture, it is celebrated for its fantastic acoustics, which were first acclaimed in May 1891, when Carnegie Hall was opened with a five-day festival featuring, amongst others, the Russian composer Peter Tchaikovsky as a guest conductor. Since then it has been the forum for important jazz events, historic lectures, noted educational forums, as well as many concerts. Carnegie Hall actually consists of three concert halls, namely the Isaac Stern Auditorium (seating 2,800), the Joan and Sanford I. Weill Recital Hall (seating 268), and the Judy and Arthur Zankel Hall (seating 599).

THE HIGHLIGHTS:
MIDTOWN MANHATTAN

TIP Shopping Mall

However much the traffic rumbles around him, Columbus remains unmoved (below), and no wonder – he's made of marble (and was a gift to the city from the Italian-American community). The square is dominated by the 229-m (751-foot) high twin towers of the Time Warner Center.

All kinds of wares bring consumers to the shopping mall on the lower floors of the Time Warner Center. Go up the escalator to find a sensational view over Columbus Circle and Central Park, extending right across to the Upper East Side.
10 Columbus Circle; Tel (212) 823 63 00.

COLUMBUS CIRCLE, TIME WARNER CENTER 44

Midtown's north-western tip is formed by Columbus Circle, the gateway to the Upper West Side. In the middle of the roundabout there is a statue of Columbus by Gaetano Russo, which was erected in 1892 to commemorate the 400th anniversary of the "discovery" of America. The statue is also the reference point for the measurement of all distances to and from New York. It is a major landmark and point of attraction in the city. It is also a good place to arrange to meet people. The angular glass edifice of the Time Warner Center, built in 2004 to a design by the architect David Childs, continues the traditions of the twin towers built on the west side of Central Park. Situated inside the complex, which cost $1.8 billion, are the headquarters of Time Warner Inc., CNN's studios, luxury apartments, a Mandarin Oriental Hotel, as well as several restaurants, stores, and a wholefood market.

THE HIGHLIGHTS:
MIDTOWN MANHATTAN

The harmonious setting of the Grand Army Plaza has even inspired artists (below). A night in the Plaza Hotel (which would be as pleasant as it is expensive) is not in everyone's budget, but even the less well-off can treat themselves to an afternoon cup of tea in the Palm Court (below right).

TIP Plaza Champagne Bar

This successor to the historic 1907 Plaza Champagne Bar has a pleasant view of Fifth Avenue, and you can select from the finest wines and champagnes with which to wash down your caviar.
Fifth Ave/Central Park South; Tel (212) 759 30 00; Sun–Tues 6.00–24.00, Fri–Sat 6.00–1.00.

Fifth Avenue comes to a worthy end with Grand Army Plaza by Central Park, at whose south-east entrance horse-drawn buggies begin their pleasure trips. Built in 1915, the Pulitzer fountain in the middle commemorates the famous publisher, and the plaza's north-ern half boasts an equestrian statue of William Tecumseh Sherman, the Civil War General. Built by Henry J. Harden-berg in 1907 in the style of a French chateau, the legendary Plaza hotel was once advertised with the slogan "Noth-ing boring ever happens at the Plaza". Some $400 million was spent on restorations between 2005 and 2007, and the slogan still applies. Today the site is no longer "just" a hotel (some of the area is now turned over to private homes, with stores, bars, and restau-rants that are open to the public).

CENTRAL PARK,
UPPER EAST SIDE,
EAST HARLEM

North of 59th Street, Central Park divides Manhattan into the Upper East Side and the Upper West Side. The park is a green oasis in the centre of the urban mass, and people who live right on it can count their blessings: a view that looks out over some form of green space rather than other buildings is these days virtually unaffordable in New York. Madonna's own townhouse located on the Upper East Side is said to have changed hands for a cool $40 million. Running along the eastern edge of Central Park, Fifth Avenue turns into "Museum Mile" with some of the best museums in the city.

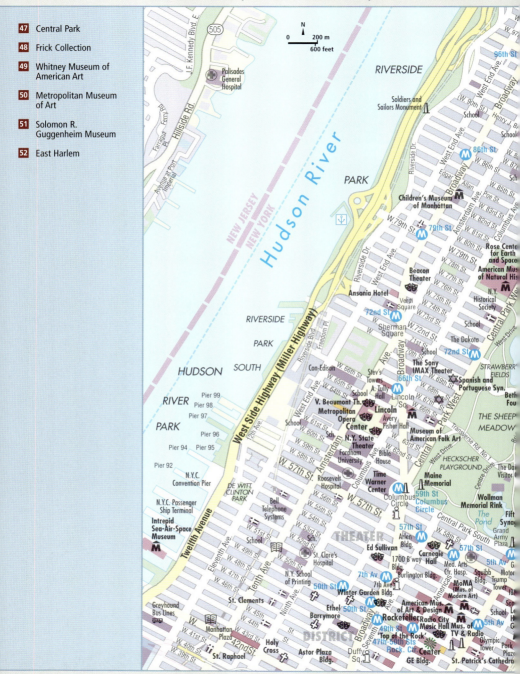

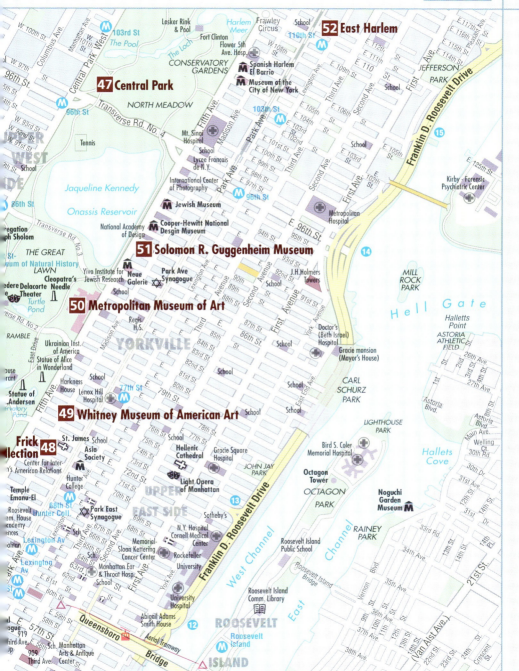

47 Central Park

52 East Harlem

51 Solomon R. Guggenheim Museum

50 Metropolitan Museum of Art

49 Whitney Museum of American Art

48 Frick Collection

Designed by man rather than nature, the result is nonetheless quite beautiful (below, the cast iron Bow Bridge). On Sundays and during the summer months the park is turned into a vast stage for New Yorkers (right and below, inset), who come to exercise, socialize, or just relax and watch the rest of the city go by.

INFO Zoo

Just a few paces from Fifth Avenue, this spot is a paradise on earth – Ida and Gus, the two polar bears, are the public's favourites. Tropical animals can be found in the rainforest pavilion, and sea lions and pandas in the temperate zone.
64th St/Fifth Ave; Tel (212) 439 65 00; 10.00–17.00, daily.

Construction began on Central Park in north Manhattan in 1858, realizing a lifelong dream for American landscape architect Frederick Law Olmsted and his partner, British-born Calvert Vaux. Together they created a "green lung" in the ever-expanding city, extending from 59th to 110th Street and covering a vast 340 ha. (1,016 acres), representing 6 percent of Manhattan's total area. It became the second-largest park in the city after Jamaica Bay Park in Queens (1,150 ha. 3,440 acres). Free open-air concerts are held here in the summer. Information on these Summer Stage performances and other events is at the Visitors' Center, located in a neo-Gothic building designed by Olmsted and Vaux called The Dairy. The park also contains a zoo, a large lake called The Reservoir (between 71st and 78th streets), where row boats can be hired, and Belvedere Castle, from where there are panoramic views over the park.

Jewish influence on the life of the city is unmistakeable – public schools, for example, are closed on Jewish as well as Christian holidays. Day-to-day Jewish life is now no longer just the preserve of orthodox hardliners who seek to retain the traditions of the *schtetl* in their appearance and lifestyle, but also of largely secularized Jews, who are identifiable only because they wear a *kippah* on festive occasions. The Museum of Jewish Heritage remembers the Holocaust (right).

KOSHER IS HIP: NEW YORK AND THE JEWISH AVANT-GARDE

New York has the largest Jewish community in the world. Around a million Jews live here – more even than in Jerusalem. Descendants of the Jews expelled from Spain in 1492, the first 23 refugees of Sephardic origin reached the New World in 1654, landing their ship at what was to become Battery Park, where a memorial to "The Jewish Plymouth Rock" stands to this day. German, Eastern European, Russian, and Ukrainian Jews followed in several waves of immigration throughout the 19th and 20th centuries. Their descendants have long since become an intrinsic part of American society, allowing the young Jewish avant-garde the freedom to move on from inherited stereotypes and traditions.

Founded in 2002, the magazine "Heeb" (once an anti-Semitic term of abuse, from "Hebe", an abbreviation of "Hebrew") has become the organ of this new consciousness, expressing its sense of irony with t-shirts reading "Jews Kick Ass". Film director Steven Spielberg was one of its early backers. Aimed at a primarily young readership, its approach is satiric and no-holds-barred. Hip hop artists such as Aviad Cohen ("the artist formerly known as 50 shekels"), and filmmakers like Jonathan Kesselman, the "godfather of Jewxploitation", whose The Hebrew Hammer depicts the first Jewish action hero fighting evil (in this case, Father Christmas' son), are some of the new protagonists of Jewish pop culture.

THE HIGHLIGHTS: CENTRAL PARK, UPPER EAST SIDE, EAST HARLEM

Henry Clay Frick even had an organ built in the stairwell of his imposing villa (below). Among the works of art are pieces by Jean-Honoré Fragonard (right), Jan Vermeer and Georges de La Tour (below, inset left and right), and James Abbott McNeill Whistler (below right). The collection also holds several special temporary exhibitions a year.

INFO Sketching in the Galleries

An exceptional ruling applies to visitors to the Frick Collection: sketching is allowed in the exhibition rooms, although only with pencil or charcoal on pads up to A3 size.

1 East 70th St; Tel (212) 288 07 00; Tues–Sat 10.00–18.00, Sun 11.00–17.00.

In 1905, Pittsburgh steel magnate Henry Clay Frick (1849–1919) and his wife moved to New York to live out their twilight years. An avid art collector, for $5 million Frick built an imposing French neo-classical townhouse on the corner of Fifth Avenue and 70th Street to a design by Carrère & Hastings; it was to become a very worthy setting for his great collection. Frick later bequeathed the house, which covers a full city block, and its valuable contents to the nation and in 1935, after the death of his widow, Adelaide Frick, it was turned into a museum that is now one of the best small art museums in the country. The museum houses a collection of Old Masters, as well as French furniture, enamelwork from Limoges, Italian Renaissance bronzes, and oriental carpets. Highlights include Holbein the Younger's beautiful *Portrait of Sir Thomas More* and *The Polish Rider* by Rembrandt.

THE HIGHLIGHTS: CENTRAL PARK, UPPER EAST SIDE, EAST HARLEM

The Whitney Museum (right) displays contemporary American art in individual exhibitions: shown here are works by Mark Handforth (below); Sol LeWitt (below right, above and middle); and Daniel Joseph Martinez (below right, bottom) as part of the "Whitney Biennale of American Art".

INFO Whitney After Hours

On Friday evenings between 18.00 and 21.00 the museum hosts an innovative schedule of performance art, avant-garde exhibitions, live performances, and art events where visitors pay what they can afford to attend.
945 Madison Ave/75th St; Tel (212) 570 36 00; Tues–Thurs, Sat, Sun 11.00–18.00, Fri 13.00–21.00.

In 1918, Gertrude Vanderbilt Whitney (1875–1942), a respected sculptor in her own right, opened an art gallery in her studio in Greenwich Village. She concentrated on American contemporary art and by the end of the 1920s had amassed a collection of about 700 canvases and sculptures, which she intended to donate to the Metropolitan Museum of Art. Her gift was refused, however, because the museum was more interested in European art, and so in 1931 she founded the Whitney Museum of American Art, which is now considered one of the most significant collections of 20th- and 21st-century American art. All the big names – including Edward Hopper, Jasper Johns, Roy Lichtenstein, and Andy Warhol – are represented here. Today the Whitney makes a point of exhibiting living artists, and its annual and bi-annual exhibitions are known for displaying the work of lesser known artists.

THE HIGHLIGHTS: CENTRAL PARK, UPPER EAST SIDE, EAST HARLEM

The museum welcomes more than five million visitors a year from all over the world. Below, *House III* by native New Yorker Roy Lichtenstein on the roof terrace; below right, a statue by Randolph Rogers depicting the blind flower girl of Pompeii; right, the famous Egyptian Collection with the Temple of Dendur.

INFO Concerts & Lectures

The Met offers a superb schedule of classical and modern concerts, lectures, and film showings throughout the year, which are listed by month at www.metmuseum.org

1000 Fifth Ave/82nd St; Tel (212) 570 39 49; Tues–Thurs 9.30–17.30, Fri, Sat 9.30–21.00, Sun 9.30–17.30.

Besides the British Museum in London, the Louvre in Paris, and the Hermitage in St Petersburg, the Metropolitan Museum of Modern Art, known as the "Met" for short, is one of the greatest art museums in the world. Designed by Calvert Vaux and Jacob Wrey Mould, and expanded several times since its construction in 1870, it houses more than two million exhibits from five millennia of art history. It was founded by wealthy New Yorkers and leading artists of the day who wanted to make art accessible to the people. First-time visitors are often overwhelmed by the museum's sheer scope – where else can you see an Egyptian temple, a Rembrandt self-portrait, and Frank Lloyd Wright's studio under the same roof? And talking of roofs: along with all its other highlights the Met has a sculpture garden on its roof terrace, with a fantastic view of Central Park and the Manhattan skyline.

THE HIGHLIGHTS: CENTRAL PARK, UPPER EAST SIDE, EAST HARLEM

Impressive, whether seen from inside or outside, Frank Lloyd Wright's unconventional museum building is home to the great collection of abstract art amassed by the millionaire Solomon R. Guggenheim. The ramp, angled at 5 degrees, completes five revolutions of the 28.5-m (93-foot) high rotunda.

INFO Free Public Tours

Free tours are offered once a week (on either a Monday or a Friday), illustrating various aspects of the museum, such as Frank Lloyd Wright's much-discussed design.

1071 Fifth Ave/89th St; Tel (212) 423 36 18; Fri, Sun–Wed 10.00–17.45, Sat 10.00–19.45.

Neither Frank Lloyd Wright, the architect who designed the museum's original building (it was his last major work), nor Solomon R. Guggenheim, the coal and steel industrialist who commissioned it, lived to see this iconic building's inauguration in 1959. They were thus spared the initially scathing criticism the museum attracted: John Canaday, the art critic of the *New York Times*, is recorded as saying: "The Solomon R. Guggenheim Museum is a war between architecture and painting in which both come out badly maimed". Resembling an inverted snail shell from the outside, the building took 16 years to complete. Lit from above by a glass skylight, a central spiral ramp runs through the interior from the main level to the top of the building. Internationally renowned, the Guggenheim houses a collection of Impressionist, Post Impressionist, and contemporary art.

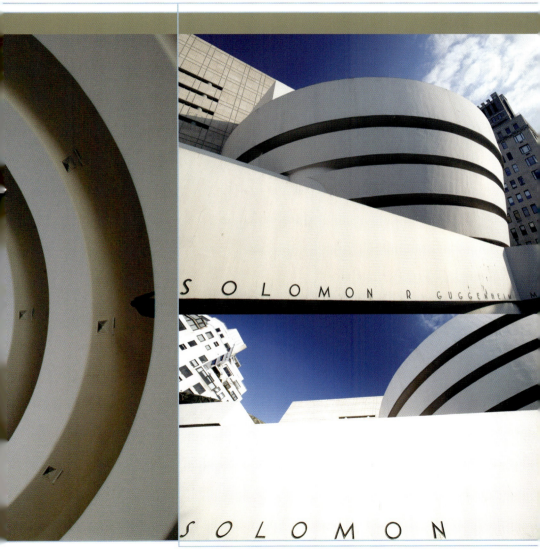

THE HIGHLIGHTS: CENTRAL PARK, UPPER EAST SIDE, EAST HARLEM

Day-to-day East Harlem: dreams of Puerto Rico at the market (below), children playing with a fire hydrant (below, right) and enjoying a parade (right). Founded by a group of socially-minded artists and civic leaders, the Museo del Barrio (below, inset) is not only a museum, it has also become a hip Latino cultural venue.

TIP Rao's Restaurant

The jukebox, the quirky décor, the warm welcome, and the Neapolitan cooking have made this Spanish Harlem classic one of the most desirable restaurants for miles around. Early booking is essential.

455 East 114th St; Tel (212) 722 67 09; Mon–Fri, evenings only.

Known as "Spanish Harlem" or simply "El Barrio" (Spanish for "district"), this famous area east of Fifth Avenue between 96th and 125th Streets is home to the largest Latino community in New York, consisting largely of Puerto Ricans, but also with many Dominicans, Cubans, and Mexicans. In the 1960s and 1970s, East Harlem was one of the poorest parts of New York and even today the difference between this part of the city and the smart Upper East Side is unmistakable. Conditions have improved markedly, nonetheless, and Latinos are rightly proud of their neighborhood which has brought forth musicians such as Ray Barretto, Eddie Palmieri, and Tito Puente. Mount Sinai Hospital is considered one of the finest in the United States, Latino art and culture is on display at the Museo del Barrio, and no street parades are more exuberant than the ones held here.

UPPER WEST SIDE, MORNINGSIDE HEIGHTS, HARLEM, THE NORTH

Much like its counterpart on the East Side, a district principally inhabited by well-off New Yorkers, the Upper West Side is an upscale area, bounded by Central Park, the Hudson River, 59th, and 125th Streets. The adjacent district of Morningside Heights is home to churches, colleges, and institutions such as The Jewish Seminary of America, Columbia University (known as the "Acropolis of the academic world"), and the still unfinished Cathedral of Saint John the Divine. Named after Haarlem in Holland, and originally a Dutch settlement, Harlem is today a bastion of black consciousness and it underwent some rapid gentrification in the 1990s.

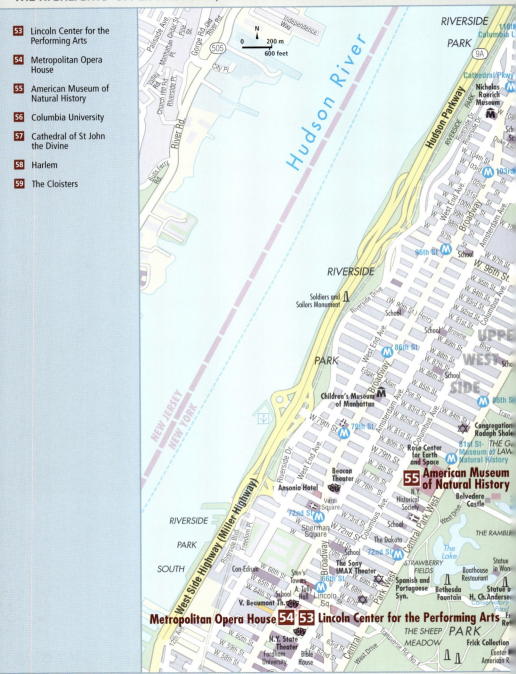

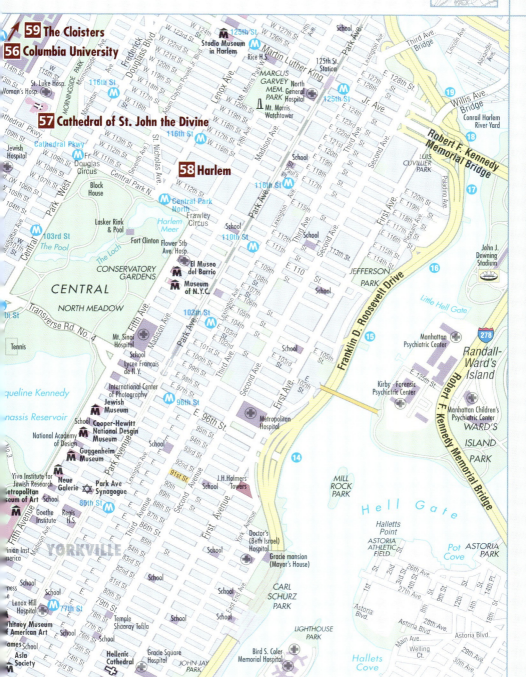

59 The Cloisters
56 Columbia University

Studio Museum in Harlem

Martin Luther King

57 Cathedral of St. John the Divine

58 Harlem

El Museo del Barrio

Museum of N.Y.C.

CENTRAL

NORTH MEADOW

CONSERVATORY GARDENS

Jacqueline Kennedy Onassis Reservoir

International Center of Photography
Jewish Museum

Cooper-Hewitt National Desgin Museum

National Academy of Design

Guggenheim Museum

Yivo Institute for Jewish Research
Neue Galerie
Park Ave Synagogue

Metropolitan Museum of Art

Goethe Institute
Regis H.S.

YORKVILLE

Lenox Hill Hospital

Whitney Museum of American Art

Asia Society

Temple Shaaray Tefila

Hellenic Cathedral

Gracie Square Hospital

JOHN JAY PARK

Robert F. Kennedy Memorial Bridge

Conrail Harlem River Yard

LUIS CUVILLER PARK

Paladino Ave

John J. Downing Stadium

JEFFERSON PARK

Little Hell Gate

Manhattan Psychiatric Center

Randall-Ward's Island

Kirby - Forensic Psychiatric Center

Manhattan Children's Psychiatric Center
WARD'S ISLAND PARK

MILL ROCK PARK

Hell Gate

Halletts Point
ASTORIA ATHLETIC FIELD

Pot Cove
ASTORIA PARK

CARL SCHURZ PARK

Gracie mansion (Mayor's House)

Doctor's (Beth Israel) Hospital

Astoria Blvd.

LIGHTHOUSE PARK

Bird S. Coler Memorial Hospital

Welling Ct.

Hallets Cove

Willis Ave. Bridge

Robert F. Kennedy Memorial Bridge

THE HIGHLIGHTS: UPPER WEST SIDE, MORNINGSIDE HEIGHTS, HARLEM, THE NORTH

The Metropolitan Opera House is located in the middle of the cultural center (below), next to the David H. Koch Theater and the Avery Fisher Hall, home of the New York Philharmonic (left and right respectively in the image). Above: Leonard Bernstein conducted the Met's inaugural concert in 1959.

INFO Tour of Jazz

Take a guided tour behind the scenes of the great jazz and swing events held in the Lincoln Center, including the Frederick P. Rose Hall and the House of Swing, with amazing views of both Central Park and the Manhattan Skyline.
70 Lincoln Center Plaza; Information line Tel (212) 875 53 50.

Situated on Columbus and Amsterdam Avenues between 62nd and 66th Streets, The Lincoln Center for the Performing Arts is a cultural complex housing the Metropolitan Opera, the New York City Ballet, and the New York Philharmonic Orchestra. Planned on the initiative of a group of civic leaders, including John D. Rockefeller III, most of the complex was built in the 1960s under the direction of the architect Wallace K. Harrison. Rockefeller was a major fund raiser and made a significant contribution from his own funds. The chosen site was a former slum area called "San Juan Hill"; it had been the scene of fights between rival street gangs that inspired Leonard Bernstein to write the musical *West Side Story*, filmed in 1961. The complex forms part of the comprehensive series of renovations that was designed to improve conditions in this otherwise infamous part of the Upper West Side.

THE HIGHLIGHTS: UPPER WEST SIDE, MORNINGSIDE HEIGHTS, HARLEM, THE NORTH

INFO Open Air Concerts

The Met seats 3,800 (right) opera lovers, who appreciate the auditorium's excellent acoustics for performances such as Wagner's *Rheingold* (below). Guest performances by famous ballet companies (below right, the legendary Bolshoi Ballet performing scenes from Yuri Grigorovich's *Spartacus*) also entrance the audience.

Open-air concerts at the Met are among New York's most popular traditions; in July and August performances take place in various parks, to which admission is usually still free.

Information: Tel (212) 362 60 00; www.metopera.org/parks

The "Met" is one of the world's greatest opera houses – singing here is like qualifying for the opera equivalent of the Olympics. The façade of the opera house, built in 1966 to a design by Wallace K. Harrison, also has an Olympic feel. Five strikingly high arched windows allow a view into the foyer where two murals by Marc Chagall, both some 10 m (33 feet) square, proclaim the origins and triumphs of music. With an estimated value of $20 million, these paintings are not only objects of beauty but also collateral for a loan that the Met was forced to take out in the spring of 2009 as a result of the global credit crunch. Luciano Pavarotti achieved world fame here, and Placido Domingo is an established member of the Met's roster. The original opera house, the Old Met, where Caruso and Callas once sang, was on Broadway. It opened in 1883 with a performance of *Faust*, but was demolished in 1967.

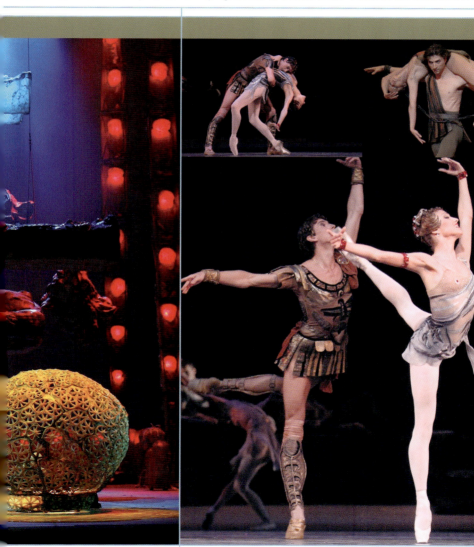

Originating in Poland, bagels have long been served in New York with cream cheese and smoked salmon. Along with Porterhouse steaks and burgers, they are now firmly established as a classic of US cuisine. The cheese counter at Zabar's, the legendary delicatessen on the Upper West Side, is the place to be: they have (almost) everything there and it's better than (almost) anywhere else.

BAGELS, BURGERS, & ZABAR'S: CULINARY NEW YORK

Are you in the mood for something a little different? The Wall Street Burger Shoppe will sell you a hamburger for a cool $175. Not a run-of-the-mill burger, of course, but a "Richard Nouveau Burger", named after the mascot of a New York internet site. This tasty snack consists of 280 grams (half a pound) of the finest Kobe steak mince, 25 grams (1 oz) of black truffles, and 60 grams (2.5 oz) of aged Gruyère, topped with a slice of goose liver and a pinch of gold leaf. This three-star establishment in the Flatiron District has kept ahead of the competition for more than 15 years, which in New York is almost an eternity. Zagat (the equivalent to the European Michelin Guide) has acclaimed the place as the "Best Restaurant in New York" four times in a row. Head chef Danny Meyer serves up many surprises with the strangest ingredients. However, New York cuisine is not all bagels and burgers – and Meyer is not the only innovative chef. There is talk on the Upper West Side of a culinary revolution, which started with the celebrity chef Tom Valenti ("the flavor king of New York") whose restaurant has been meeting the needs of even the most demanding gourmets since 2001. The best delicatessen in New York and an institution on the Upper West Side, Zabar's has also featured in its fair share of films and TV sitcoms, with mentions in *Sex and the City*, among others.

THE HIGHLIGHTS: UPPER WEST SIDE, MORNINGSIDE HEIGHTS, HARLEM, THE NORTH

INFO Spotlight Tours

The films starring Ben Stiller as a night watchman show what can happen during a *Night at the Museum* – the museum in the films was based on the AMNH – but dinosaur skeletons can excite the imagination during the day as well. The Rose Center for Earth and Space (below, left) includes a new entrance to the museum.

The admission price can also include surprise tours dealing with a themed aspect of the museum's activities. If you are less keen on surprises, a one-hour tour through the highlights of the whole museum can be booked.
Central Park West/79th St; Tel (212) 769 51 00; daily 10.00–17.45.

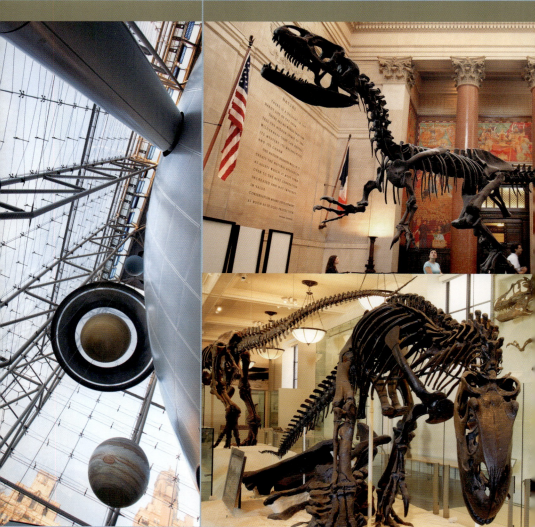

Founded on 6 April 1869, construction work on the monumental Roman triumphal building of the American Museum of Natural History began in 1874 to a design by Calvert Vaux and Jacob Wrey Mould, and the museum was officially opened in 1877. It is the oldest and still one of the largest natural history museums in the world, with 35 million specimens, only a small percentage of which can be displayed at any one time. The museum consists of 15 buildings that are interconnected, housing its many exhibition halls and research laboratories. Comprehensively informative about the history of our world and the cosmos, it boasts mighty dinosaur skeletons, a life-size replica blue whale, and a 19-m (63-foot) long Haida Native North American canoe made of cedar. The Rose Center for Earth and Space, which also houses the Hayden Planetarium, has extended the exhibition space by a quarter.

Alma Mater, the "nourishing mother", guards Columbia University's Low Library (below). The Cathedral of St John the Divine (below right, the entrance on the west façade; above, a hidden treasure, the now-destroyed Twin Towers depicted in a relief on the capital of a pillar in the interior).

INFO Vertical Tour

A climb of 124 steps is rewarded with fascinating views of the cathedral's architecture. The high point of the one-hour tour is the wonderful view from the roof over to Manhattan's Morningside Heights. Booking recommended.

1047 Amsterdam Avenue; Tel (212) 932 73 47; Sat 12.00 and 14.00.

COLUMBIA UNIVERSITY 56
CATHEDRAL OF ST JOHN THE DIVINE 57

"Think big": when the Cathedral of St John the Divine on 112th Street is finally completed, it will go down in the history of sacred architecture as the largest cathedral in the world. Begun in a Byzantine-Romanesque style by Heins & La Farge, the foundation stone was laid on 27 December 1892. Although a neo-Gothic extension was added by Cram & Ferguson in 1911, even today this church is only two-thirds finished. Both construction, and now also renovation, are an ongoing process. With 20,000 students, Columbia University, founded in 1754 as King's College and later renamed, is one of the oldest, largest, and, with Harvard, Princeton, and Yale, one of the most respected universities in the country and a member of the Ivy League. Columbia's faculties of law, medicine, and journalism are particularly renowned and today the university can proudly boast more than 50 Nobel Prize-winners amongst its graduates.

THE HIGHLIGHTS: UPPER WEST SIDE, MORNINGSIDE HEIGHTS, HARLEM, THE NORTH

INFO Apollo Theatre

Harlem's main artery, 125th Street. The images on the left page give an idea of this somewhat different world. Right: Immediately after Michael Jackson's death on 25 June 2009, many of his fans assembled in front of the Apollo Theater where "Jacko" got his big break (below left).

All the showbiz greats have appeared at the Apollo, and many began their careers at the amateur nights here. All this is recounted in the hour-long Historical Tour.

253 West 125th St; Tel (212) 531 53 37; Mon, Tues, Thurs, Fri 11.00, 13.00, 15.00, Wed 11.00, Sat, Sun 11.00, 13.00.

In 1658 Peter Stuyvesant established a trading-post near modern-day 125th Street, naming it "Nieuw Haarlem". German and Irish immigrants first settled here, followed by Italians. It was not until the beginning of the 20th century, when the subway was built, that African-Americans from Lower Manhattan also moved in. More African-Americans from the southern states and the West Indies followed during World War I, and since then Harlem has become the most famous black district in the United States. A focus for the development of an independent black culture, it has also become a byword for the integration problems experienced by the country's various communities, despite being in the supposed "melting pot" of New York. Religion has played an important role in Harlem's community – there are over 400 churches of many different denominations and several mosques.

Bounded by 110th Street, the Harlem River, 5th Avenue, and Morningside and St Nicholas Avenues, Harlem is now on the move, both musically, in its night clubs and gospel churches, and socially, as much of the district is being redeveloped: Harlem is b(l)ack – and beautiful! A range of building and renovation projects are now taking place in many parts of the "hood".

HARLEM SHUFFLE: FAITH, HOPE, AND JAZZ

"Take the 'A' Train", once the Duke Ellington Band's signature tune, was an invitation people were more than happy to take up, as line A of the New York subway goes from Brooklyn directly to Harlem, right into the jazz-filled heart of the black community. Such artists as Sarah Vaughan, James Brown, and the Jacksons all got their big breaks here at the legendary Apollo Theater amateur nights. As the Jazz Museum on East 126th Street points out, no other community has nurtured jazz more faithfully apart from New Orleans. Even today the district is living off the times when the seductive blue notes of jazz would enthral and enslave many a music lover. In her novel *Jazz*, Toni Morrison, Nobel Prize-winner for Literature, had to resort to drastic measures to end a jazz party: a shot rings out, ending not just the party but also the life of an eighteen-year-old beauty. It soon turns out that love is involved, and jazz too, of course, the two inextricably entwined. It was also Toni Morrison who described not Barack Obama but saxophone-playing Bill Clinton, who has an office in Harlem to this day, as "America's first black president", an indication that the holy trinity of faith, hope, and jazz is not just a question of skin tone. The legendary pianist and composer Willie "The Lion" Smith said, "I'd rather be a fly on a lampost in Harlem than a millionaire anywhere else", which really says it all.

Medieval Europe in Manhattan: the museum includes not only parts of cloisters, abbeys, and chapels, and a tranquil monastic garden, but also medieval works of art, such as these busts from an altar made in Baden-Württemberg around 1470 (below).

INFO Garden Tours

The guided tour pointing out the botanical and architectural highlights shows the monastery garden at its best. The informative garden walks are available from May to October.
99 Margaret Corbin Drive; Tel (212) 923 37 00; Mar–Oct Tues–Sun 13.00.

The Cloisters is a museum of medieval art of a kind unique in the United States. Its central building incorporates fragments from cloisters and other medieval buildings that were collected in Europe by the sculptor George Gray Barnard, and then assembled and expanded into a museum by the archi-tects Allen, Collins & Willis in the 1930s. Thanks to the financial support of John D. Rockefeller Jr, the museum, located high above the Hudson River in Fort Tyron Park in the wooded north of Manhattan, has been a branch of the Metropolitan Museum of Modern Art since 1925. Its holdings of medieval art include the "Unicorn Tapestries", price-less wall-hangings depicting a hunt for a mythical white unicorn, which comes back to life when it is killed, and a medieval Book of Hours. As you walk through the reconstructed monastic rooms and peaceful chapels, the expe-rience is as much religious as historic.

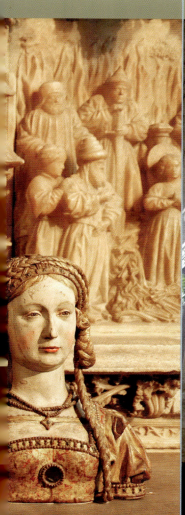

BROOKLYN, QUEENS, THE BRONX, STATEN ISLAND

Although doubtless the most popular and famous of the five boroughs, Manhattan is not all there is to New York. The Bronx, Brooklyn, Queens, and Staten Island are all familiar names, but in reality few visitors to New York venture far beyond Manhattan. It is true that these boroughs have been noted for their urban decay, Staten Island is sometimes known as "the forgotten borough", and most people only know Queens from travelling through from the airport. But little by little things are looking up for all these less famous parts of New York, with their diverse range of ethnic cultures. If you have some time to spare, why not venture a little further afield and see for yourself?

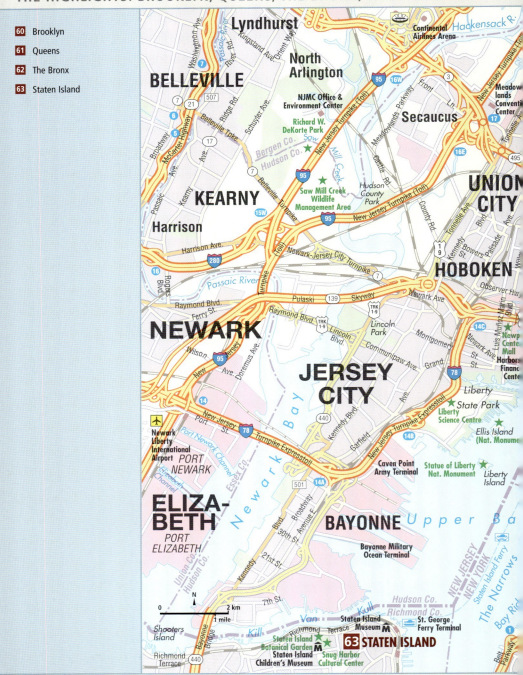

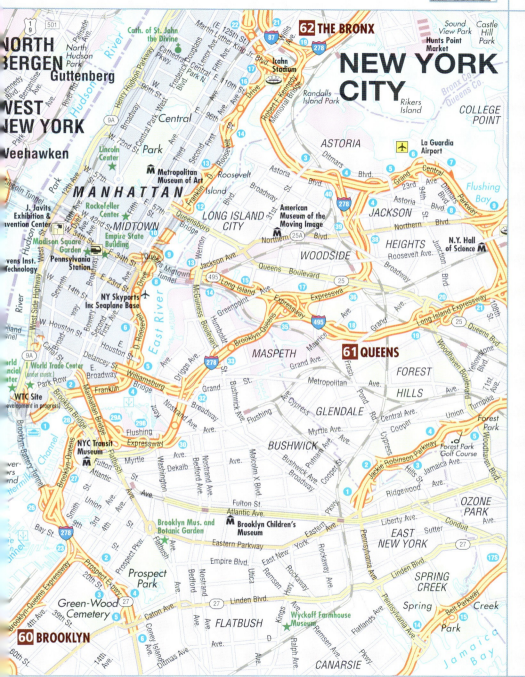

THE HIGHLIGHTS: BROOKLYN, QUEENS, THE BRONX, STATEN ISLAND

Brooklyn offers the nicest route into Manhattan: the Brooklyn Bridge (below left),a brownstone house (below right), the impressive Brooklyn Museum (right), fascinating streets, bustling markets, a charming waterfront, and an imposing public library (below right).

INFO Boat tours

The *April Lynn* departs from Bay End Marina on fishing trips (with a catch guaranteed), sightseeing tours across New York Bay, or a cocktail cruise at sundown: the choice is yours.

Fish NYC, Bay End Marina, Mill Basin; Tel (718) 629 36 15; Apr–Dec.

Brooklyn is New York's most populous borough, with some 2.5 million residents. Until the five boroughs were incorporated in 1898, Brooklyn was the fourth-largest city in the United States, and it still has something rather metropolitan about it: 93 different ethnic groups from 150 countries lived here at the end of the 1990s, with their identities emphasized by enclaves such as Little Odessa and Little Arabia. Brooklyn, originally named Breukelen after the town near Utrecht, started life as a Dutch settlement. Brooklyn Heights, an idyllic – and expensive – residential area at the mouth of the East River between Brooklyn Bridge and the Atlantic River, is now listed as a national monument. The Brooklyn Museum is one of the largest art museums in the country, with exhibits from the ancient world to the present day. But history can be found in the streets as well; many are lined with the famous Brownstone row houses.

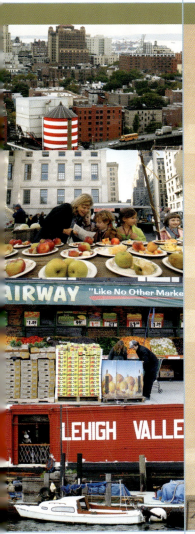

THE HIGHLIGHTS: BROOKLYN, QUEENS, THE BRONX, STATEN ISLAND

You might well find yourself humming a few lines of "Under the Boardwalk" by the Drifters, their much-covered 1964 Motown hymn of praise to the Coney Island boardwalks. The nearby fairground also gets a mention. A wooden rollercoaster (right).

INFO The Cyclone

After more than 80 years, the chains of the giant rollercoaster are still rattling. Despite its deceptively harmless appearance, a ride on the Cyclone is a test of nerve, a unique mixture of nostalgia and adrenalin.

834 Surf Ave; Tel (718) 265 21 00; from 12.00, daily.

Three bridges connect Brooklyn and Manhattan over the East River, their mnemonic being "BMW": starting from the north, Brooklyn, Manhattan, and Williamsburg. Entirely aware of its charms, Brooklyn Bridge, the urbane eldest brother, delivers the best views, including over the Brooklyn Promenade (also known as the Esplanade), which runs along the East River. One of Brooklyn's oldest public attractions, Prospect Park, was laid out in the 1860s. Its creators, Frederick Law Olmsted and Calvert Vaux, considered it a greater artistic success than Central Park, which they had just completed. It includes a zoo, a wildlife area, a lake, and sports areas among its other facilities. The famous Coney Island peninsula in south Brooklyn, with its long beach and fairground, was a major resort in the early 20th century. Today it has a slightly faded, nostalgic feel, with a hint of salt in the air from the nearby Atlantic.

INFO American Museum of the Moving Image

The quay, below, is a reminder that Queens is on Long Island. Graffiti art *à la* Queens (below right and right) is artistic and whimsical rather than aggressive, and many a tagger has dreamt of a career like Keith Haring's, who displayed his art in subway stations before it was acclaimed in museums.

The AMMI is not just for movie fans. With over 70,000 exhibits on display, this museum in the Paramount Pictures studios tells the history of New York in film. You can also see modern film and TV techniques, and even try some of them out.
35th Ave/37th St, Astoria; Tel (718)784 45 20.

Covering an area of 313 sq. km (120 sq. miles), Queens is New York's largest borough and there are supposedly more languages spoken here than anywhere else on earth. About half of the 2.2 million residents are of different ethnicities, so it seems appropriate that John F. Kennedy International and LaGuardia airports, two of New York's three international hubs, are located in this borough. Resonant names for sports fans include Shea Stadium (the home of the New York Mets baseball team until April 2009, when the new Citi Field Stadium was opened) and the Arthur Ashe Stadium in Flushing Meadows Park, where the US Tennis Open is held. Art fans might be drawn to MoMA's P.S.1 Contemporary Art Center, while the work of Japanese–American artist Isami Noguchi, known for his sculpture as well as classic furniture designs that are still on sale today, is on show at the Isami Noguchi Garden Museum.

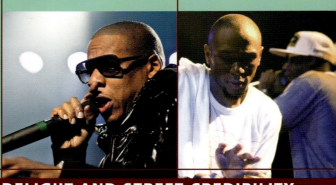

Hip hop history in the making: the annual VH1 Hip Hip Honors feature performances from stars like rappers Chuck D and Flavor Flav (below, left and right) from Public Enemy. Below, inset left from top: pioneers of hip hop, Run-D.M.C., who were also the first crew to win a gold disc; the Beastie Boys, who began as a hardcore punk band in 1979; and a breakdancer. Other major stars on the scene are Jay-Z, Mos Def, and Talib Kweli (right, from left).

HIP HOP: RAPPER'S DELIGHT AND STREET CREDIBILITY

When Kool DJ Herc, a Jamaica-born disc jockey who moved to New York at the age of 13, started mixing the reggae and raps of his old home with the funk and soul of his new one in the South Bronx, little could he have realized that he was inventing a whole new music genre. Within a few months the spark had ignited in Harlem and the black ghettos of other cities; everybody was dancing and singing in the new "hip hop" style. DJs combined song samples from the 1970s with modern R&B rhythms, scratching old vinyl records to a new rhythm and decrying the social poverty of the black ghettos in their raps. The Sugarhill Gang had the first hip hop hit with *Rapper's Delight*, and Grandmaster Flash, Run-D.M.C., and other artists subsequently took over the charts. Groups like Public Enemy (*Fight the Power*) went on extended world tours, attracting enormous attention with their politically charged lyrics. "Street cred" is still a deciding factor for success: an authenticity won on the streets of places like the South Bronx, rapping about everyday life, which the rappers themselves had experienced – even if they're now millionaires. Rap today can be broken down into many different substyles that have evolved from the Old School rap of the early 1980s, but the essence remains the same – a rhythmic vocal delivery of poetry and rhyme, over a beat or even without accompaniment.

THE HIGHLIGHTS: BROOKLYN, QUEENS, THE BRONX, STATEN ISLAND

INFO City Island

Below: A street scene; below inset: A tram depot. The Bronx is renowned as being the home of the New York Yankees, a Baltimore baseball team founded in 1901, which moved here in 1923. Since April 2009 the Yankees have been playing in their new Yankee Stadium, which cost $1.5 billion (right).

This little island in Long Island Sound is like a romantic fishing village and has a great selection of seafood restaurants. Visitors wishing to see live fish are welcome aboard the boats of the Island Current Fleet, amongst others.
Captain Chris; Boat Livery Marina; Tel (917) 417 75 57, in season.

The only borough of New York to have a definite article and an indefinite future – or so the joke went when the South Bronx ("SoBro") was a byword for urban decay with the highest rates of criminality in the United States. That was in the 1960s, but it had not always been the case. In 1639, when the Swedish seafarer Johan Bronck landed on the peninsula that was to be named after him, he felt he had discovered "a land of virgin forest and limitless opportunities". And fortunately, it has not remained the case either. People walk with a little more swagger in the Bronx than elsewhere; this is as true of local hip hop heroes as of the heroes in blue and white striped uniforms, the New York Yankees, the baseball team that is the Bronx's pride and joy. As in other boroughs, after seeing a decline in the 1970s, recently there has been a good deal of renovation, much of it in the South Bronx.

One of the nicest places that New York-ers seeking nature get away to is Long Island. Its eastern tip is marked by the lighthouse at Montauk (below). The Hudson River Valley is also idyllic – the Vanderbilts (right and below, inset top left) and the Roosevelts (below, inset bottom left) lived in Hyde Park, on the eastern shore of the river. Long Island's North Shore is also the setting for F. Scott Fitzgerald's classic novel of the Jazz Age, *The Great Gatsby*.

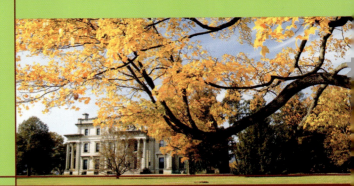

SMALL EXCURSIONS FROM THE BIG CITY

New York is on the same latitude as Naples, so it is no wonder that the summer months particularly see hundreds and thousands of overheated city-dwellers leaving the asphalt canyons of the streets and escaping into Nature, which in Manhattan is essentially limited to Central Park. A trip to Long Island, whose western tip is formed by the boroughs of Queens and Brooklyn, is quite literally a hop over the river. You would be happy enough to own a beach house at the far eastern end of this 190-km (120-mile) long island; for a few dollars more you could live in the "Hamptons" (named after former whaling villages such as East Hampton, Bridgehampton, and Hampton Bays), next door to the likes of Calvin Klein. Or you could go right to the eastern tip of Montauk Island, where the surfers congregate. North of Manhattan, the Hudson River widens into a mighty torrent, and time seems to have stood still in many places along its valley. Many affluent people chose to make their home in the country here – the Roosevelts, for example, in whose villa the 32nd president of the United States was born. A little further along the Hudson Valley, at West Point, the legendary military academy was founded 80 years previously. The list of its notable alumni is long and includes two US presidents, Ulysses S. Grant and Dwight D. Eisenhower, as well as a certain George Armstrong Custer.

THE HIGHLIGHTS: BROOKLYN, QUEENS, THE BRONX, STATEN ISLAND

INFO Staten Island Ferry

The New York City Marathon goes through all five boroughs and begins on Staten Island's 1,330-m (4,265-foot) long Verrazzano Narrows Bridge (below), which was opened in 1964. Historic Richmond Town is a museum village illustrating the island's colonial past (right and below right).

There has been a non-stop ferry service between Staten Island and Manhattan since 1810. You can enjoy views of the Manhattan skyline, the Statue of Liberty, and Ellis Island for free on the 25-minute journey by both day and night.
South St/State St; by day every 30 mins, by night hourly.

This is where our brief trip beyond Manhattan ends. Some people say that you don't need to leave the ferry to see the sights – just take some photos as you pass Lady Liberty, enjoy the views of the glittering skyline of Manhattan, and then come straight back. Fewer than 500,000 people live on Staten Island and they may view the island differently. Admittedly the island once had Fresh Kills Landfill, the largest landfill site in the world, on its doorstep, but it's closed now anyway. The situation sounds even better when you learn that the site has been treated and cleaned up; it is now being turned into a park that will be three times the size of Central Park. The area is part of a significant tidal ecosytem with creeks and wetlands. Staten Islands boasts a zoo, a botanical garden, and several museums, including the Sandy Ground Historical Museum, which explores the island's old communities.

Is New York for culture lovers? Of course – there are museums and theaters galore. Is it a good city for shopping? No doubt – the variety of shops, from luxury boutiques to discount outlets, is enormous. A dream destination for gourmets? Certainly – world-renowned top chefs will take you on a culinary voyage of exploration. A haven for night owls? Absolutely – the "city that never sleeps" has clubs, bars, and discos for every taste. And if you need to rest, there's everything from the finest luxury hotel to the simplest hostel. In the following pages, you will find expert tips on some of the best-known and must-see addresses to help you make the most of your stay in one of the world's most exciting cities.

Museums, music, and drama

American Numismatic Society

This museum and research institute is devoted to the study of coins from all periods and cultures; it boasts a comprehensive collection of over 800,000 coins from all over the world, dating from the ancient world to the present day. Specific enquiries can also be accommodated. A perfect spot to inspire a passion for coins and collecting.
75 Varick St;
Tel 571 44 70;
Mon–Fri 9.30–16.30.
www.numismatics.org

The Fraunces' Tavern Museum

A merchant's house, built in 1719, which was to witness historic events in 1763, during its time as a tavern; it was reconstructed in 1928 in a complex with four other, 19th-century buildings, and all illustrate different aspects of American history.
54 Pearl St;
Tel 968 17 76;
Mon–Sat 12.00–17.00.
www. frauncestavern-museum.org

George Gustav Heye Center (Museum of the American Indian)

Dedicated to American Indian culture from North, South and Central America (see p. 30), the museum has been housed in the old Custom House building since 1994. It has one of the most extensive collections of Native American arts in the world. It's a fascinating museum.
1 Bowling Green;
Tel 514 37 00;

10.00–17.00, daily, Thurs 10.00–20.00, closed 25 Dec.
www.nmai.si.edu

The Grey Art Gallery

New York University's gallery in the old NYU Silver Center concentrates on late 19th- and 20th-century art, including works by Picasso, Miró, and Matisse; it also specializes in works by American artists.
100 Washington Sq E.;
Tel 998 67 80;
Tues, Thurs, Fri 11.00–18.00,
Wed 11.00–20.00,
Sat 11.00–17.00,
closed public hols.
www.nyu.edu/greyart/

The Merchant's House Museum

A of townhouse of 1831 preserved in its original condition, affording a glimpse into another world: the life of a 19th-century New York merchant's family.
29 E. 4th St;
Tel 777 10 89;
Thurs–Mon 12.00–17.00,
closed public hols.
www.merchantshouse.com

Museum for African Art

The venue was founded in 1984 and features changing displays. The small museum, whose premises are still being refurbished, is dedicated to African art.
593 Broadway;
Tel 966 13 13;
Tues–Fri 10:30–17.30,
Sat, Sun 12.00–18.00.
www.africanart.org

Museum of American Finance

A glimpse into the world of American financial history and the stock exchange (see p. 36). It celebrates the spirit of entrepreneurship and the

democratic free market tradition that has made New York City such a financial world capital.
48 Wall St;
Tel 908 41 10;
Tues–Sat 10.00–16.00,
closed public hols.
www.moaf.org

Museum of Jewish Heritage

Opened in 1997 in a six-sided, tiered building, the museum's photos, videos, documents, computer games, and exhibits are mostly concerned with the Holocaust. However, they also deal with Jewish culture and lifestyle from the 19th century to the modern day.
36 Battery Pl.;
Tel (646) 437 42 00;
Sun–Tues, Thurs 10.00–17.45, Wed 10.00–20.00, Fri 10.00–15.00 (winter)/17.00 (summer), closed Thanksgiving and Jewish holidays.
www.mjhnyc.org

New Museum of Contemporary Art

Founded in 1977, the museum features the latest trends in art. A great spot for those interested in contemporary movements and in new artists.
535 Broadway;
Tel 219 12 22; Wed, Sat, Sun 12.00–18.00, Thurs, Fri 12.00–21.00, closed Thanksgiving, 25 Dec, 1 Jan.
www.newmuseum.org

New York City Fire Museum

Housed in a fire station built in 1904, the museum has a wide range of exhibits, including fire apparatus, tenders, hoses, protective clothing, and parade uniforms etc, and lots of inter-

esting information about the New York Fire Department since the 18th century. Boys of all ages will love it.
278 Spring St;
Tel 691 13 03;
Tues–Sat 10.00–17.00,
Sun 10.00–16.00, closed public hols.
www.nycfiremuseum.org

New York City Police Museum

Three hundred years of the history of the famous police departments are brought to life here. A special display is devoted to the harrowing events of 11 September 2001.
100 Old Slip;
Tel 480 31 00;
Mon–Sat 10.00–17.00.
www.nycpolicemuseum.org

Skyscraper Museum

The history and development of skyscraper construction techniques, from their early beginnings up to the modern day, are illustrated in this museum. It also examines current notions of the future of high-rise building.
39 Battery Pl;
Tel 968 19 61;
Wed–Sun 12.00–18.00.
www.skyscraper.org

South St Seaport Museum

Old businesses and warehouses in the original heart of New York's docks on the east shore of Manhattan have been partly converted into museums, and there are vintage sailboats, such as the *Pioneer*, the *Wavertree*, and the *Peking*, galleries, and pretty restaurants and cafés. The district, which has recently been laboriously refurbished, recalls a time when this was a hub of overseas trade; the rise of the

DOWNTOWN MANHATTAN

These pages give additional information for the area of New York described in the "Highlights" section (pp. 156–173). Please note that the area code for New York is **212**.

steamship in the mid-19th century saw a shift of business to the deeper Hudson River on Manhattan's West Side (see p. 44).
East River, 12 Fulton St;
Tel 748 87 25;
Apr–Dec Tues–Sun 10.00–18.00, Jan–Mar Fri–Sun 10.00–17.00, sailings 12.00–16.00 depending on weather.
www.southstreetseaport-museum.org

Tenement Museum
A working family's home from 1863, giving an idea of the far-from-ideal living conditions endured by immigrants of the period. It really brings the period alive.
97 Orchard St;
Tel 431 02 33;
10.15-17.00, daily, by guided tour only, closed Thanksgiving, 25 Dec, 1 Jan.
www.tenement.org

Trinity Museum
A small museum in the left nave of Trinity Church, dealing with the history of the local community since the 17th century and the construction of the current neo-Gothic church (see p. 32).
Trinity Pl;
Tel 602 08 00;
Mon–Fri 9.00–17.30, Sat, Sun 9.00–15.45, closed during services.
www.trinitywallSt.org

Ukrainian Museum
Admire works by Ukrainian artists such as Alexander Archipenko and Alexis Gritchenko, as well as Ukrainian folk art, including lace-making, Easter eggs, ceramics, and marriage customs.
222 E 6th St;
Tel 228 01 10;

Wed–Sun 11.00–17.00, closed public hols.
www.ukrainianmuseum.org

Festivals and events

Halloween Parade
The country's biggest Halloween celebrations take place on the streets of Greenwich Village, especially Sixth Avenue. The participants' gruesome costumes vary from quirky but imaginative to the decidedly odd. The noisy after-party is held on Washington Square every year. It's an interesting event with puppets, dancers, and artists of all kinds. Great photo opportunity!
31 Oct, from 19.00.
www.halloween-nyc.com

Howl! Festival
A week-long festival presenting visual arts, drama, dance, film, and literary readings at various venues in the East Village; the event is named after the poem "Howl!" by Allen Ginsberg, who was one of the principal members of the Beat generation.
Tel 673 54 33, Aug.
www.howlfestival.com

Independence Day Fireworks
The highlight of the US Independence Day celebrations is the great firework display on the East River, which is occasionally accompanied by a long procession of boats. It starts at 21.00 and good views are to be had from higher roofs in Manhattan with a view to the east, or from the Lower East Side waterfront, Williamsburg, and Brooklyn.
Tel 484 12 00; 4 Jul.
www.nycgo.com

River to River Festival
New York's biggest open-air festival comprises more than 500 events spread throughout the whole summer. The varied schedule includes live concerts ranging from classical to pop and jazz, dance and theatre performances, film showings, and much more. The concerts in the parks and gardens between Battery Park and City Hall are particularly popular.
Jun-Aug.
www.rivertorivernyc.org

Washington Square Music Festival
Free classical, jazz, and swing concerts held in the open air and performed by musicians from Carnegie Hall, the Lincoln Center, the Metropolitan and the New York City Operas, and the Brooklyn Academy of Music, as well as many other budding musicians. It is worth arriving early to get a good seat for the free concerts.
Tel 252 36 21;
mid-Jun to mid-Jul.
www.washingtonsquaremusicfestival.org

Sport and leisure

Bunya City Spa
This spa venue in SoHo offers Far Eastern-style relaxation, such as a papaya body polish (a delicate skin treatment), Japanese shiatsu, or a four-handed massage with Asiatic medicinal herbs, conducted by two well-qualified practitioners. It's an amazing experience. You will emerge refreshed and rejuvenated.
474 West Broadway/Prince St; Tel 388 12 88;
Mon-Sat 10.00–21.00, Sun 10.00–19.00.
www.bunyacityspa.com

Great Jones Spa
This temple to relaxation promises that an afternoon spent in their Wet Lounge is better relaxation from daily stress than a week's holiday. In any case this is pure relaxation, whether in the hot tubs of the Water Lounge, the sauna, or the Cold Plunge. You can also have a massage, facial, and much more, of course.
29 Great Jones St./Lafayette St;
Tel 505 31 85;
Mon 16.00–22.00, Tues–Sun 9.00–22.00.
www.gjspa.com

Jivamukti
For many this is the best place for yoga in Manhattan. Jivamukti yoga is taught to music, including pop and house, not just Indian or Far Eastern sounds. At the end of the session, as many pupils as can be accommodated are given a mini massage, and you can also have Sanskrit tuition if you are interested.
841 Broadway/Union Sq;
Tel 353 02 14;
Mon–Thurs 8.00–20.00, Fri 8.00–18.45, Sat–Sun 9.15–17.00.
www.jivamuktiyoga.com

Madison Square Garden
Both the New York Rangers' ice-hockey season and the New York Knicks' baseball season begin at the end of summer, and both teams are very popular in the city, even if their recent sporting achievements have left much to be desired. Tickets for Rangers games start at $40 and for Knicks games at $34.50. It's an exciting game to watch, and worth trying to get tickets for.

Rangers: Tel 465 67 41;
Sep–Apr.
www.rangers.nhl.com
Knicks: Tel 465 71 71;
Oct–Jun.
www.nba.com/knicks

Real Pilates

Pilates guru Alycea Ungaro offers courses for beginners and advanced students alike. The exercises range from therapeutic treatments to sports training. The weekend courses last from six to twelve hours and are led by various Pilates teachers.
177 Duane St;
Tel 625 07 77;
Mon–Fri 8.00–19.00, Sat 9.00–13.00, Sun 9.15–14.00.
www.realpilatesnyc.com

Ringling Bros and Barnum & Bailey Circus

The audience holds its breath at this exciting show, with daring acrobats on the trapeze and high wire, and the tigers and bears, while America's best clowns always raise a laugh with their hilarious antics. The Ringling Brothers put on one of the finest circuses in America.
Madison Square Garden;
Mid-Mar to the beginning of April.
www.ringling.com

Sydney's Playground

Probably the largest playground in New York, with mini-skyscrapers, on which children can climb to their hearts' content, and toy vehicles to race round a replica highway. Sidney' Café nearby has all kinds of sweet and savory refreshments.
66 White St;
Tel 431 91 25;
Mon, Wed, Fri 8.30–18.00,
Tues, Thurs, Sat 10.00–18.00.

Shopping

Boucher

The quirky design of the accessories made here by the store owner, Laura Mady, has attracted plenty of customers to the Meatpacking District: her necklaces and earrings are especially popular. Gold, pearls, and gemstones (garnets, sapphires, etc.,) are used in the design of her attractive products. There are some great designs for brides and bridesmaids in particular. It's a gem of a shop…
9 9th Ave/Little West St;
Tel 206 37 75;
Mar–Dec Mon–Sat 12.00–19.00, Sun 12.00-18.00, Jan–Feb closed Mon.

Century 21

The fashion discount store has four floors of designer clothes for him and her, from Armani and DKNY to Marc Jacobs, etc. Except for the early mornings, the store is always full as there are decent reductions (sometimes up to 50 percent) on clothes, accessories, shoes, and perfumes. If you want to shop in peace and avoid the long queues at the fitting rooms, come early and have breakfast later.
22 Cortland St/Church St;
Tel 227 90 92;
Mon–Wed and Fri 7.45–20.00, Thurs 7.45–20.30, Sat 10.00–20.00, Sun 11.00–19.00.
www.c21stores.com

Daffy's

Two floors of designer clothes and accessories for men, women, and children at exceptionally low prices (mostly reduced by 50 percent). A good rummage here is usually rewarded with unbelievable bargains. This discount chain also has several other branches in the city (see website).
462 Broadway/Grand St;
Tel 334 74 44;
Mon–Sat 10.00–20.00, Sun 12.00–19.00.
www.daffys.com

Dean & Deluca

A SoHo delicatessen stocking Italian delights and provisions, and a wide range of kitchen utensils and gift ideas. The in-house espresso bar is very popular with patrons. This is a must-see spot for lovers of all things culinary and kitchen-based.
560 Broadway/Prince St;
Tel (800) 221 77 14;
Mon–Fri 7.00–20.00, Sat, Sun 8.00–20.00.
www.deananddeluca.com

Economy Candy

Candy for young and old in a shop with jars full of gummi bears, licorice, and malt sweets, as well as almost antique chewing gum dispensers. Whether you're looking for jellied candy, fruit-tasting snakes or sugared almonds, ginger and papaya cubes or hand-made pralines, you'll find something to suit every taste. Perfect for the sweet-toothed visitor.
108 Rivington St/Essex St;
Tel 254 15 31;
Sun–Fri 9.00–18.00, Sat 10.00–17.00.
www.economycandy.com

J&R Music & Computer World

J&R is the first port of call for a lot of computer nerds looking for spare parts, memory components, or PC accessories. This store, not far from the City Hall, also has cameras, stereos, VCRs, and a good range of CDs and DVDs.
23 Park Row;
Tel 238 90 00;
Mon–Sat 9.00–19.30, Sun 10.30–18.30.
www.jr.com

Prada

Along with the current collections you can also admire pieces from previous Prada epochs, but it's not just the fashion that will draw your attention. The building's interior is a real experience: the Dutch architect Rem Koolhaas has re-fashioned the old Guggenheim headquarters in SoHo into the renowned designer's flagship store with a giant showroom.
575 Broadway;
Tel 334 88 88;
Mon–Sat 11.00–19.00, Sun 12.00–18.00.
www.prada.com

The Original Firestore

If you're looking for souvenirs of the New York Fire or Police Departments, this is the place. Along with the usual articles, such as caps, t-shirts, and jackets, there are special items relating to 9/11.
17 Greenwich Ave/Christopher St;
Tel (800) 229 92 58;
Mon–Thurs 11.00–19.00, Fri–Sat 11.00–20.00, Sun 12.00–18.00.
www.nyfirestore.com

Eating and drinking

Amaya

A reliable Thai restaurant in the East Village. Don't let the somewhat kitschy atmosphere put you off: the crunchy pork ribs will make the trip worthwhile, and the duck

DOWNTOWN MANHATTAN

These pages give additional information for the area of New York described in the "Highlights" section (pp. 156–173). Please note that the area code for New York is 212.

pancakes with hot sauce are a delight. Freshly-baked banana tastes especially good here. Definitely worth a try.
234 E. 4th St (near Ave B);
Tel (646) 313 19 87;
Mon–Thurs 12.00–23.00,
Fri–Sun 12.00–24.00.

Angelica Kitchen
One of Manhattan's few vegetarian restaurants, with imaginative and creative cooking. Amongst the recommended dishes are the walnut and lentil pasties and the "Dragon Bowls", influenced by Asiatic and Latin American cuisine. Cash only, and seat availability is on a first come, first served basis. And you can buy her book when you leave.
300 E. 12th St
(corner of Second Ave);
Tel 228 29 09;
11.30–22.30, daily.
www.angelicakitchen.com

Aroma
Not much more than a classic diner with a few tables – but what a diner! No snacks from around the world, just the finest Italian dishes, such as Sicilian meatloaf and homemade pasta. Casual but friendly atmosphere with delicious food. What more could you want?
36 E. 4th St;
Tel 375 01 00;
Sun–Thurs 17.00–23.30,
Fri, Sat 17.00–24.00.
www.aromanyc.com

Arturo's
The best wood-oven pizza in town, according to dyed-in-the-wool Italians. Fresh salads and good wine, and it's worth the wait in the evenings. The tastiest variants are "shrimp marinara" and

"veal parmesan", and there are even very smart pizzas topped with lobster.
106 W. Houston St, corner of Thompson St;
Tel 677 38 20;
Mon–Thurs 16.00–1.00,
Fri, Sat 16.00–2.00,
Sun 15.00–12.00.

Babbo
One of the best Italians in Manhattan. Mario Batali, the head chef, indulges his guests with dishes such as goat cheese tortellini with dried oranges and wild fennel pollen and mussel linguini with hot chilli. The lamb sausage is served with a purée of sweet peas.
110 Waverly Pl.
(near Sixth Ave);
Tel 777 03 03;
Mon–Sat 17.30–23.30,
Sun 17.00–23.00.
www.babbonyc.com

Belcourt
Matt Hamilton, the head chef, worked for a while on a Tuscan farm in order to get the right feel for traditional Italian cooking. He has invested his knowledge in the fine home-made food in this restaurant, complemented by its antique furniture. Try the French toast for breakfast.
84 E. 4th St;
Tel 979 20 34;
Sun–Thurs 10.00–23.00,
Fri, Sat 10.00–12.00.

17 Bleecker
A competitor with Starbuck's for internet and email junkies who wish to go about their business in peace and yet don't want to forego a coffee shop atmosphere. The coffee tastes light and good, and there are sandwiches and wraps. Check your mail and

enjoy a delicious coffee at the same time. Caffeine, catch-up, and correspondence. Result!
17 Bleecker St;
Tel 529 39 14;
Mon–Fri 7.00–23.00,
Sat, Sun 8.00–23.00.

Blt Fish
Proprietor and top chef Laurent Tourondel has described his fish restaurant as a "mixture of a Paris brasserie and a New England fish shack". The snacks in the Fish Shack in the cellar are especially tasty, but expensive.
21 West 17th St;
Tel 691 88 88;
Mon–Thurs 11.45–14.30,
17.30–23.00, Fri 11.45–14.30,
17.30–23.00, Sat 17.30–
23.30, Sun 17.00–22.00.
www.bltfish.com

Bondi Road
The photos of Bondi Beach on the high walls here conjure up an Australian holiday feeling, and fish and chips, and other solid seafood dishes, are served up on rustic tables. The fish and the beer come from Australia and the bar is lively in the evenings. You can almost smell the sea. Don't forget your surfboard!
153 Rivington St
(near Suffolk St);
Tel 253 53 11; Mon 16.00–
22.00, Tues, Wed 16.00–
24.00, Thurs 16.00–1.00, Fri
16.00–2.00, Sat 11.00–4.00,
Sun 11.00–22.00.
www.thesunburntcow.com

Boqueria
Inspired by the Boqueria market in Barcelona, this hip restaurant serves the apotheosis of Spanish cooking; it's traditional yet innovative. The tapas and raciones taste better than in Catalunya. Seamus

Mullen, the chef, researched for two years in Spain before opening the restaurant.
53 West 19th St (between 5th and 6th Aves);
Tel 255 41 60;
Mon–Thurs 12.00–24.00,
Fri, Sat 12.00–2.00.
www.boquerianyc.com,

Café Cordadito
One of the few Cuban family restaurants with first-class, home-made food. A well-known critic has described the place as serving "good portions of tasty and reasonably-priced food". The menu is dominated by meat with rice and beans in all their varieties.
210 E. 3rd St (near Ave B);
Tel 614 30 80;
Mon 17.00–23.00,
Tues–Fri 12.00–23.00,
Sat, Sun 11.00–23.00.

Café Katja
Erwin Schrottner, an Austrian, has fulfilled a dream with this home-from-home bar. The menu offers dishes like Bernerwurstel (sausages stuffed with Emmental), beetroot, and freshly baked pretzels. There is also imported beer from Europe and Linzertorte for afterwards.
79 Orchard St
(corner of Grand St);
Tel 219 95 45;
16.00–1.00, daily.
www.cafe-katja.com

Cherin Sushi
A good-value sushi bar in the East Village – exceptional in expensive Manhattan. If you turn up for happy hour in the early evening, you'll even get a discount. The inventive sushi rolls (such as cheps roll with yellowtail, eel, tempura sprinkles, and avocado) are well worth sampling.

*306 E 6th St
(near Second Ave);
Tel 388 13 48;
Mon–Thurs 17.00–24.00,
Fri, Sat 17.00–1.00.*

Cones
An Argentinean ice-cream bar with especially creamy ice-cream in more than 20 varieties, the most popular of which are hazelnut, tiramisu, and yerba maté (Argentinean tea). There are also lots of variations of sorbet (such as water melon and bilberry).
*272 Bleecker St
(near Morton St);
Tel 414 17 95;
Sun–Thurs 13.00–23.00,
Fri, Sat 13.00–1.00.*

Dogmatic Dogs
There are hot dogs on every corner in Manhattan, but these are especially good. The sausage meat is from free range cattle from Violet Hills Farm in Sullivan County and is served in crunchy rolls. You'll find mustard and hot sauces, too. Hot dog fans will be in heaven here.
*26 E 17th St
(near Broadway);
Tel 414 06 00;
Mon–Thurs 11.00–20.00,
Fri, Sat 11.00–21.00,
Sun 12.00-19.00.*

Eat-pisode
A jewel amongst the many Thai restaurants in New York. Wara Spulchai, the owner, has dispensed with any fussiness and relies on family recipes. The curry comes in five grades of hotness, and the green curry with chicken is one of the best dishes. Authentic and fantastic.
*123 Ludlow St
(near Rivington St);
Tel 677 76 24;*

*Mon–Thurs 12.00–23.00,
Fri, Sat 13.00–24.00,
Sun 14.00–23.00.
www.eat-pisode.com*

El Rinconcito
A small Spanish-American diner with a family atmosphere. Salsa music gets you in the mood to eat roast chicken and enchiladas or stew with pig's feet. Some of the dishes are very hot, but they will all fill you up.
*408 E 10th St (near Ave C);
Tel 254-1381;
9.00–21.00, daily.*

EN Japanese Brasserie
The first branch of a Japanese restaurant chain. Instead of the usual sushi and noodles they swear by fresh tofu here. It comes in lots of variations and is served with ingredients like shrimp or thinly sliced meat (yuba). Yuba sashimi is served with grated horseradish and shiso salad.
*435 Hudson St
(corner of Leroy St);
Tel 647 91 96;
Sun–Thurs17.30–23.00,
Fri, Sat 17.30–24.00.
www.enjb.com*

Eva's
Tasty health food with a Mediterranean touch. The omelet shows how seriously the owners take things – it is only made with egg whites and is baked. Lovers of substantial fare swear by the turkey burgers or the baked tofu. The fresh fruit juices are especially tasty. It's also available "to go".
*11 West 8th St
(near Fifth Ave);
Tel 677 34 96;
Mon–Sat 11.00–23.00,
Sun 11.00–22.00.
www.evassupplements.com*

Festival Mexicano Restaurant
Forget the Tex-Mex food you get in most American "south of the border" restaurants – they have authentic Mexican cooking here, the best example of which is the hot chicken broth with chicken pieces and avocado. The meat and chicken tacos are also very good, and they have tasty milkshakes to soothe your palate. Come here for the real thing.
*120 Rivington St
(near Essex St);
Tel 995 01 54;
Sun–Thurs 11.00–23.00,
Fri, Sat 11.00–24.00.*

Frank
One of the best Italians in the East Village. Famous for his hot sauces, Frank Prisinzano serves up home-made surprises like "Uncle Michael's Meatloaf" and "Grandma Carmela's Ragout". If you are in the mood for a Mediterranean meatloaf, this is mandatory.
*88 Second Ave
(near Fifth St);
Tel 420 02 02;
Mon–Thurs 10.00–1.00,
Fri, Sat 10.00–2.00,
Sun 10.00–24.00.
www.frankrestaurant.com*

Georgia's Eastside BBQ
The name of the restaurant comes from Alan Natkiel, the owner, having learnt the secret art of the barbecue in Georgia. The ribs are marinated in beer before being grilled and are wonderfully tender. There is also coleslaw, sweet vegetables, and cornbread.
*192 Orchard St
(near Stanton St);
Tel 253 62 80;
Mon 17.00–22.00,*

*Tues–Sun 12.00–23.00.
www.georgiaseastsidebbq.com*

Hong Kong Station
A Chinese noodle restaurant of the first order. The egg or rice noodles are cooked in tasty chicken stock before the addition of mushrooms, broccoli or other treats, including cow's stomach and pig's blood, which take a bit of getting used to. The curried fish balls are well recommended. Excellent value for money.
*128 Hester St (near Bowery);
Tel 966 93 82;
7.30–20.30, daily.*

JoeDoe
An atmospheric restaurant with a rustic feel. The tiny kitchen produces Irish dishes such as pork belly with red beans, stuffed peppers, and cod in beer sauce. And the beer doesn't taste bad either.
*45 E. 1st St;
Tel 780 02 62;
Mon, Wed, Thurs
17.00–23.00, Fri 17.00–24.00,
Sat 11.00–16.00, 17.00–
24.00, Sun 11.00–16.00,
17.00–23.00.
www.chefjoedoe.com*

Joe's Pizza
An institution in Greenwich Village for years. Joe Pasquale, the owner, swears by original Italian thin-crust pizza with a balanced mixture of cheese and other toppings. You won't find fancy pizzas with lobster and other weird and wonderful toppings at Joe's, everything here is completely traditional. Authentic and satisfying.
*7 Carmine St (near Sixth Ave);
Tel 366 18 82;
9.00–5.00, daily.
www.famousjoespizza.com*

DOWNTOWN MANHATTAN

These pages give additional information for the area of New York described in the "Highlights" section (pp. 156–173). Please note that the area code for New York is **212**.

La Paella

A Spanish atmosphere with cheerful music in an authentic *bodega*, serving Spanish dishes such as the famed paella, five different versions of which are available. The ingredients, especially the mussels, fish, and chorizo, are liberally portioned. The far-too-easy-to-drink sangria is also recommended.
214 E 9th St (near Third Ave);
Tel 598 43 21,
Sun–Thurs 12.00–22.30,
Fri, Sat 12.00–23.30.

Lavagna

A romantic Italian in an unremarkable side street. The house dishes include crispy Margherita pizza from a wood oven, and the fish dishes are pretty respectable, too. A friendly and welcoming atmosphere awaits, along with tasty Italian dishes.
545 E Fifth St;
Tel 979 10 05;
Mon–Thurs 18.00–23.00,
Fri, Sat 18.00–24.00, Sun
17.00–23.00.
www.lavagnanyc.com

Moustache

Near East cooking in a relaxed atmosphere. The salads are generous and fresh, and the pitzas and falafel will satisfy even the greatest hungers; the baba ghannouj (aubergine purée with sesame seeds) is a delight.
265 E.10th St
(near First Ave);
Tel 228 20 22;
12.00–24.00, daily.

Nyonya

The very best Malaysian cuisine, arguably better and more interesting than so many Thai and Chinese restaurants. Amongst the excellent fare on offer are roti canai (crispy pancakes), oyster omelette, steamed fish, and mango shrimp.
194 Grand St
(near Mulberry St);
Tel 334 36 69; Sun–Thurs
11.00–23.30, Fri, Sat
11.00–24.00.

Pastis

Typical Meatpacking District: this 1930s Paris brasserie has surprisingly authentic décor. Oysters, fish soup, artichokes, and first-class cocktails are amongst the regular customers' favourites. A great spot to eat after a hard day on the hoof.
9 Ninth Ave;
Tel 929 48 44;
Mon–Wed 8.00–1.00, Thurs
8.00–2.00, Sat 10.00–3.00,
Sun 10.00–1.00.
www.pastisny.com

Peking Duck House

Even the Chinese rate the Peking Duck, which tastes better than anywhere else in Chinatown. It is served here with little pancakes, spring onions, gherkins, and Hoisin sauce. The chicken with pine kernels and Shanghai shrimp taste excellent, too.
28 Mott St;
Tel 227 18 10;
Sun–Thurs 11.30–22.30,
Fri, Sat 11.45–23.00.
www.pekingduckhousenyc.
com

Prune

One of the best places to go for an original lunch or weekend brunch. The sensational burgers and spaghetti carbonara are especially recommended, and there is a great range of cocktails and drinks, including 12 different kinds of Bloody Mary. Perfect for a refreshing cocktail after a day spent shopping.
54 E. First St;
Tel 677-6221
www.prunerestaurant.com
Mon–Thurs 11.30–15.00,
18.00–23.00, Fri 11.30–15.00,
18.00–24.00, Sat
10.00–15.30, 18.00–24.00,
Sun 10.00–15.30,
17.00–22.00

Pylos

Home-made Greek food which compares favorably with the pseudo-Greek food in a lot of places. Lamb and chicken are cooked in a clay pot, there is Greek salad, and a wide range of Greek wines. Very authentic.
128 E.7th St (near Ave A)
Tel 473-0220
www.pylosrestaurant.com
Mon, Tues 17.00–24.00,
Wed, Thurs Sun
11.30–16.00, 17.00–24.00,
Fri, Sat 11.30–16.00,
17.00–1.00

Rai Rai Ken

A credible alternative to the many sushi bars in the East Village: noodles are the main event in this little bar. Soba, udon, and ramen feature in all their variations, and tasty gyoza (pork dumplings).
214 E. 10th St
(near Second Ave);
Tel 477 70 30;
Mon–Sat 12.00–2.30,
Sun 12.00–23.30.

Red Egg

The owner is the son of a Chinese father and a Peruvian mother and combines the best of each country's cuisine in an interesting fusion. Shrimp, chicken pieces, pork, and vegetable float in the curry broth of the "curry bread bowl", and you have to try the coconut pudding for dessert. Delicious and unusual.
202 Centre St
(corner of Howard St);
Tel 966 11 23;
10.00–23.00, daily.
www.redeggnyc.com

Sapporo East

A small Japanese bar without the elegance of the new East Village, and yet the slack feel is deceptive: the noodle dishes are excellent and the sushi here is pretty good too, especially the imaginative California rolls. Extremely good value for money.
245 E. 10th St
(corner of First Ave);
Tel 260 13 30; 17.00–0.45,
daily.

26 Seats

The name comes from the 26 different chairs, but it is popular principally for its French-influenced food, such as onion tart, fish with maize cakes and champagne vinaigrette, and calamari. Delicieux! Bon appetit!
168 Ave B;
Tel 677 47 87;
Tues– Thurs Sun 17.30–
23.00, Fri, Sat 17.30–23.30.

Su Ra

A hot tip for lovers of Korean food. Most visitors rave about the red snapper with mushrooms; the bibimbop (rice with vegetables and raw egg) and the noodle dishes are also excellent. For a little more than $30 you can have a "King's Meal" with various house specials.
105 E. 9th St
(near Fourth Ave);
Tel 982 63 90;
Mon–Thurs 12.00–23.00;
Fri, Sat 12.00–24.00.
www.suranyc.com

STK

A trendy steak house in the Meatpacking District, decorated in black and silver and (as it says itself) aimed at a female clientele. The steaks taste great, and there is a bustling bar area, but avoid the cocktails at the bar. It is a new style steakhouse with a good atmosphere and often great music.
26 Little W.12th St
(near Ninth Ave);
Tel (646) 624 24 44;
17.30–2.00, daily.
www.stkhouse.com

Sweet Rhythm

Excellent jazz of every kind, especially on Mondays when the New School University ensemble shows its mettle. Tuesday is vocals night. The few tables available also have a good view. Reductions for students.
88 7th Ave;
Tel 255 36 26;
19.00–2.00, daily.
www.sweetrhythmny.com

11th St Bar

A traditional Irish pub with original Guinness and the usual alcoholic drinks. There is live Irish music session on Sunday evenings from 21.00 and bluegrass groups play on Tuesdays and Wednesdays .
510 E. 11th St (near Ave A);
Tel 982 39 29;
Mon–Fri 16.00–4.00,
Sat, Sun 13.00–4.00.

Table 8

Govind Armstrong, an experimental cook from California and a student of Wolfgang Puck's, serves up surprising combinations of ingredients: the duck is accompanied by candied kumquats, the red snapper has a fine lobster sauce, and the filet mignon comes with roast leeks.
25 Cooper Sq. (near 6th St);
Tel 475 34 00;
7.00–11.00, 12.00–15.30,
18.00–23.00, daily.
www.thecoopersquarehotel.com

Tree

A rustic bistro without the elegance of many New York restaurants, and the hearty food is down-to-earth, too. Spicy onion soup, ribs with pasta, steak with first-class fries, and an intimate garden that is still an insider tip.
190 First Ave (near 12th St);
Tel 358 71 71;
Mon–Thurs 17.00–24.00,
Fri, Sat 17.00–1.00, Sun
11.00–16.00, 17.00–24.00.
www.treenyc.com

TriBeCa Grill

Top American cooking with an Asiatic and Italian touch, and the historic Tiffany bar is a good place to hang out in as well. Robert de Niro is the co-owner and there are portraits of his father hanging on the walls (see p. 54).
375 Greenwich St/corner of Franklin St;
Tel 941 39 00;
Mon–Thurs 11.30–17.00,
17.30–23.00, Fri 11.30–17.00,
17.30–23.30, Sun
11.30–15.00, 17.30–22.00.
www.myriadrestaurant group.com

Wd-50

Wylie Dufresne, a celebrity chef with a love of experimentation, serves up surprising combinations of ingredients in striking forms. Pork belly and fish dishes are amongst the most popular choices, and the best thing to do is order the "tasting menu". The desserts are also deliciously rich and unusual, for example goat's cheese panna cotta with maple syrup and cashew nuts.
50 Clinton St (near Rivington St); Tel 477 29 00;
Mon–Sat 18.00–23.00, Sun 18.00–22.00.
www.wd-50.com

Zoé

A well-known place to meet and be seen in SoHo. Modern American cuisine in Californian surroundings and a leisurely atmosphere. See and be seen here!
90 Prince St, between Broadway and Mercer St;
Tel 966 67 22; Mon 12.00–15.00, Tues–Thurs 12.00–22.00, Fri 12.00–23.00, Sat 11.30–15.30, 17.30–22.00.
www.zoerestaurant.com

Accommodation

Cosmopolitan Hotel

A small hotel located in TriBeCa which is good value (for New York) at under $200, although you have to make certain allowances for the size and furnishing of the rooms; no problem if you are just looking for somewhere to sleep – at least the rooms have a window.
95 West Broadway (near Chambers St);
Tel 566 19 00.
www.cosmohotel.com

Duane St Hotel

A simple boutique hotel with sparsely decorated rooms that are mostly intended for business travellers, as are the large desks; there is also an office space for guests next to the lobby. Guests can also take advantage of free admission to the nearby Tribeca Health & Fitness Club.
130 Duane St (corner of Church St);
Tel 964 46 00.
www.duanestreethotel.com

Hampton Inn

Manhattan-SoHo
Hampton is one of the cleanest and most reliable hotel chains in the USA. Usually reasonably priced, the location in Manhattan means you will have to dig a little deeper here. The rooms are decorated in a modern style and the beds are extremely comfortable. The terrace on the 19th floor offers visitors a great view of New York.
54 Watts St (near Sixth Ave);
Tel 226 62 88.
www.hamptonsohonyc.com

Holiday Inn Express Downtown

You know what you are getting with Holiday Inn Express, one of the best-value and most reliable hotel chains in the USA: large rooms, comfortable beds, simple design – everything you need for a good night's sleep. Familiar, efficient, and you know where you are...
126 Water St,
Tel 747 92 22.
www.hiexpress.com

Hotel on Rivington

A futuristic-looking hotel in a glass and aluminium highrise. The rooms were styled by the designer India Mahdavi and have strikingly large windows. The rooms and furnishings are mainly black and white, with flat-screen televisions built into the wall.
107 Rivington St;
Tel 475 26 00.
www.hotelonrivington.com

The Blue Note is a top class jazz club; a view of the Cosmopolitan Hotel; live it up in a penthouse at boutique hotel 60 Thompson; nice and smart in the Hampton Inn Manhattan-SoHo (from left)

DOWNTOWN MANHATTAN

These pages give additional information for the area of New York described in the "Highlights" section (pp. 156–173). Please note that the area code for New York is **212**.

Lafayette House

An unassuming guest house in a historic 1840s brownstone house. The variously decorated rooms make you feel like an ordinary tenant spending an extended time in New York and you would hardly recognize the place as a hotel; there isn't even a lobby. The rooms are luxurious, the beds comfortable, and there is a welcoming open fire.
38 E. 4th St (near Bowery);
Tel 505 81 00.
www.lafayettenyc.com

The Mercer

Film stars, models, and other celebrities discovered this hotel in SoHo long ago. The rooms are elegantly decorated with striking flowing lines, and dark African wood and warm mauves create a refined atmosphere. The showers are enormous, the bathtubs are big enough for two, and the bottles in the bathrooms are from a Swedish cosmetics firm. You can hire a trainer for your daily gym session, if you are feeling exceptionally energetic during your stay.
147 Mercer St
(near Prince St);
Tel 966 60 60.
www.mercerhotel.com

Second Home on Second Avenue

Five astonishingly large rooms in a simple guest house in the East Village. The Peruvian owner has drawn on the folklore of his South American homeland for the décor. The beds are comfortable, the service extremely friendly, and you wouldn't recognize it as a bed and breakfast from the outside.

221 Second Ave
(near 14th St);
Tel 677 31 61.

SoHotel

You have to make a lot of allowances for the room rates at this hotel: the rooms are small and sparsely furnished, the corridors narrow, and the service limited, but the prices are great. Students especially are fans of the low prices. SoHotel prides itself on being "the oldest hotel in New York", and even William Waldorf is supposed to have stayed here. However, you won't meet any celebrities in the SoHotel nowadays.
341 Broome St
(near Bowery);
Tel 226 14 82.
www.thesohotel.com

60 Thompson

A modern boutique hotel located in SoHo that isn't just for rich brokers and beautiful models. The design incorporates dark wood and soft tones and the tiles in the bathroom are marble; the somewhat severe feel is perhaps something for younger people. The top floor is taken up with "a60," a Moroccan-themed club with great views over the city.
60 Thompson St
(near Broome St);
Tel 219 20 00.
www.60thompson.com

Washington Square Hotel

Writers, singers, and painters lived in this hotel in the West Village in the 1960s; even Bob Dylan and Joan Baez are said to have stayed here. The hotel has since been renovated and the deluxe rooms will certainly meet the highest expectations.

103 Waverly Pl
(near MacDougal St);
Tel 777 95 15.
www.washingtonsquare-hotel.com

Nightlife

2A

This popular bar in the East Village has been here since the 1980s. The drug dealers have moved out of the area and now there are restaurants and bistros with a middle-class clientele. You get two drinks for the price of one between 16.00 and 20.00.
25 Ave A (corner of 2nd St);
Tel 505 24 66;
16.00–4.00, daily.

Blue Note

Since opening in 1981, Blue Note has become one of the most successful jazz clubs in the world. Danny Bensusan, the founder and owner, had wanted to present artists like Lionel Hampton, Sarah Vaughan, Dizzy Gillespie, and Oscar Peterson in intimate surroundings and the club fulfilled his dream.
131 West Third St;
Tel 475-8592;
from 20.00, daily.
www.bluenote.net

5C Café and Cultural Center

A health food restaurant by day and a jazz club by night, this has remained an insider tip despite the successful concerts here. The avant-garde is well represented at 5C and the admission prices are low, rarely rising above $10.
68 Ave C (corner of 5th St);
Tel 477 59 93;
Tues–Thurs 17.00–21.00,
Fri, Sat 17.00–1.00.
www.5ccc.com

Entwine

A surprisingly spacious wine bar in the West Village. The club covers two floors and a patio, and its brick walls and seemingly randomly placed upholstered furniture give it a homely feel. Excellent selection of wines from all over the world and an amazing range of cocktails.
765 Washington St
(near 12th St);
Tel 727 87 65;
Sun–Thurs 15.00–24.00,
Fri, Sat 15.00–2.00.
www.entwinenyc.com

Fat Cat

A cellar pool hall, but unlike the billiards rooms of yesteryear. This establishment's rooms are intimate and dimly lit; an hour of pool costs less than $10. There's other games available too, like ping pong and shuffleboard, as well as live jazz every evening on the small stage, with late night jam sessions to 4 a.m.
75 Christopher St
(near Seventh Ave);
Tel 675 60 56;
Mon–Thurs 14.00–5.00,
Fri, Sat 12.00–5.00.
www.fatcatmjazz.com

White Horse Tavern

The Welsh poet and writer Dylan Thomas's former hangout, and still a shrine for fans and followers of the famous alcoholic. A great spot for Thomas lovers, although unfortunately his death was related to the18 whiskies he had previously drunk in this bar. Take your notebook in case you are inspired to follow in his poetic footsteps…
567 Hudson St
(corner of 11th St);
Tel 243 92 60;
11.00–3.00, daily.

Museums, music, and drama

Museum of Arts & Design (formerly American Craft Museum)

The museum provides an interesting overview of American arts and crafts, especially from the 20th century, including a great many beautiful textiles and some stunning pieces in wood and metal. Fabulous jewelry and an interactive website.
2 Columbus Circle;
Tel (212) 956 3535;
Tues–Sun 11.00–18.00, Thurs
11.00–21.00, closed Mon
and major holidays;
www.madmuseum.org.

American Folk Art Museum

Housed in a spectacular new building by Tod Williams and Billie Tsien, the museum is devoted to American life from the colonial period to the present day. Exhibits include drawings, paintings, sculpture, photographs, and everyday objects from all walks of life, including some beautifully made fabrics and textile items, especially quilts, for which American folk art is justifiably renown.
45 West 53rd St;
Tel 265 10 40;
Tues–Sun 10.30–17.30, Fri
10.30–19.30.

American Museum of the Moving Image

Founded in 1988 in a building belonging to Astoria Studios, the museum exhibits film and video pieces by contemporary artists as well as giving an overview of the origins and history of cinema. The museum's treasures include technical equipment, movie requisites, and some nostalgic

curios from the history of the silver screen.
35th Ave, 37th St, Astoria;
Tel (718) 784 45 20/784 00 77;
Tues–Fri 10.00–15.00,
closed Thanksgiving, 25 Dec;
www.movingimage.us

Carnegie Hall

A neo-Renaissance building with three concert halls used for jazz concerts, educational forum, and historic lectures, including the largest, the Issac Stern Auditorium, containing almost 2,800 seats and with excellent acoustics. It was built in 1891 thanks to a generous donation from Andrew Carnegie, the steel magnate, and was once the home of the New York Philharmonic, which has since moved on to the Lincoln Center. The halls are still used for rock and pop gigs as well as classical concerts. The Rose Museum on the second floor of the hall is dedicated to its history. It also contains interesting items such as a ring owned by Beethoven and a jacket worn by Judy Garland.
881 7th Ave (at 57th St);
Tel 632 05 40.

International Center of Photography Museum

The ICP Museum opened in 1974. The temporary exhibitions that it frequently holds are drawn from its stock of over 10,000 photographs, from daguerrotypes to contemporary photo art. The emphasis is on photojournalism from 1930 to 1990.
1133 Avenue of the Americas;
Tel 857 00 00;
Tues–Thurs, Sat, Sun
10.00–18.00, Fri 10.00–20.00,
closed public hols;
www.icp.org

Intrepid Sea Air Space Museum

The aircraft carrier USS *Intrepid*, which saw service in World War II, has been used as a museum ship since 1982. On board you can see military aircraft, helicopters, and objects from the US space program. The museum also has a nuclear submarine, the *Growler*, and a British *Concorde*. The interactive elements and the flight simulator also make the museum a draw for children. If you have little ones in your group, it's a good place to spend a few happy hours, especially on wet days.
Pier 86, 12th Ave/46th St;
Tel (877) 957 74 47 (ship);
Apr to Sep Mon–Fri
10.00–17.00, Sat, Sun, public
hols, 10.00–18.00, Oct–Mar
Tues–Sun 10.00–17.00;
www.intrepidmuseum.org

Japan Society Gallery

Temporary exhibitions offering an interesting insight into Japan's art and culture from prehistory to the present day. Events and lectures related to all things Japanese are also held here.
333 East 47th St;
Tel 832 11 55;
Tues–Fri 11.00–18.00,
Sat, Sun 11.00–17.00,
closed public hols;
www.japansociety.org

Madison Square Garden

Built above the old platforms of Pennsylvania Station, this famous multi-purpose complex featured in the film classic *Godzilla* and contains a large sports arena where rock concerts and sporting events such as basketball, ice hockey, and boxing matches all take place. There is also a theater,

a bowling alley, a movie theater, exhibition spaces, and a conference center with restaurants and stores.
4 Pennsylvania Plaza;
Tel 465 67 4;
www.thegarden.com

The Museum at FIT

The museum is part of the State University of New York's Fashion Institute of Technology and takes visitors on a fascinating stroll through the history of fashion from the 18th century to the present day. The contemporary star designer are also featured. With more than 50,000 exhibits, it is the world's largest fashion collection.
Tel 217 45 58;
Tues–Fri 12.00–20.00,
Sat 10.00–17.00,
closed public hols.

The Paley Center for Media

The museum was founded in 1976 and is housed in a Philip Johnson and John Burgee building equipped with projection rooms and video consoles. The 50,000 exhibits have much to interest both the professional student of broadcasting and television in America and the general consumer. The center's mission – it also has a location in Los Angeles – is to look at the social significance of television, radio, and the emerging new media technologies.
25 West 52nd St;
Tel 621 68 00;
Tues–Sun 12.00–18.00,
Thurs 12.00–20.00;
www.paleycenter.org

The Morgan Library & Museum

This library building was opened to the public in 1924 as a gift from J.P.Morgan, one

Times Square; the American Craft Museum's collection contains the finest arts and crafts; the P.S.1 Contemporary Art Center – home of the avant-garde; the giant Christmas tree at the Rockefeller Center (from left).

MIDTOWN MANHATTAN

These pages give additional information for the area of New York described in the "Highlights" section (pp. 88–141). Please note that the area code for New York is **212**.

of America's richest men. Themed temporary exhibitions and the permanent exhibition drawn from its own holdings give an overview of the world of medieval manuscripts and incunabula. One of the highlights of its many gems is a genuine Gutenberg Bible. There are also manuscripts by Charles Dickens, Mozart, Lord Byron, and Robert Burns, among many others. The permanent exhibition includes artists' sketches, paintings, and fine sculpture, including work by Rembrandt, Gainsborough, and Picasso.
225 Madison Ave/36th St;
Tel 685 00 08;
Tues–Thurs 10.30–17.00,
Fri 10.30–21.00, Sat
10.00–18.00, Sun
11.00–18.00, closed
Thanksgiving, 25 Dec, 1 Jan;
www.themorgan.org

P.S. 1 Contemporary Art Center
After extensive refurbishment, Public School 1, an 1890 junior high school, has become an important center for contemporary art, showing a prestigious series of works curated by the Museum of Modern Art. The fast turnover of new exhibitions provides a good indicator of the most up-to-date trends in contemporary art.
22–25 Jackson Ave/
46th Ave, Long Island;
Tel (718) 784 20 84;
Thurs–Mon 12.00–18.00,
closed Thanksgiving,
25 Dec, 1 Jan.

Rubin Museum of Art
Opened in 2004 in an old department store, the museum is devoted to Himalayan culture; with more than 2,000 exhibits, including paintings, sculpture, and textiles, it provides a considered and very informative overview. Although works of art range in date over two millennia, most reflect major periods and schools of Himalayan art from the 12th century onward.
150 W 17th St;
Tel 620 50 00;
Mon, Thurs 11.00–17.00,
Wed 11.00–19.00, Fri
11.00–22.00, Sat, Sun
11.00–18.00;
www.rmanyc.org

Theodore Roosevelt Birthplace
An early 20th-century reconstruction of the original brownstone, the house is full of mementos of the president, who was born in New York in 1858. The original house was unfortunately demolished, but the reconstruction has been furnished with many original items provided by Roosevelt's widow and his sisters.
28 East 20th St;
Tel 260 16 16;
Tues–Sat 9.00–17.00;
www.nps.gov

Yeshiva University Museum
This museum provides a comprehensive and fascinating overview of Jewish history, beliefs, and culture.
15 West 16th St;
Tel 294 83 30;
Sun, Tue, Wed, Thurs
11.00–17.00;
www.yumuseum.org

Festivals and events

9th Avenue International Food Festival
Every year, up to a million visitors are drawn to the culinary delights offered by the festival. The delicacies on offer range from fish and seafood dishes, falafel and grilled cheese to kebabs, satay, suckling pig, and even elephant's ears (conservationists don't worry, it's actually a kind of biscuit). There is also a flea market, bric-a-brac, market stalls, and live music. This is a paradise for foodies!
9th Ave from West
5th–37th St;
Tel 484 12 00;
mid May.
http://nycgo.com

Columbus Day Parade
Celebrating themselves: more than 500,000 spectators gather along Fifth Avenue to remember explorer Christopher Columbus and to commemorate the discovery of America. Participants in the colorful ceremonial procession include the mayor of New York, delegations from various Italian regions, cities, and villages, Broadway stars, a number of international folklore groups, plus plenty of marching bands.
5th Ave from East 44th to
79th St; around 12 Oct.

Easter Parade
Hundreds of participants flock to St Patrick's Cathedral for this special Easter event, showing off their magnificent, and occasionally rather daring, Easter hats, bonnets, and other headgear.
5th Ave between East 50th
and 51st St; Easter Sunday,
10.00–16.00.

Fleet Week
A week-long celebration of the Navy, Marine Corps, and Coast Guard which sees New York invaded by hundreds of sailors looking for a party; the city resembles a 1940s film set (think *On the Town*) for the duration. You can inspect the ships at anchor on the Hudson River and much more besides. The climax of Fleet Week is the remembrance service for fallen US service personnel, which is held on the aircraft carrier *Intrepid* on Memorial Day.
West 46th St/12th Ave;
Tel 245 00 72;
late May.

Gay and Lesbian Pride Parade
The lesbian and gay pride parade moves down Fifth Avenue in a five-hour spectacle with dancers, entertainers, and members of the gay and lesbian community. The glittering parade, cheered on by up to a million spectators, is considered the highlight of Gay Pride Week. The festivities commemorate the so-called Stonewall Riots, when gays and lesbians first fought back against police raids in Greenwich Village in June 1969.
From Columbus Circle via
5th Ave to Christopher St;
Tel 807 74 33;
last Sun in May;
www.nycpride.org

Christmas Tree Lighting Ceremony
The lights on the gigantic Christmas tree at the Rockefeller Center are lit in a solemn ceremony. Hundreds of spectators of all ages come along to see the official beginning of Christmas in New York.
5th Ave between
West 49th and 51st St;
Tel 632 39 75;
late Nov/early Dec.

New Year's Eve

New Year's Eve celebrations begin at 19.00 in Times Square where a few glasses are raised despite the (usually) intense cold. The countdown until the Waterford crystal ball raised on a pole over One Times Square is dropped at midnight has become world-famous. Other parts of the city hold events that are also worth seeing, such as the midnight run through Central Park. New York on New Year's Eve is an exciting place. New Year in New York is an occasion that you will never forget.
midnight run:
Tel 860 44 55;
New Year's Eve.

Puerto Rican Day Parade

Thousands of dancing and flag-waving spectators line Fifth and 3rd Avenues to see the Puerto Rican parade with its traditional dance troupes and musicians. Loud Latin American music from meter-high speakers or thumping out from houses along the route celebrates the rhythms of bomba, meringue, plena, and salsa.
5th to 3rd Ave from
East 44th–86th St;
second Sun in May.

St Patrick's Day Parade

Spectators descend on Fifth Avenue in their thousands to cheer on the world-famous Irish procession of bagpipers and magnificent floats. It is thought that up to 100,000 people attend the event, with some of them taking the opportunity to enjoy to the full the beer that flows in considerable quantities.
5th Ave from East 44th St;
17 Mar.

Sport and leisure

Annual Empire State Building Run Up

The annual run up the stairs of the Empire State from the lobby to the 86th floor comprises 1,576 steps. Trained runners can do it in about nine to eleven minutes. Plenty of video cameras are installed in the stairwells so that the spectators can follow the action on big screens, silently relieved that they only watching rather than taking part.
350 5th Ave/34th St;
Tel 736 31 00; Feb.

Bird Watching

Part of the national society named after the famous 19th-century ornithologist, The New York City Audubon Society holds bird watching tours in various parks in the city throughout the year, as well as excursions to the heron colonies on Long Island Sound, ornithology and butterfly courses for beginners, and much more. Some of the events are free. The three-hour tours of Central Park during the migration season (Apr to May and Sep to Oct) are especially popular. There is also a bird information hotline.
NYC Audubon Society
71 West 23rd St;
Tel 691 74 83;
mid-Aug–Oct, Mon,
Wed, and Sat from 7.30,
Tues from 9.00;
Starr Saphir: Tel 304 38 08.

Bliss49

You can switch off from daily stress here, either in the sauna, under a steam shower, or with a massage. All this costs, however, but a 90-minute body treatment with carrot mulch and a rub-down with unguents and oils can be had for under $200. There are two other branches of Bliss in Manhattan. If you are in need of some post-shopping/sightseeing bliss, this is where to come.
541 Lexington Ave/
East 49th St;
Tel 219 89 70;
8.00–22.00, daily;
www.blissworld.com

Chelsea Piers Sports and Entertainment Complex

If you are regretting some of that NYC pizza and cheesecake, a trip to the city's largest leisure and sports complex might tempt you – there are facilities for ball games (baseball, soccer, golf) and martial arts (boxing!), along with swimming, yoga, climbing, and much more. There are also two rinks for skating and ice hockey which are open throughout the year. There is an outdoor rollerblading area and you can relax in the in-house spa or on the sunbathing terrace.
Pier 59–62, 23nd St/
West Side Highway;
Tel 336 66 66;
www.chelseapiers.com

Elizabeth Arden's Red Door

If you have a big budget, you should treat yourself to the famous US cosmetic firm's "Red Door Salon & Spa". The range of treatments includes facials, bathing, massages, manicures, and pedicures. Spa packages start at around $99 dollars and the spa is open every day from 8.00 (9.00 on Sunday). There is another branch a little to the south, further down Fifth Avenue.
691 5th Ave/54th St;
Tel 546 02 00.

Okeanos

"A day in the banya is a day you don't age" is the motto of this smart Russian spa in Midtown East. Along with the usual facilities you can indulge in a Russian sauna with the traditional birch twig mortification. Even ice hockey players come to Okeanos to be restored to fitness with vigorous massages.
211 East 51st St/3rd Ave;
Tel 223 67 73;
Tues–Fri 12.00–22.00, Sat
11.00–20.00, Sun
12.00–17.00.

Roosevelt Island Tram

Just like San Francisco, New York has cable cars as well: the aerial tram, generally just known as "the tram", starts in Manhattan at the intersection of 2nd Avenue and 60th Street, crosses the East Channel of the East River at a height of 40 meters (130 feet) and terminates on Roosevelt Island after a journey of about a kilometer (half a mile). The four-minute journey offers panoramic views of the Manhattan skyline, while Roosevelt Island itself has several historic buildings which are best inspected as part of a gentle stoll around the island.
Roosevelt Island Operating Corporation:
Tel 832 45 55;
Rambling: www.riwalk.com

Shopping

Christie's

Auctions at Christie's are considered a big social event. The objects up for auction can be viewed beforehand and a visit is always worthwhile, even if you don't intend to buy anything.

MIDTOWN MANHATTAN

These pages give additional information for the area of New York described in the "Highlights" section (pp. 88–141). Please note that the area code for New York is **212**.

20 Rockefeller Plaza/
West 49th St;
Tel 636 20 00;
Mon–Fri 9.30–17.30;
www.christies.com

Emporio Armani

If you like Armani designer clothes and have sufficient funds, this is the place to be. Relax in the café on the sixth floor and enjoy the view of the city from the roof terrace.
601 Madison Ave/
East 56th St;
Mon–Sat 10.00–19.00,
Sun 12.00–18.00.

Lord & Taylor

The most traditional retailer of ladies' and gentlemen's clothing in the US is based near the Empire State Building. This respected department store sells mainly branded goods by US designers – at reduced prices. The end-of-season sale has clothes, shoes, and bags with even greater reductions.
424 5th Ave;
Tel 391 33 44;
Mon–Fri 10.00–20.30,
Sat 10.00–19.00,
Sun 11.00–19.00.

Manolo Blahnik

It has to be high heels: platforms and quirky design had made this Spanish designer's shoes a status symbol long before the *Sex and the City* TV series. Bianca Jagger was wearing stacked and pointy Blahnik creations in 1977 when she famously rode a white horse into New York's Studio 54 club. If shoes are your thing, Manolo Blahnik on 5th Avenue is your destination. It doesn't get much better than this...
31 West 54th St/5th Ave;
Tel 582 30 07;

Mon–Fri 10.30–20.00,
Sat 10.30–17.30,
Sun 12.00–17.00..

NBA Store

A world of experiences for basketball fans in the National Basketball Association's (NBA) only store in the city. They stock sports clothes for men, women, and children, as well as balls and accessories from key rings to drinks coolers.
666 5th Ave/West 52nd St;
Tel 515 62 21;
Mon–Sat 10.00–19.00
(summer 10.00–20.00),
Sun 11.00–18.00;
www.nba.com

The Original Levi's Store

The right place to stock up on original Levi's, starting with classics like button fly 501s and ending with pieces from the current collection. As well as jeans there are shirts, T-shirts, pullovers, jackets, and accessories.
750 Lexington Ave/59th St,
Tel 826 59 57,
Mon–Sat 10.00–20.00,
Sun 12.00–18.00;
www.levi.com

Tourneau Time Machine

They call themselves the world's largest watch store. The three floors of this veritable temple to time are stocked with more than 8,000 models, with 90 brands on offer. There's bound to be something for almost every visitor. Time is of the essence here, in more ways than one.
12 East 57th St/5th Ave;
Tel 758 73 00;
Mon–Wed and Fri–Sat
10.00–18.00, Thurs
10.00–19.00, Sun
11.30–17.30;
www.tourneau.com

Toys 'R' US

The largest US branch of this toy chain is chock full of children in a buying mood – hoping their parents are also – especially in the run-up to Christmas. Apart from the stuffed toy aisle and the big wheel there are three floors of very technically complicated toys, arranged by type, and the basement houses a giant video and computer games section.
1514 Broadway;
Tel (800) 869 77 87;
Mon–Sat 10.00–22.00,
Sun 11.00–20.00;
www.toysrus.com

Eating and drinking

Abboccato

Head chef Jake Addeo has a predilection for extraordinary Italian food, conjuring exquisite Italian nouvelle cuisine from quite rustic ingredients. Special tips: quail stuffed with mortadella, soft gnocchi, and sea urchin with candied lemon. Not quite the food that your average Italian mama makes...
136 West 55th St
(near 6th Ave);
Tel 265 40 00;
Mon 7.30–10.30,
12.00–15.00, 17.00–22.00,
Tues–Sat 7.30–10.30,
12.00–15.00, 17.00–23.00,
Sun 7.30–10.30, 16.00–22.00.
www.abboccato.com

Adour Alain Ducasse

This gourmet paradise in the St Regis Hotel is decorated in mahogany and burgundy tones inspired by the wine list. Alain Ducasse has won Michelin stars and can turn simple root vegetables into a delicacy. His greatest successes are duck breast and

fish – you rarely find something so perfectly cooked in New York.
2 East 55th St
(corner of 5th Ave);
Tel 710 22 77;
Sun–Thurs 17.30–22.30,
Fri, Sat 17.30–23.00.

Alonso's Steakhouse

This tiny steak and seafood restaurant is not out of the ordinary just because of the stuffed ox, elk, and bear heads. It has become well-known for its excellent and juicy Porterhouse steaks. Regular diners are fans of the onion rings and the excellent spinach as accompaniments.
265 West 20th Ave
(near 8th Ave);
Tel 675 77 49;
17.00–23.00, daily.

Aquavit

Hypermodern surroundings which are not perhaps quite to everyone's taste, but the aquavit in this smart Scandinavian restaurant is excellent. The specialities (of course) include herring served with vodka and "beef Rydberg" (steak with onions served with a raw egg).
65 East 55th St
(near Madison Ave);
Tel 307 73 11; Sun–Thurs
12.00–14.30, 17.30–22.30, Fri
12.00–14.30, 17.15–23.00,
Sat 17.00–23.00;
www.aquavit.org

Ariana Afghan Kebab House

One of the smallest but one of the best kebab restaurants in Midtown. More than 20 varieties of kebab make choosing difficult, but they are all delicious. The exotic-tasting dishes include the spiced pumpkin, the milk

pudding with almonds and pistachios, and the yoghurt drink with grated cucumber.
787 9th Ave (near 52nd St);
Tel 262 23 23;
12.00–22.45, daily.

Artisanal
A high-ceilinged bistro with a very French feel, making you feel like you're in the middle of Paris. The focus here is on cheese, with over 200 differently prepared varieties from all over the world, served as a starter, main course, or dessert. The tempting fondues are better than in Swiss restaurants. Paris comes to Park Avenue. Bon appetit!
2 Park Ave
(corner of 32nd St);
Tel 725 85 85;
Mon–Fri 10.45–22.45,
Sat 10.30–22.45,
Sun 10.30–22.00;
www.artisanalcheese.com

Bao Noodles
Co-owner Michael Huynh has brought the recipes of his youth to New York. The stir fries, noodles, and salads taste just like they do in the Far East. He also has tasty dressings for meat, fish, and shellfish. The interior design is reminiscent of a French bistro.
391 2nd Ave (near 23rd St);
Tel 725 77 70; Sun–Wed
11.30–23.00, Thurs–Sat
11.00–24.00.
www.baonoodles.com

Beacon
All the dishes are cooked or grilled over an open fire: trout, duck, oysters, even the bread is baked before the customers' eyes. There is a reassuringly large selection of liquid mixes for cocktail fans to enjoy and the Sunday brunch is very tasty.

25 West 56th St
(near 5th Ave);
Tel 332 05 00;
Mon–Thurs 12.00–14.30,
17.00–22.00, Fri 12.00–14.30,
17.00–22.30, Sat
17.00–22.30, Sun
10.30–14.30, 16.00–20.00.
www.beaconnyc.com

Better Burger
Even in Manhattan you can get fast food for vegetarians and the health-conscious. The meat is of course from organic cattle and the poultry from free-range turkeys and chickens, and harmful fats are left out of the cooking process. They also have healthy vegetable dishes..
561 3rd Ave (near 37th St);
Tel 949 75 28;
Mon–Sat 11.00–22.30,
Sun 11.00–22.00.

BLT Steak
BLT stands for bacon, lettuce, and tomato, but these ingredients have only supporting roles. The main part is played by the excellent steak. The astonishingly tender filet mignon tastes best but you can't go wrong with a gigantic Porterhouse either.
106 East 57th St
(near Park Ave);
Tel 752 74 70;
Mon–Thurs 11.45–14.30,
17.30–23.00, Fri 11.45–14.30,
17.30–23.30, Sat
17.30–23.30.

Boi
This Vietnamese restaurant has an excellent menu and has won praise from Vietnamese customers. As well as expertly spiced dishes such as "Buddhist Sweet and Sour" and grilled aubergine there are desserts such as tamarind cake with red papaya.

246 East 44th St
(near 2nd Ave);
Tel 681 65 41;
Mon–Wed 11.30–15.00,
17.30–22.00, Thurs, Fri
11.30–15.00, 17.30–23.00,
Sat 17.30–23.00, Sun
17.00–21.00.

Bread Market Cafe
Organic ingredients are rare in new York bakeries and coffee shops. This café swears by fresh ingredients for its sandwiches, wraps, and salads, which are in a class of their own. Business people often opt for tasty burritos and hearty soups for lunch.
485 5th Ave;
Tel 957 56 77;
Mon–Fri 6.30–19.00.
www.breadmarket.com

Burger Joint
No longer an insider tip: the burgers in this smart burger place in the lobby of the Parker Meridien Hotel still taste as they should, and are good value as well.
119 West 56th St
(near 6th Ave);
Tel 708 74 14;
Sun–Thurs 11.00–23.30, Fri,
Sat 11.00–24.00.

Carve Unique Sandwiches
IA sandwich shop in the Theater District for the upper crust, as it were: the sandwiches, filled with fine pork, turkey breast, and fresh ingredients like tomatoes, onions, and lettuce taste delicious.
760 8th Ave
(corner of 47th St);
Tel 730 49 49;
7.00–17.00, daily.

Cookshop
The open-plan kitchen of this trendy restaurant in Chelsea serves up hearty fare such as

grilled chicken and steamed fish. All the ingredients are sourced locally and the fruit and veg is served seasonally. The smoked fish is from their own smoker.
156 10th Ave
(corner of 20th St);
Tel 924 44 40;
Mon–Fri 11.30–15.00,
17.30–24.00, Sat 11.00–
15.00, 17.30–24.00, Sun
11.00–15.00, 17.30–22.00;
www.cookshopny.com

Darbar Grill
The atmosphere is reminiscent of an up-market steak house, but head chef Simon Gomes cooks Indian cuisine with an international feel. The scallops are served with a delicious coconut and mint sauce, the giant shrimps are spicy and hot, and the rice has just the right consistency.
157 East 55th St
(near 3rd St);
Tel 751 46 00;
Sun–Thurs 11.30–22.30,
Fri, Sat 11.30–23.00.
www.darbargrillny.com

DB Bistro Moderne
Daniel Bouloud ("DB"), the head chef here, serves up an exclusive alternative to the usual burgers and "whoppers": his "DB" burger is stuffed with delicious truffle and goose liver and is priced to match. For slightly more adventurous tastes.
55 West 44th St
(near 5th Ave);
Tel 391 24 00;
Mon 7.00–10.00,
12.00–14.30, 17.00–22.00,
Tues–Fri 7.00–10.00,
12.00–14.30, 17.00–23.00,
Sat 8.00–11.00, 12.00–14.30,
17.00–23.00, Sun 8.00–11.00,
17.00–22.00;
www.danielnyc.com

MIDTOWN MANHATTAN

These pages give additional information for the area of New York described in the "Highlights" section (pp. 88–141). Please note that the area code for New York is **212**.

Django
The name is deceptive, there's no spaghetti Western food here, but rather small tapas and Italian snacks, matched with first class wine, while crusty bread is served with Mediterranean dips. Django is like a cross between a French bistro and a New York after-work bar.
480 Lexington Ave
(corner of 46th St);
Tel 871 66 00;
Mon–Fri 11.30–14.00,
17.30–22.30;
www.djangorestaurant.com

Estiatorio Milos
Fine fare from Greece in pleasant surroundings. The fish is on ice, ready to be picked out and bought by weight. First class sea bass, which, like all the other fish, is served baked, grilled, or steamed. Try one of their excellent Greek wines to accompany your meal.
125 West 55th St
(near 6th Ave);
Tel 245 74 00;
Mon–Fri 12.00–14.45, 17.00–23.45, Sat 17.00–23.45,
Sun 17.00–22.45;
www.milos.ca

Go! Go! Curry
The Japanese baseball star Hideki Matsui wore the number 55 on his jersey and has named his Asian restaurant accordingly: "Go! Go!" means "55" in Japanese. Even the opening times are based on the number. Curry is the order of the day in this snack bar and the pork is a real improvement on the usual. Go, go... it's worth it!
273 West 38th St
(near 8th Ave);
Tel 730 55 55;
10.55–21.55, daily.

Hallo Berlin
German cuisine that actually tastes like German cuisine is a rarity in the States. This restaurant is one of the honorable exceptions, with Wiener schnitzel, sausage dishes, dumplings, and pickled herring – almost like being in Germany itself.
626 Tenth Ave
(near 44th St);
Tel 977 19 44;
Sun–Thurs 12.00–23.00,
Fri, Sat 12.00–1.00.
www.halloberlinrestaurant.com

99c Fresh Pizza
The name says it all: Abdul's pizzas do indeed cost only 99c. And they taste very good. The tomato sauce and cheese prove a very tasty combo – Abdul's can certainly hold its own against Pizza Hut. If you have a pizza craving while out shopping, you can't do better than this.
151 East 43rd St
(near 3rd Ave);
Tel 922 02 57;
Mon–Sat 9.00–2.30,
Sun 12.00–2.30.

Klee Brasserie
The Vienna roast chicken doesn't taste quite as good as in Vienna, but even so: this bistro has an interesting selection of German and Austrian dishes, with beer from Cologne and Belgium. Absolutely recommended: roast lamb and the varied poultry dishes.
200 Ninth Ave (near 22nd St);
Tel 633 80 33;
Tues–Fri 12.00–15.00,
17.30–24.00, Sat
11.00–15.30, 17.30–24.00,
Sun 11.00–15.30,
17.00–22.00;
www.kleebrasserie.com

Kurumazushi
Sinfully expensive, but worth every cent. Toshihiru Uezu's unassuming portion of sushi heaven is famous for its excellent tuna sashimi, its incomparable uni (sea urchin), and other Japanese specialities, such as white Kuruma shrimp.
7 East 47th St (on the second floor of an office block);
Tel 317 28 02;
Mon–Sat 11.30–14.00,
17.30–22.00.

La Grenouille
This restaurant is in a smart room filled with bright flower arrangements where you immediately feel at home. Charles Masson, the owner, is celebrating French cuisine to the max and until recently didn't feel the need to translate the menu into English. The fish dishes are wonderfully tender – but unfortunately also extremely expensive. If your wallet is bigger than your appetite, this is the place for you.
3 East 52nd St (near 5th Ave);
Tel 752 14 95;
Tues–Sat 12.00–15.00,
17.00–23.00.
www.la-grenouille.com

La Petite Auberge
A real insider tip amongst the better French restaurants. You'll get a good value, top-class three-course meal here, such as with the excellent duck à l'orange. Home cooking of the better sort, ensuring that the Auberge gives the city's award-winning restaurants a run for their money.
116 Lexington Ave
(corner of 28th St);
Tel 689 50 03;

Oct–May Mon–Fri 12.00–23.00, Sat 17.00–23.00, Sun 16.30–22.00, May–Sep Tues–Fri 12.00–23.00, Sat 17.00–23.00;
www.lapetiteaubergeny.com

Lazzara's Pizza Café
A slightly out-of-the-way restaurant but a favourite with pizza fans since 1985. The gas lamps and vents in the high ceiling are reminiscent of the 19th century. The pizza here is as thin and crispy as they eat it in Sicily and the choice of toppings is wide ranging. "Lazzara's Special Pizza", for example, is served with ham, black olives, and tomatoes.
221 West 38th St
(near 7th Ave);
Tel 944 77 92;
Mon 11.30–16.30,
Tues–Fri 11.30–21.00;
www.lazzaraspizza.com

Le Périgord
A smart French restaurant with fine cooking. Amongst the dishes to be recommended here are classics like veal escalope with mushroom sauce or fillet of salmon. The "Floating Island Dessert" is very popular (and very full of calories).
405 East 52nd St;
Tel 755 62 44;
Mon–Fri 12.00–15.30, 17.30–22.00, Sat, Sun 17.30–22.00;
www.leperigord.com

Le Zie
Italian home cooking as it should be: hearty spaghetti with meatballs, lasagne, linguini, and wonderful fish dishes are all on the menu in this sparely decorated restaurant. Regulars rave about the calves' liver with onions.

172 7th Ave (near 20th St);
Tel 206 86 86;
Mon–Fri 12.00–23.30, Sat,
Sun 12.00–23.00.
www.lezie.com

Los Dos Molinos
Fans of spicy Mexican food
have picked the right place
when if come here. "I don't
know how to make mild
sauces" says the chef, and
promptly challenges the
palate with jalapenos and
other chillies. The pork ribs
with rice and beans are highly
recommended:. A culinary hot
spot in more ways than one.
119 East 18th St
(near Park Ave South);
Tel 505 15 74;
Tues–Thurs 12.00–14.30,
17.00–22.30, Fri 12.00–14.30,
17.00–23.30, Sat 15.00–
23.30, Sun 12.00–17.00;
www.losdosmolinosnyc.com

Mia Dona
A tiny and rather cramped
restaurant but with first-class
Mediterranean cuisine. The
grilled lamb and quail bro-
chette and roasted rabbit are
the best choices, and the fish
and mussel dishes are good
too. The lamb spare ribs are
especially tasty.
206 East 58th St
(corner of 3rd Ave);
Tel 750 81 70;
Mon–Thurs 12.00–14.30,
17.00–22.00, Fri 12.00–14.30,
17.00–23.00, Sat 17.00–
23.00, Sun 11.00–14.30,
17.00–21.00;
www.miadona.com

Norma's
The breakfast and lunch
menu at the Le Parker Merid-
ian hotel has gained notoriety
for its legendary $1,000
omelette (served with lobster
and any amount of beluga

caviar). The generous breakfast (such as pancakes with
blueberries and whipped
cream or eggs Benedict with
artichokes) is rather better
value for money. You won't
need lunch afterwards.
118 West 57th St
(near 6th Ave);
Tel 708 74 60;
7.00–15.00, daily;
www.normasnyc.com

Omai
A very good Vietnamese in
Chelsea where the head chef
cooks for demanding fans of
Asian cooking – his tofu with
lemon grass crust and the
excellently spiced spare ribs
are amongst the real specialities. All in all, the prices are
still pretty reasonable.
158 9th Ave (near 19th St);
Tel 633 05 50;
12.00–14.30, 17.30–22.00,
daily;
www.omainyc.com

Park Blue
First impressions are deceptive: the modern dining
lounge doesn't just serve oysters and odd cocktails – other
favourites include the relatively cheap and very juicy
cheeseburgers and other
small dishes.
158 West 58th St
(near 7th Ave);
Tel 247 27 27;
Sun–Tues 17.00–2.00,
Wed–Sat 17.00–3.00.
www.parkbluenyc.com

Pom Pom Diner
This diner is a regular stop for
hungry strollers and night
owls. Traditional American
fast food such as cheeseburgers and club sandwiches are
amongst the most ordered
specialities. Low-calorie salads are less popular here.

610 11th Ave (near 45th St);
Tel 397 83 95;
Mon–Sat 24 hours.

Prespa
Most customers prefer to sit
at the long bar. A relaxed
atmosphere and pleasant gui-
tar music accompany great-
tasting and inventive dishes
such as tuna tartare with avocado relish and red snapper
wrapped in thinly sliced ham
on a bed of asparagus. All the
food has a touch of the
Mediterranean about it.
184 Lexington Ave
(near 31st St);
Tel 810 43 35;
12.00–23.00, daily;
www.prespanyc.com

Prime Burger
A diner from the 1960s, as if
time had stood still; and the
same is true of the menu.
Classics such as burgers,
sandwiches, and "chicken in a
basket" are amongst the
favourites. The burgers are
good – the meat is lean and
the burgers are hand-made.
5 East 51st St (near 5th Ave);
Tel 759 47 29;
Mon–Fri 7.00–19.00, Sat
7.00–17.00, Aug closed Sat;
www.primeburger.com

Quality Meats
There's a good selection of
first class steak houses in
Manhattan, and this is one of
them. The giant steaks are
excellent but some of the
more unusual things here
take a bit of getting used to:
the roast chicken is floating in
sweet kumquats, and the
steak tartare is accompanied
with a little dish of seasoning.
Rather expensive.
57 West 58th St
(near 6th Ave);
Tel 371 77 77;

Mon–Wed 11.30–15.00,
17.00–22.30, Thurs, Fri
11.30–15.00, 17.00–23.00,
Sat 17.00–23.00, Sun
17.00–22.00.

The Red Cat
An artists' café decorated in
shades of red. The head chef
serves up a mixture of American and Mediterranean cuisine and even the vegetables
taste delicious here, especially the courgette, which is
served with toasted almonds.
227 10th Ave (near 23rd St);
Tel 242 11 22;
Mon 17.00–23.00,
Tues–Thurs 12.00–14.30,
17.00–23.00, Fri, Sat
12.00–14.30, 17.00–24.00,
Sun 17.00–22.30;
www.theredcat.com

Sparks
One of the best steak houses
in Manhattan. The atmos-
phere is rather reminiscent of
a busy station bar, but the
steaks are as meltingly tender
as is otherwise found only in
cowboy country. You should
nonetheless have an accom-
modating credit card, as the
prices can be rather steep.
210 E 46th St, between
2nd and 3rd Ave;
Tel 687 48 55;
Mon–Thurs 12.00–23.00,
Fri 12.00–23.30, Sat
17.00–23.30.

Accommodation

Algonquin Hotel
This venerable establishment
in the Theater District has
been one of the city's most
respected hotels since 1902.
During the 1920s it was a
meeting-place for New York
intellectuals and literary figures such as Dorothy Parker,
Alexander Woollcott, and

The Four Seasons Hotel represents unadulterated luxury: the lobby and Joël Robuchon's L'Atelier; the Algonquin Hotel has a famous literary tradition; the Red Cat is a good place for experimental cuisine (from left).

MIDTOWN MANHATTAN

These pages give additional information for the area of New York described in the "Highlights" section (pp. 88–141). Please note that the area code for New York is **212**.

Robert Benchley, who met around the famous Algonquin Round Table. The paneled lobby alone is worth a visit.
59 West 44th St
(near 6th Ave);
Tel 840 68 00.
www.algonquinhotel.com

Casablanca Hotel
Stand in the lobby and it feels like you have been transported onto the set of the legendary Humphrey Bogart movie. Tropical plants, rattan furniture, and Moroccan mosaics and murals conjure up a North African feel and the rooms are luxuriously appointed. The tea room is called "Rick's Café" (of course) and you can borrow books about Bogart from the lounge to completely immerse yourself in the whole experience.
147 West 43rd St
(near Broadway);
Tel 869 12 12;
www.casablancahotel.com

Four Seasons Hotel
Stars like Marilyn Monroe have stayed in this legendary hotel. One of the best in the world, its spacious rooms have every conceivable extra and it regularly features in "Best of" lists about New York. Luxury of this standard has its price, however, and the room rates start at $1,000.
57 East 57th St
(near Park Ave);
Tel 758 57 00.
www.fourseasons.com

Hilton Times Square
Completed in 2000, the Hilton on Times Square prides itself on having the largest standard rooms in the city. Despite its central location, the hotel is extremely quiet.

The Sky Lobby on the 21st floor has a magnificent view of the heart of the city.
234 West 42nd St
(near 8th Ave);
Tel 840 82 22;
www.timessquare.com

Millennium Broadway
This smart art deco hotel is only two blocks from Times Square and has many extras, including large beds, comfortable bedlinen, and free internet access. The excellent service makes the high room rates halfway bearable.
145 West 44th St
(near 6th Ave);
Tel 768 44 00;
www.millenniumhotels.com

Le Parker Meridien
Apart from an excellent restaurant, this hotel has lots of other extras – such as ergonomically designed chairs and giant televisions with integrated DVD and CD players. The speedy lifts have cartoons playing on built-in television screens in case you get bored between floors.
118 West 57th St
(near 6th Ave);
Tel 245 50 00;
www.parkermeridien.com

Renaissance Times Square
Blue and gold are the defining shades in the refurbished rooms and the recently completed upgrade has introduced new extras such as large LCD televisions with all the technical advantages that come with them. The One Room Suites are recommended for families. All this comes at a price, of course – be prepared to dig deep.
714 7th Ave (near 48th St);
Tel 765 76 76;
www.renaissancehotels.com

Salisbury Hotel
This simple hotel is situated opposite Carnegie Hall and is only a few minutes away from the stores on Fifth Avenue. The rooms are quite large for such a budget price hotel. There are various special "corporate rooms" with computer connections and the like for business travellers. A few dollars will buy you the continental breakfast.
123 West 57th St;
Tel 246 13 00;
www.nycsalisbury.com

Sofitel
The rooms here are small for a luxury hotel, but the many extras and the atmospheric art deco surroundings make up for the cramped conditions. The new rooms on the upper floors are the best – with private balconies and impressive views of the city.
45 West 44th St
(near 5th Ave);
Tel 354 88 44;
www.sofitel.com

Nightlife

Failte Irish Whiskey Bar
An Irish pub as it should be: you can warm yourself at the fire, or at the bar, with Guinness and whiskey – Irish, of course – and play pool in the side room. A bar to relax in, and better than the themed replica pubs of recent years.
531 2nd Ave (near 30th St);
Tel 725 94 40;
12.00–4.00, daily.

Marquee
To get past the bouncers guarding this trendy pub you need to be "young and beautiful". If you pass their scrutiny, you will find techno remixes blasting out of the

speakers and a giant chandelier over the dance floor reflecting a myriad of lights.
289 10th Ave (near 26th St);
Tel (646) 473 02 02;
Tues 22.00–4.00, Wed–Sat 22.30–4.00;
www.marqueeny.com

Niagara
A retro bar, reminiscent of old New York: the speakers pump out dance tracks from the last 30 years and the walls are hung with cigarette posters from a time when you could still smoke inside buildings in the Big Apple.
112 Ave A (corner of 7th St);
Tel 420 95 17;
16.00–4.00, daily;
www.niagarabar.com

PDT
Entered through a phone booth in "Crif Dogs" where the hot dogs are wonderful, at PDT there are cocktails on the menu, which is not unnatural given that it is an underground speakeasy. You can order from the hotdog menu to accompany your cocktail – an odd combination, but it makes a change from olives.
113 St Marks Place
(near 1st Ave);
Tel 614 03 86;
Sun–Thurs 18.00–2.00,
Fri, Sat 18.00–3.00.

Secret Lounge
An insider tip on the gay scene since 2005. A chandelier and candleabras add to the atmosphere in this Victorian room. Vodka and other hard liquor are popular with the regulars and the music is mainly European house.
525 West 29th Ave
(near 10th Ave);
Tel 268 55 80;
Thurs–Sat 22.00–4.00.

Museums, music, and drama

Asia Society Museum

The museum has a significant collection of East Asiatic art and cultural objects from the 11th to the 19th centuries, most of which were once owned by magnate John D. Rockefeller III; it also specializes in modern Asiatic and American-Asian art. Changing exhibitions, lectures, dance performances, concerts, and film showings complete the schedule.
725 Park Ave/70th St;
Tel 288 64 00;
Tues–Sun 11.00–18.00,
Fri 11.00–21.00, closed
Independence Day,
Thanksgiving, 25 Dec, 1 Jan.
www.asiasociety.org

Cooper Hewitt Museum (National Museum of Design)

Since its 1967 acquisition of one of the world's largest design and crafts collections, the Smithsonian Institution has been exhibiting it in steel king Andrew Carnegie's old townhouse. The core of the collection was amassed by the sisters Sarah, Eleanor, and Amy Hewitt, granddaughters of the steel magnate Peter Cooper, before 1897. The collection includes objects from history as well as contemporary design icons.
91st St/Fifth Ave;
Tel 849 84 00;
Mon–Fri 10.00–17.00,
Sat 10.00–18.00, Sun
12.00–18.00, closed
Thanksgiving, 25 Dec, 1 Jan.
www.cooperhewitt.org

Delacorte Theater

Shakespeare in the Park Productions has been performing free shows, which always include one play by Shakespeare, on its open-air stage in Central Park every summer since 1962. It is invariably hot, and tickets are much sought-after but well worth trying to get hold of. Seeing Shakespeare in Central Park won't be something that you'll easily forget.
Mid-Park, Central Park
West, 81st St;
Tel 861 72 77.
www.centralpark.com

El Museo del Barrio

Founded in 1969, the museum exhibits Central and South American art from pre-Columbian cultures to the present day. It's a really interesting spot.
1230 5th Ave;
Tel 831 72 72;
Wed–Sun 11.00–17.00.
www.elmuseo.org

The Jewish Museum

Founded in 1904, the museum has one of the largest collections of Judaica in the world, spanning four thousand years of Jewish history. This is a fascinating museum and well worth adding to your schedule.
1109 Fifth Ave/92nd St;
Tel 423 32 00;
Sun–Tues, Thurs, Sat
11.00–17.45, Fri 11.00–16.00/
17.45, closed Thanksgiving
and on Jewish holidays.
www.thejewishmuseum.org

Mount Vernon Hotel Museum (formerly Abigail Adams Smith Museum)

A legendary hotel, located in a 1799 coach house since 1826, and once a secluded retreat for already stressed New Yorkers back in the days when the city only went as far as 14th Street. Original furniture and fixtures give a good idea of life in the period.
421 E. 61st St;
Tel 838 68 78;
Tues–Sun 11.00–16.00,
closed August, Independence Day, Thanksgiving,
25 Dec, 1 Jan.
www.mvhm.org

Museum of American Illustration (Society of Illustrators)

Founded in 1901, the society promotes the work of illustrators and its gallery has a collection of more than 2,000 original works by famous American illustrators. The sketch nights, with jazz and models, are well-known. Try your hand too…
128 E. 63rd St;
Tel 838 25 60;
Tues 10.00–20.00, Wed–Fri
10.00–17.00, Sat 12.00–
16.00, closed public hols.
www.societyillustrators.org

Museum of the City of New York

This is the place to witness an overview of the city's three-hundred-year history and its development from discovery through the settlement of Nieuw Amsterdam to the present day, looking at lifestyles from other periods, the city's cultural life, and even old toys.
1220 Fifth Ave/103rd St;
Tel 534 16 72;
Tues–Sun 10.00–17.00,
closed Thanksgiving,
25 Dec, 1 Jan.
www.mcny.org

Neue Galerie New York

Housed since 1994 in a neo-classical building on the Museum Mile, the collection, which partly belongs to Ronald S. Lauder, heir to the cosmetic firm, exhibits Austrian art from the turn of the 20th century, including Gustav Klimt's *Adele Bloch-Bauer* and some German expressionism. Lauder, a former American ambassador to Austria, was much involved in the restitution of stolen Jewish art, which he often bought at auction. It's a wonderful collection, don't miss it.
1048 5th Ave;
Tel 628 62 00;
Thurs–Mon 11.00–18.00.
www.neuegalerie.org

Whitney Museum of American Art

The most important collection of 20th-century American art is located in a Marcel Breuer building, housing works by the Ashcan School, Alexander Calder, Keith Haring, Edward Hopper, Jasper Johns, Franz Kline, Edward Kienholz, Willem de Kooning, Barnett Newman, Jackson Pollock, and George Segal, amongst others. It was founded in 1931 by the heiress, artist, and sculptor Gertrude Vanderbilt to promote contemporary American art. There is a branch of the museum with a sculpture garden in Philip Morris Park which is worth seeing (see p. 148).
945 Madison Ave/75th St;
Tel 570 36 00;
Wed–Thurs 11.00–18.00,
13.00–21.00, Sat–Sun
11.00–18.00, closed
Thanksgiving, 25 Dec, 1 Jan.
www.whitney.org

Festivals and events

Central Park Summerstage

This summer festival offers a variety of different and interesting cultural events: music,

A trip to the Park in the fall: The Whitney Museum exhibits American art; the Cooper Hewitt Museum concentrates on design; El Museo del Barrio is devoted to Latin American culture (from left).

CENTRAL PARK AND UPPER EAST SIDE

These pages give additional information for the area of New York described in the "Highlights" section (pp. 156–173). Please note that the area code for New York is 212.

dance, film, and readings by famous artists. Many of the events are free, some ask for a small donation, and others are ticketed (see p. 140).
Jun–Aug
www.summerstage.org,

Macy's Thanksgiving Day Parade

New York's biggest department store puts on this gigantic show for young and old alike on Thanksgiving Day. Brightly painted floats, marching bands, cheerleaders, and troupes of clowns and dancers all make the atmosphere relaxed, but the parade is most famous for the large collection of giant gas-filled inflatables in the forms of famous comic or toy characters. The last float in the parade is always occupied by Macy's Santa Claus.
From the Museum of Natural History (Central Park) via Broadway to Herald Sq.; fourth Thurs in Nov, from 9.00.
www.macys.com

Philharmonic in the Park

In the summertime, the world-famous New York Philharmonic orchestra gives free evening concerts at various locations in every borough of the city. There are open-air events in Central Park, Prospect Park in Brooklyn and in parks in Queens, the Bronx, Staten Island, as well as other districts. Many visitors take a picnic to enjoy during the performance.
Tel 875 56 56; Jul.
www.nyphil.org

Shakespeare in the Park

In the summer the Delacorte Theater is given over to Shakespeare, performing the master's works for free. Demand is high, so get your free tickets early on the day of the performance from the Delacorte Theater in Central Park or the Public Theater (425, Lafayette St).
Jun–Aug, performances begin at 20.30.
www.publictheater.org

Steuben Day Parade

A German-American parade which attracts thousands of spectators who cheer on the brightly painted floats, groups in traditional folk costume, choirs, dancing troupes, marching bands, dignitaries, and lots of cultural societies. The spectacle has been held since 1957 to commemorate the Prussian general von Steuben, a hero of the American War of Independence.
5th Ave from E. 63rd-86th St; third weekend in Sep.
www.germanparadenyc.org

Sport and leisure

Asphalt Green

You can learn to do proper butterfly stroke or the like in the pool of this not-for-profit organisation, and the trainer will observe your technique through windows in the pool wall. The smaller pools have other programs (such as for muscle strengthening) and there are lots of courses aimed at children. The sports and fitness schedule is pretty comprehensive – there are indoor and outdoor sports facilities in the complex, including a gymnasium and gymnastics rooms.
555 E. 90th St/York Ave; Tel 369 88 90; Mon–Fri 5.30–22.00, Sat–Sun 8.00–20.00.
www.asphaltgreen.org

Central Park Bicycle Tours

You can rent bikes here (including a lock and a helmet) and take a tour through Central Park. The tours take place between two and five times daily and on average last two hours.
203 West 58th St (near Columbus Circle), Tel 541 87 59; Mon–Sun 9.00–18.00.
www.centralparkbiketours.com

Jogging

Central Park, not to mention the many other parks in the city, is a haven for joggers. The paths in the parks are especially suited for running during the times they are cleared of cars, although you will be also sharing them with cyclists and rollerbladers. If you would prefer to run in a group, you can call an organization such as the New York Road Runners Club. Make sure you pack your running shoes.
New York Road Runners Club, Tel 860 44 55, www.nyrrc.org
Car-free periods: Mon–Fri 10.00–15.00, 19.00–7.00, Sat, Sun 24 hours.

Loeb Boathouse

If the weather is cooperative you can hire rowing boats here (priced at $10 for an hour) and explore Central Park Lake. If you prefer the luxury of someone else doing the rowing, you can hire a gondola with a gondolier ($30/half hour), but only in the summer months. The Boat House restaurant has a fantastic view of the lake.
Park Drive North/E. 72nd St; Tel 517 22 33; Apr–end of Oct, 9.30–17.30

(depending on weather). www.thecentralpark-boathouse.com

Paul Labrecque East

This is a store for stars and those who want to be seen with them. Renée Zellweger, Reese Witherspoon, Helen Mirren, and Naomi Watts, to name but a few, are all customers, and Sting treated himself to a $90 shave in the men's salon. If you wish to be attended to by Mr Paul, the owner, you will have to pay a little more.
171 E. 65th St/Lexington Ave; Tel 988 78 16; Mon–Fri 8.00–21.00, Sat 9.00–20.00, Sun 10.00–20.00.
www.paullabrecque.com

Shopping

Calvin Klein

The designer's biggest store in New York has four floors of clothes, shoes, and household goods. Enjoy browsing or shopping. It's an experience.
654 Madison Ave/E. 60th St; Tel 292 90 00; Mon–Wed, Fri–Sat 10.00–18.00, Thurs 10.00–19.00, Sun 12.00–18.00.
www.calvinklein.com

Donna Karan New York (DKNY)

Donna Karan's flagship store is a small establishment selling fashion (especially women's clothes) and accessories by the world-famous designer. The vegetarian café is a good place for a rest between bouts of shopping.
819 Madison Ave/E. 69th St; Tel 866 240 4700; Mon–Wed, Fri–Sat 10.00–18.00, Thurs 10.00–19.00, Sun 12.00–17.00.
www.donnakaran.com

Little Shop of Crafts

Not only can you buy materials in New York's biggest craft store, you can also get involved creatively in the workshops here. You can choose a range of crafts from painting ceramics through to making pearl jewellery and sewing stuffed animals.
431 E. 73rd St;
Tel 717 66 36;
Mon–Tues 11.00–18.30,
Wed–Fri 11.00–22.00, Sat
10.00–20.00, Sun
10.00–18.30.
www.littleshopny.com

Sotheby's

Just as at Christie's there are almost daily auctions of antiques, art objects, carpets, jewels, coins, books, and more. It's worth dropping in even if you're not interested in buying anything, although many a casual visitor has been swept up into the bidding frenzy.
1334 York Ave/E. 72nd St;
Tel 606 70 00;
Mon–Sat 10.00–17.00, Sun
12.00–17.00, mid-Jul to early
Sep: closed Sat, Sun.
www.sothebys.com

Eating and drinking

Accademia di Vino

Two bars located in a pleasant restaurant decorated in brown and ochre tones. Kevin Garcia, the head chef, offers an astoundingly wide range of Italian dishes, including good pizzas, salads, and antipasti. There are more than 500 bottles in the wine cellar. Well worth a visit.
1081 Third Ave
(near 64th St);
Tel 888 63 33;
12.00–24.00, daily.
www.accademiadivino.com

Barking Dog

A dog-orientated bar – there is even a "doggie bar" with water bowls near the entrance for man's best friend. Two-legged guests will enjoy the good breakfasts and American classics like meatloaf. There are queues for the excellent weekend brunch. Perfect for canine-friendly folk.
1678 Third Ave
(corner of 94th St);
Tel 831 18 00;
8.00–23.00, daily.

Beyoglu

A very friendly Turkish bar, offering good value for money, which has been described by some critics as "the best Turkish restaurant in the city". The doner kebab is made from the best meat and all the specials are very inviting, especially the fish dishes which are made with fresh herbs.
1431 Third Ave
(corner of 81st St);
Tel 650 08 50,
12.00–23.30, daily.

California Pizza Kitchen

Founded in California in 1985, this restaurant chain has since spread right across the USA. Crispy pizzas with quirky toppings such as Peking duck are a trademark of this fast food outlet and are popular particularly with young people.
201 E. 60th St;
Tel 755 77 73;
Sun–Thurs 11.30–22.00,
Fri, Sat 11.30–23.00.
www.cpk.com

40 Carrots

The girls from *Sex and the City* might just have dropped in here; the frozen yogurt is low in calories and just the right refreshment after a hard afternoon's shopping at Bloomingdale's. Relax, refresh, rejuvenate.
1000 Third Ave,
(Bloomingdale's basement);
Tel 705 30 85;
Mon–Fri 10.00–19.00, Sat,
Sun 10.00–18.00.

Centolire

A rustic atmosphere somewhat reminiscent of a trattoria in Tuscany. Pino Luongo, the head chef, serves up astonishingly authentic Italian cuisine, in particular from Tuscany and northern Italy. The Tuscan fish stew is especially recommended.
1167 Madison Ave
(near 86th St);
Tel 734 77 11;
Mon–Sat 12.00–15.00,
17.30–22.30, Sun
11.30–15.00, 17.00–21.00.

Cinema Café

The posters and pictures on the walls here recall such legendary films as *Casablanca*. There is "cinema popcorn" on the menu, of course, but this little restaurant also serves delicious sandwiches and wraps with original fillings such as turkey breast and mango. The crispy pizza is quite delightful.
45 E. 60th St
(near Madison Ave);
Tel 750 75 00;
Mon–Fri 11.00–22.00, Sat
9.00–21.00, Sun 10.00–18.00.
www.cinemarestaurants.com

David Burke Townhouse

Located in an unassuming townhouse, David Burke's restaurant is renowned principally for its original and elaborate presentation. It has won a prize for being the best lobster restaurant, and the salmon and tuna parfaits and the butterscotch panna cotta are also tipped for awards.
133 E. 61st St
(near Lexington Ave),
Tel 813 21 21;
Mon–Fri 11.45–14.30,
17.00–23.00, Sat 12.00–
14.30, 17.00–23.00, Sun
11.00–14.30, 16.30–21.00.
www.dbdrestaurant.com

Delmonico Gourmet

A characterful lunch bar on the Upper East Side; most of the regulars take their lunch "to go", usually pasta and seafood salads, Chinese and Japanese fare, steamed vegetables with exotic dressings, and of course every variety of sandwich you could possibly think of or hope for. Drop in and enjoy the choice.
55 E. 59th St
(near Madison Ave);
Tel 751 55 59;
Mon–Fri 24 hours.

Fig & Olive

Mediterranean charm on the Upper East Side. As the name suggests, good quality olive oil is added to almost every dish, and the fig and olive salad has a unique taste. The store next door has an exceptional selection of wines.
808 Lexington Ave
(near 62nd St);
Tel 207 45 55;
11.00–23.00, daily.
www.figandolive.com

Gajyumaru

A tiny sushi bar, and one of the best on the Upper East Side. The toro (tuna) and the uni (sea urchin) are best – and the most expensive. If you prefer your fish cooked, try one of the spicy noodle dishes. Splash out…

CENTRAL PARK AND UPPER EAST SIDE

These pages give additional information for the area of New York described in the "Highlights" section (pp. 156–173). Please note that the area code for New York is 212.

Sotheby's, the legendary auction house; the Cinema Brasserie serves small delicacies – this is the dining room; Fig & Olive makes dreams of the Mediterranean come true (from left).

1659 First Ave (near 87th St);
Tel 860 88 57;
Tues–Sat 12.00–14.30,
17.00–23.00, Sun
12.00–14.30, 17.00–22.30.

Hokkaido Sushi

An excellent sushi bar which sets great store by design. The Manhattan rolls (with tempura shrimp) and the spicy tuna are arranged to resemble the New York skyline. The sushi is of above average quality and your choice is best left to the sushi chef.
1817 Second Ave
(corner of 94th St);
Tel 289 19 02;
Mon–Sat 11.00–15.00,
17.00–23.30, Sun
13.00–23.30.
www.hokkaidosushi.com

I Vandali

Here they give you chalks and ask you to "vandalize" the walls by brightening them up with graffiti. It's only a gimmick, and the food is good anyway. Marco Sanmartino, the head chef, serves first-class antipasti and creative pasta dishes. Something to write home about, even on the walls!
1590 First Ave
(near 83rd St);
Tel 585 33 39;
Sun–Thurs 17.00–23.00, Fri,
Sat 17.00–23.30.
www.ivandalinyc.com

Le Refuge

Authentic French cuisine served up in a small restaurant with a generally older clientele. The fillet of beef melts in the mouth, and the house specials include duck with green beans and almonds, and lamb ratatouille.
166 E. 82nd St
(near Lexington Ave);

Tel 861 45 05;
17.00–23.00, daily.
www.lerefugenyc.com

Le Train Bleu

A top tip for Bloomingdale's customers: next to the household goods section you'll find a pleasant little bar located in a recreated 1920s railway carriage – and your shopping bags go in the luggage rack. The food is excellent with delicacies like pheasant pâté with Cumberland sauce and Japanese soba noodles. Enjoy the journey.
1000 Third Ave
(corner of 59th St);
Tel 705 21 00;
Mon–Wed, Fri, Sat 10.30–
17.00, Thurs 10.30–19.00,
Sun 10.30–16.30.

Maya

Although the name might suggest something else, Maya is one of the best and most up-to-date Mexicans in town. Richard Sandoval, the owner, serves traditional Mexican food without the Tex-Mex additions you usually find in the US. Authentic and tasty.
1191 First Ave
(near 64th St);
Tel 585 18 18;
Sun–Thurs 17.00–22.00,
Fri, Sat 17.00–23.00.
www.modernmexican.com

Mustang Grill

Mexican food lovers are looked after in this little cantina until late into the night. The house specials include quesadilla and spicy chicken with jalapeños, but most people come here for the excellent margaritas. There are over 100 kinds of tequila here for the discerning diner.
1633 Second Ave

(corner of 85th St),
Tel 744 91 94;
Mon–Wed 11.30–1.00,
Thurs Fri 11.30–3.00, Sat
10.00–3.00, Sun 10.00–1.00.
www.mustanggrill.com

Nica Trattoria

A Sicilian tratttoria with an authentic family feel. The owners swear by fresh ingredients and their first-class (and calorie-laden) gnocchi with various sauces is excellent. The classic pasta dishes are recommended, of course.
354 E. 84th St
(near First Ave);
Tel 472 50 40;
17.30–22.30, daily.
www.nica-nyc.com

Orsay

It feels like you're in Paris in this French bistro. The atmosphere seems authentic even if the waiters don't speak French, and particularly the little dishes like lobster salad and the smoked salmon appetizers are a real treat for the palate. A little corner of French paradise in the heart of New York.
1057 Lexington Ave
(corner of 75th St);
Tel 517 64 00;
Mon–Fri 12.00–15.00,
17.30–23.00, Sat 12.00–
15.30, 17.30–23.00, Sun
11.00–15.30, 17.30–2.00.
www.orsayrestaurant.com

Parlor Steakhouse

One of the city's newest and best steakhouses. The quality of the steaks is high, particularly the filet mignon, and the fish dishes are tender and spicy too. The oysters and the giant shrimp cocktail starters are recommended.
1600 Third Ave
(corner of 90th St);

Tel 423 58 88;
Mon–Thurs 11.45–23.00,
Fri 11.45–24.00, Sat
11.00–24.00, Sun
11.00–22.00.
www.parlorsteakhouse.com

Peri Ela

Don't be put off by the gloomy drawing-room atmosphere; Peri Ela is one of the few restaurants in New York with authentic Turkish food, as guaranteed by the owners, Silay and Jill Ciner and their family. The kebabs and the meze taste fantastic.
1361 Lexington Ave
(near 90th St);
Tel 410 43 00;
12.00–16.00, 17.00–23.00,
daily.

Pio Pio

More than fast food: the grilled chickens in this little Peruvian bar have got very little to do with KFC and the other chicken chains. Before the pullets are placed on the grill at Pio Pio, they are marinated in Peruvian beer and other (secret) ingredients to give them the right kick.
1746 First Ave
(near 90th St),
Tel 426 58 00;
11.00–23.00, daily.

Primola

A refined lounge ambience in one of the most popular Italians on the Upper East Side. Giuliano Zuliani swears by fine Italian cooking and his fish and mussel dishes are particularly well-realized. Regulars also praise the spicy veal and the scampi.
1226 Second Ave
(near 64th St);
Tel 758 17 75;
Mon–Fri 12.00–15.00, 17.00–
23.00, Sat, Sun 17.00–23.00.

Sala Thai

An unassuming Thai restaurant located on the Upper East Side; it's nothing special, but has very good curry recipes. The vegetables are fresh and crunchy, the rice is well-cooked and the sauces hot. The spicy shrimps come especially highly recommended. Authentic and delicious food.
1718 Second Ave
(near 89th St);
Tel 410 55 57;
Mon–Sat 17.00–23.00, Sun 17.00–22.30.

Sasabune

"Today's special – trust me" boasts the menu, and you can put your faith in Kenji Takahashi, the sushi chef here. The tasting menu uses only the finest raw fish and features such creative starters as salmon wrapped in seaweed and albacore sashimi with ponzu sauce. The fish simply melts in the mouth. Easily the best sushi bar in north Manhattan.
401 E. 73rd St (near First Ave);
Tel 249 85 83;
Tues–Fri 12.00–14.00, 17.30–22.00, Sat 17.30–22.00.

Sfoglia

It's just like eating with a real Italian family – there are only ten tables in this tiny but respectable Italian restaurant. Just as in the main restaurant located on the island of Nantucket, the strongest influence here is delicious, pepped-up but authentic Italian home cooking.
1402 Lexington Ave
(corner of 92nd St);
Tel 831 14 02;
Mon 17.30–22.30, Tues–Sat 12.00–14.30, 17.30–22.30.
www.sfogliarestaurant.com

Shanghai Pavilion

It's not just Chinatown that has first-class Chinese restaurants. The Shanghai Pavilion on the Upper East Side has a surprisingly authentic selection of first-class dishes, including carp dumplings in red pepper sauce and tender chicken nuggets.
1378 Third Ave
(near 78th St);
Tel 585 33 88;
Mon–Fri 11.30–22.30,
Sat, Sun 12.00–22.30.

Slice, the Perfect Food

It's not just vegetarians who swear by this unusual pizza restaurant on the Upper East Side. Only organic vegetables and free-range beef is used on the crisply bases, and they have vegan cheese on request. Guests can assemble their own combinations of pizza toppings. Get ready to be creative.
1413 Second Ave
(near 74th St);
Tel 249 43 53;
Mon–Wed 11.00–22.00,
Thurs–Sun 11.00–23.00.
www.sliceperfect.com

Southern Hospitality

Justin Timberlake, the co-owner, attracts a few fans, but most of the patrons come here because of the hearty spare ribs and the BBQ chicken. These calorie-laden delicacies taste just as good as in St Louis or Memphis. Have fries, beans, and biscuits with them. The food is the star here too.
1460 Second Ave
(near 76th St);
Tel 249 10 01;
Mon–Fri 16.00–2.00,
Sat, Sun 11.30–2.00.
www.southernhospitalitybbq.com

Swifty's

A somewhat loud and rather uncomfortable restaurant, but that doesn't seem to bother any of the diners here. The tasty food makes up for everything and they serve both traditional American and European specialities – treat yourself to the delicious soft-shell crab or the scallops. There is also a fixed price pre-theater menu.
1007 Lexington Ave
(near 72nd St);
Tel 535 60 00;
Mon–Fri 12.00–15.30, 17.30–23.15, Sat, Sun 12.00– 16.00, 17.30–23.15.
www.swiftysnyc.com

Taco Taco

Regulars swear by the margaritas and the guacamole here. The tacos, always made with fresh ingredients and first-class meat, are also excellent. The pork is marinated in a tasty jalapeño sauce and is as hot as might be expected. The atmosphere transports you all the way across the border to Mexico.
1726 Second Ave
(near 90th St);
Tel 289 82 26;
Sun–Thurs 11.30–23.00,
Fri, Sat 11.30–24.00.

Tiramisu

As you might guess, the tiramisu tastes particularly good here, of course, but both the thin-crust oven pizza and the pasta dishes are also recommended, including the ravioli alla Cardinale, ricotta and spinach ravioli with shrimps, and zucchini in tomato sauce.
1410 Third Ave
(corner of 80th St);
Tel 988 97 80;
12.00–23.30, daily.

Viand

This diner, which opened in 1976, has always been a good place to stop off after a shopping trip. The turkey sandwich is almost legendary – the turkey is always fresh from the oven. The desserts, such as the cinnamon rice pudding, are also very tasty. If you are in the mood for a turkey sandwich, this is the place to go.
673 Madison Ave
(corner of 61st St);
Tel 751 66 22;
6.00–22.00, daily

Zebú Grill

The caipirinhas are delicious in this first-class Brazilian restaurant, one of the few located in Manhattan, but that's not all. The mixed grill with South American spicy meat is a winner and the rustic décor is reminiscent of houses in rural Brazil. There's also a delicious brunch menu, so take a late breakfast here.
305 E. 92nd St
(near Second Ave);
Tel 426 75 00;
Mon–Sat 17.00–23.30,
Sun 16.30–22.00.
www.zebugrill.com

Accommodation

Affinia Gardens

The junior suites in this "all-suites" hotel located on the Upper East Side are all equipped with a kitchen and will save you many an expensive restaurant visit. The décor is simple with a warm atmosphere, and guests have free access to the gym and the laundry.
215 E. 64th St
(near Third Ave);
Tel 355 12 30.
www.affinia.com

CENTRAL PARK AND UPPER EAST SIDE

These pages give additional information for the area of New York described in the "Highlights" section (pp. 156–173). Please note that the area code for New York is 212.

The Carlyle
Named after the British essayist Thomas Carlyle, this hotel has been one of the finest on the Upper East Side since the 1930s. A timeless classic, the spacious rooms here resemble private apartments and feature lots of extras, including wireless internet access, and DVD and iPod inputs. A sophisticated place to stay that is a true New York landmark.
35 E. 76th St
(corner of Madison Ave);
Tel 744 16 00.
www.thecarlyle.com

The Franklin Hotel
The rooms in this hotel recall the 1950s, and some of them are pretty small. They don't skimp on the extras, however, and there's wireless internet access as well as plasma televisions and free newspapers. A European breakfast is included in the price.
164 E. 87th St
(near Lexington Ave);
Tel 369 10 00.
www.franklinhotel.com

The Helmsley Carlton House
A first-class hotel with an inviting lobby, bright, spacious rooms, and attentive service. The beds are extremely comfortable and the extras include wireless internet access, several telephones, and extremely friendly room service.
680 Madison Ave
(corner of 61st St);
Tel 838 30 00.
www.helmsleyhotels.com

Hotel Wales
The rooms in this lovingly decorated hotel are correct ito the last detail and give it a welcoming, homely atmosphere; the European bed linen also provides additional comfort while the gym and the business facilities are modern in appearance. The continental breakfast is included in the price.
1295 Madison Ave
(near 92nd St);
Tel 876 60 00.
www.waleshotel.com

The Lowell
You can't get a room in this elegant hotel for under $500 but you can at least see where your money is going – the spacious rooms are furnished with the finest carpets and fabrics and are reminiscent of the rooms in a European castle. The service is exceptional; if you like, the staff will even do your shopping for you. Be prepared for a spot of real pampering.
28 E. 63rd St
(corner of Madison Ave);
Tel 838 14 00.
www.lowellhotel.com

Loews Regency Hotel
Smart and expensive, like all the hotels on the Upper East Side, the Regency now has a regal shine after a programme of extensive renovations. Valuable mahogany furniture and luxurious fabrics in the rooms give it a timeless elegance. If you've forgotten your reading glasses (or your Wellington boots), it's not a problem – almost anything can be hired from the hotel for an appropriate fee. Unusually for a top-end hotel, provisions are made for pets.
540 Park Ave
(corner of 61st St);
Tel 759 41 00.
www.loewshotels.com

Nightlife

Bailey's Corner Pub
This Irish pub has been a bar of first choice for Upper East Side night owls since 1951. The counter top was originally part of a 19th-century tavern and adds to the rustic atmosphere. There is genuine Guinness on tap, and even the whiskey comes from the emerald isle.
1607 York Ave
(corner of 85th St);
Tel 650 13 41;
Mon–Sat 11.00–4.00,
Sun 12.00–4.00.

Club Macanudo
Smoking is allowed in only a few clubs in New York and this one has the best atmosphere. You can get a good cigar for just a few dollars. The noise levels are quite high, however, especially if there's live music on, as you would expect.
26 E. 63rd St
(corner of Madison Ave);
Tel 752 82 00;
Mon, Tues 17.00–1.00,
Wed–Sat 17.00-1.30.
www.clubmacanudonyc.com

Iggy's Karaoke Bar & Grill
There's singing and Irish beer here, and wannabe stars can enter the spotlight and display their vocal talents (or lack of them) to the audience as the lyrics flash across a monitor.
1452 2nd Ave;
Tel 327 30 43;
12.00–4.00, daily.
www.iggysnewyork.com

Saloon
Not a glitzy spot to go and be seen in – this place is for serious dancers. The clientele, generally in their twenties or older, strut their stuff on the enormous dance floor to top 40 hits and sounds from (average) cover bands. Also a place of interest for singles. There are three full-service bars, including a classic New York city-style pub, two DJs and a state of the art sound and lighting system.
1584 York Ave
(near 84th St);
Tel 570 54 54;
Fri, Sat 19.00–4.00.
www.saloonnyc.com

Subway Inn
Seen from the outside this is a scruffy place in a run-down area. Inside it is also scruffy, admittedly – the tables are sticky, the decor has definitely seen better days, the shelves are covered in dust – but it has been a popular rendezvous for price-conscious revellers since 1937. A real find for those seeking a laid-back atmosphere.
143 E. 60th St;
Tel 223 89 29;
Mon–Sat 11.00–4.00,
Sun 12.00–2.00.

Vudu Lounge
The giant mirror ball, the dry ice, and the flashing lights are reminiscent of a 1970s disco, and go-go girls in skimpy costumes dance on the stage. Thursdays is Latin night, with Latino couples gliding across the dance floor; on Fridays there's hip hop and R&B, Saturdays is mainstream and dance. Check ahead – the club is sometimes closed for private parties.
1487 First Ave
(near 78th St);
Tel 240 95 40;
Thurs, Fri 17.00–4.30,
Sat 22.00–4.30.
www.vudulounge.com

Museums, music, and drama

Apollo Theater

Since opening in 1913, the legendary Apollo Theater has had a tumultuous history, including the banning of black patrons in 1934, a temporary conversion into a cinema, closure in 1976, reopening in 1985, and above all the Amateur Night shows, which led to the discovery of such talents as Ella Fitzgerald, Billie Holiday, and Michael Jackson. Mainly devoted to Afro-American music, the venue also counted Duke Ellington and Louis Armstrong amongst its artists.
253 W. 125th St;
Tel 531 53 00;
Tours Mon–Fri 11.00, 13.00, 15.00 (except Thurs only 11.00), Sat, Sun 11.00, 13.00.
www.apollotheater.org

Children's Museum of Manhattan

Founded in 1973 and famed for its wide variety of very informative and entertaining activities, from fascinating scientific experiments to puppet plays and an introduction to a television studio. The museum is also a useful source of ideas for teachers.
212 W. 83rd St;
Tel 721 12 34;
Tues–Sun 10.00–17.00.
www.cmom.org

Dyckman Farmhouse Museum

Dating back to 1784 and with its original furnishings, the only remaining old farmhouse in Manhattan was made accessible to the public as a museum in 1916.
4881 Broadway/204th St;
Tel 304 94 22;
Wed–Sat 11.00–16.00, 12.00–16.00.
www.dyckmanfarmhouse.org

Hispanic Society Museum

Magnificent archaeological finds, craft pieces, sculptures, and paintings from Spain, Portugal, and South America are the core of the Hispanic Society's collection and are worth a visit. There are works by artists such as El Greco, Velazquez, Zurbaràn, Ribera, Murillo, and Goya.
Audubon Terrace,
Broadway;
Tel 926 22 34;
Tues–Sat 10.00–16.30, Sun 13.00–16.00, closed public hols.
www.hispanicsociety.org

Metropolitan Opera (Met)

Built to a design by Wallace K. Harrison in 1966, the opera house is the architectural heart of the Lincoln Center for the Performing Arts. In the foyer behind the high arcades there are two large murals by Marc Chagall, the *Sources of Music* in yellow and the *Triumph of Music* in red, and three bronzes by Aristide Maillol. The corridors are decorated with portraits of famous opera singers. One of the world's leading opera houses, the Met has been the home of the Metropolitan Opera Company and the American Ballet Theater since 1880. Almost every famous opera singer and composer has appeared here, including Enrico Caruso, Maria Callas, Arturo Toscanini, and Gustav Mahler. Opera fans and buffs should not miss this. Book well ahead for performances.
Lincoln Center,
Broadway/ 64th St;
Tel 362 60 00;

information for all events and the start of all guided tours are in the lower floor.
www.metoperafamily.org

Lincoln Center Plaza

Graced with a fountain by Philip Johnson, in August the heart of the Lincoln Center becomes a venue for street theater and other performances, which are mostly free.
Lincoln Center, Broadway.

David H. Koch Theater (formerly New York Theater)

Built by Philip Johnson and Richard Foster in the Lincoln Center in 1964, this building is now the home of the New York City Opera Company (founded in1943) and the New York City Ballet (founded in 1948). The venue was renamed after a generous benefactor in 2008.
Lincoln Center,
Broadway/ 64th St;
Tel 870 55 70.
www.lincolncenter.org

Morris-Jumel Museum

This Palladian country house, built in 1765 and once belonging to the Morris family from England, is one of the oldest houses in Manhattan and was used by George Washington as his headquarters in 1776 during the American War of Independence. A museum of American history was established here in 1904.
65 Jumel Terrace;
Tel 923 80 08;
Wed–Sun 10.00–16.00, closed public hols.
www.morrisjumel.org

The New York Historical Society Museum

Founded as a scientific institution with a large library in 1809, the Historical Society's museum offers an interesting recapitulation of the history of the city and of America. Particular highlights include enchanting paintings of birds by the artist John James Audubon, lamps by Louis Comfort Tiffany, valuable old toys, and canvases by European and American painters.
170 Central Park W./77th St;
Tel 873 34 00;
Tues–Thurs, Sat 10.00–18.00, Fri 10.00–20.00, Sun 11.00–17.45.
www.nyhistory.org

Nitchen Children's Museum of Native America

Located in an old church building, this museum offers plenty of fun activities for children to help illustrate the history of America's indigenous peoples.
550 W. 155;
Tel 694 22 40;
Mon–Fri 8.00–14.00.
www.nitchenchildrensmuseum.org

Schomburg Center for Research in Black Culture

Part of the New York Public Library, this research organization for black art, culture, and history is the largest in the world. The reading rooms and archive displays here offer visitors a wonderful glimpse of its comprehensive collection of books, manuscripts, drawings, photographs, films, and records. This is a really fascinating place to visit.
515 Malcolm X Blvd;
Tel 491 22 00;
Mon–Wed 12.00–20.00, Thurs, Fri 11.00–18.00, Sat 10.00–17.00.
www.nypl.org/research/sc/sc.html

Whole Foods – a supermarket of superlatives; the Apollo Theater: a springboard for talent; very grand opera: the Metropolitan Opera House; turn up, tune in, and get down: Midsummer night Swing (from left).

UPPER WEST SIDE AND HARLEM

These pages give additional information for the area of New York described in the "Highlights" section (pp. 160–179). Please note that the area code for New York is **212**.

Studio Museum Harlem
Established in 1970, the museum houses a series of temporary exhibitions of contemporary Afro-American art. Free admission on Sundays from noon so take advantage of that if you are in the area.
144 W. 125th St;
Tel 864 45 00,
Wed–Fri 10.00–17.00,
Sat, Sun 13.00–18.00.
www.studiomuseum.org

Festivals and events

Blessing of the Animals
Many pet-owners bring their charges to the Cathedral of St John the Divine to have them blessed on the feast of St Francis. Recordings of whales, birdsong, and wolves howling are played to the accompaniment of a human choir during the ceremony, and the whole service ends with a small party in the church grounds. If you love animals, you will love this.
1047 Amsterdam Ave/
112th St;
Tel 316 75 40;
beginning of Oct,
tickets from 9.00,
service from 11.00.
www.stjohndivine.org

Harlem Week
The highlights of this summer festival include a street festival with numerous market stalls and all sorts of tasty snacks (especially soul food) on sale, as well as concerts (jazz, soul, etc.), cabaret, and sports events such as basketball tournaments, and car shows. The event is rounded off with fashion shows presenting the newest trends in the Harlem community.
end of Jul–Sept.
www.harlemdiscover.com

New York Film Festival
Founded in 1962, the annual New York Film Festival takes place in the Alice Tully Hall in the Lincoln Center, showing the newest and best films from the US and abroad.
Columbus Ave/W. 64th–
66th St;
Tel 875 54 56;
end of Sept–mid-Oct.
www.new.lincolncenter.org
www.filminc.com

Midsummer Night Swing
"New York's biggest outdoor dance party" sees hundreds of enthusiasts dancing until late into the night. It's no wonder; there are famous big bands and DJs playing everything from swing, salsa, and tango to soul, funk, and blues. If you like dancing, this is the place for you.
Josie Robertson Plaza,
Lincoln Center; Columbus
Ave/W. 64th–66th St;
Tel 875 54 56;
Jun–Jul.
www.new.lincolncenter.org

Sport and leisure

Harlem Spirituals Tours
This agency runs a comprehensive selection of guided tours to Harlem, visiting places which have hitherto been off the beaten tourist track, such as Duke Ellington's house and the city's oldest black parish, the Mother African Methodist Episcopal Zion Church, where Sunday services are accompanied by gospel choir music.
690 8th Ave/W. 43rd–44th St;
Tel 391 09 00.
www.harlemspirituals.com

Blades, Board & Skates
Blades, Board & Skates on the Upper West Side, not far from

Central Park, hires out rollerblades throughout the year: 24-hour hire including pads costs $20, for example. There are several areas in the city dedicated to rollerblading, such as in Central Park near the Naumberg Bandshell (freestyle) or on Center Drive; otherwise in Prospect Park (Brooklyn) or on the long runs through River Side Park.
156 W. 72nd St;
Tel 787 39 11;
Mon–Sat 10.00–20.00,
Sun–19.00. (Also at 659
Broadway; Tel 477 7350)
www.blades.com

Spa in the Mandarin Oriental
If money isn't a problem, you shouldn't miss the five-star spa and gym spread over several floors of this luxury hotel. You can relax in the pool or the Thai yoga suite, or even in the separate VIP spa suite which has its own fireplace. The spa is catered, and there is also the Oriental tea lounge to provide refreshments and sustenance. Take the opportunity to pamper yourself a little or enjoy a delicious tea.
80 Columbus Circle/60th St;
Tel 805 88 00;
9.00–21.00, daily.
www.mandarinoriental.com

Shopping

Atmos
The futuristic decoration and lighting in this store make it look like a spaceship and it sells the trendy goods you might expect in such surroundings: trainers of the most garish shades, crazy t-shirts that you will find nowhere else, and weird accessories. Even established firms like Levi's and New Bal-

ance sell a few quirky lines here, and a lot of the fashion comes from young Japanese designers. Pop in for a look. It's worth it!
203 W. 125th St;
Tel 666 22 42;
Mon–Sat 11.00–20.00,
Sun 12.00–19.00.

Harlemade
A relaxed atmosphere in which to buy clothes, jewellery, and craft items from Harlem designer labels. You will also find souvenirs of Harlem with the Harlemade emblem, which is considered very "hip".
174 Malcolm X Blvd/W.
118th St;
Tel 987 25 00;
Mon–Fri 11.30–19.00,
Sat 11.00–19.00, Sun
12.00–18.00.

Harlem's Heaven Hat Boutique
Anyone who has admired the adventurous millinery of Afro-American ladies and gentlemen will find it for sale here, as well as a selection of handbags, earrings, accessories, and much more.
2538 Adam Clayton Powell
Jr Blvd/W.147th St;
Tel 491 77 06;
Tues–Sat 12.00–18.00.
www.harlemsheaven.com

Malia Mills
This store stocks elegant ladies' swimming costumes designed by the owner. Perfect one and two-piece costumes tailored from fabrics from Europe and the US.
220 Columbus Ave/
W. 70th St;
Tel 874 72 00;
Mon–Sat 11.00–18.00,
Sun 12.00–17.00.
www.maliamills.com

Nicholas
A shop to really put a back-beat in the pulse of every reggae fan, here you can buy printed t-shirts, jackets, belts, caps, scarves, and bags displaying the image of the legendary Jamaican folk hero Bob Marley. Nicholas also sells books, posters, bumper stickers, and various collectors' items.
2035 5th Ave/125th St;
Tel 289 36 28;
Mon–Sat 9.00–20.00,
Sun 12.00–18.00.
www.wholesalecentral.com/
nicholasvariety

Whole Foods
New York's biggest supermarket (and self-service restaurant) is located here in the basement of the Time Warner Building and has an overwhelming selection of fresh produce (including organic foods). If you are looking for a few unusual gift items to take home, you are bound to find something interesting here. And if you just want to buy yourself a delicious treat, you will have an amazing range to choose from.
10 Columbus Circle;
Tel 823 96 00;
8.00–23.00, daily,
restricted opening times
on public hols.
www.wholefoodsmarket.
com

Zabar's
This store is an institution amongst New York's delicatessens. Along with its gigantic array of culinary treats, Zabar's is popular for the kitchenware department on the first floor. Lovers of all things to do with the kitchen and cooking should put this on their menu.

2245 Broadway/W. 80th St;
Tel 787 20 00/46 12 34;
Mon–Fri 8.30–19.30, Sat
8.00–20.00, Sun 9.00–18.00.
www.zabars.com

Eating and Drinking

Amy Ruth's Home-Style Southern Cuisine
Possibly the best soul food in Harlem, with hearty homemade Southern food. The fried and BBQ chicken is served with potato purée, baked beans, or buttered corn, and the macaroni bake is very popular, if not particularly low in calories. If you're intending to have one of the rather lavish desserts, it may be better to forego a first course! This is a place for those who really enjoy their food, with colorful folk art from Harlem decorating the walls.
113 W. 116th St;
Tel 280 87 79;
Mon 11.30–23.00,
Tues–Thurs 8.30–23.00,
Fri 8.30–5.30, Sat 7.30–5.30,
Sun 7.30–23.00.
www.amyruthsharlem.com

Bouchon Bakery
A whiff of France in the middle of New York: Thomas Keller's boulangerie serves tasty quiches and soups as well as croissants, rolls, and other treats. Definitely not for those watching their weight, but exceptionally good food.
10 Columbus Circle (3rd floor);
Tel 823 93 66;
Mon–Fri 8.00–21.00,
Sat 10.00–21.00, Sun
10.00–19.00.

Key West Diner
One of the most popular diners in New York since 1987. Giant burgers, omelets, and

salads are popular with regulars – and even the coffee is recommended, too. The Greek salad is one of the best dishes, as you might expect from the Greek owners. Very clean and friendly.
2532 Broadway
(near 95th St);
Tel 932 00 68;
6.00–1.00, daily.

The Mermaid Inn
The ultimate in New England seafood. Oysters, shrimp, mussels, lobster, and signature dishes like fresh fish with hazelnuts, garlic, and chillies are on the menu, as is the irrepressible clam chowder, which tastes particularly creamy here and does indeed contain lots of clams. Great website. Check it out for more fishy information.
568 Amsterdam Ave
(near 88th St);
Tel 799 74 00;
Mon–Thurs 17.30–23.00,
Fri, Sat 17.00–23.30, Sun
17.00–22.00.
www.themermaidnyc.com

West Branch
A vaguely Mediterranean bistro with a club or sports bar atmosphere. The cheeseburgers are enormous and expensive, as are the Cuban pork sandwiches. The fish dishes are recommended, but the *gésier de canard* is not for everyone.
2178 Broadway
(corner of 77th St);
Tel 777 67 64;
Mon–Sun 17.00–23.00,
Fri, Sat 17.00–24.00,
Sun 17.00–22.00.

Pio Pio
A Peruvian restaurant best-known for its rotisserie chicken, which has recently

become very popular in America. The "matador Combo" (chicken, rice, beans, avocado salad, and fries with sausage) is the one to go for.
702 Amsterdam Ave
(corner of 94th St);
Tel 665 30 00;
11.00–23.00, daily.
www.piopionyc.com

Rack & Soul
Southern cooking via Harlem, with fried chicken and a first-class barbecue. Sweet waffles are served with the chicken, and there's ultra-sweet banana pudding for dessert, just like in Harlem or the Deep South. Unusually for such a place, they also stock European beer along with the Coca Cola and iced tea.
258 W. 109th St
(near Broadway);
Tel 222 48 00;
Mon–Thurs 11.00–22.00,
Fri 11.00–23.00, Sat
10.00–23.00, Sun
10.00–21.30.
www.rackandsoul.com

Accommodation

Amsterdam Inn
A good-value hotel with clean and welcoming rooms. There is unfortunately no lift, which can be an annoyance for guests in rooms on the third floor. The cheaper rooms have no en-suite bathrooms. Amongst the nice surprises are the coffee-maker and refrigerator in each room.
340 Amsterdam Ave
(corner of 76th St);
Tel 579 75 00.
www.amsterdaminn.com

Hotel Beacon
The good-value hotel was once an apartment building and a portion of the rooms

UPPER WEST SIDE AND HARLEM

These pages give additional information for the area of New York described in the "Highlights" section (pp. 160–179). Please note that the area code for New York is **212**.

are reserved for long-stay guests. Each room has a fully fitted kitchen with a cooker and a refrigerator, and the handy Fairway supermarket is located just over the road.
2130 Broadway
(near 75th St)
Tel 787 11 00.
www.beaconhotel.com

Hotel Belleclaire
A recently renovated 1903 Beaux Arts building with spacious rooms, each featuring a refrigerator (very important in expensive New York), a television, and a telephone. The beds are exceptionally comfortable and the rates are good value, with a room costing a little over $100. The best deal Uptown.
250 W. 77th St
(corner of Broadway);
Tel 362 77 00.
www.belleclairehotel.com

Excelsior Hotel
A good hotel on Central Park and a stone's throw from the American Museum of Natural History. The marble- and hardwood-decorated lobby has a European elegance, and the rooms also have Old World charm. Extras include wireless internet access.
45 W. 81st St
(near Columbus Ave);
Tel 362 92 00.
www.excelsiorhotelny.com

The Harlem Flophouse
Tiny rooms in a renovated brownstone house belonging to the artist, Rene Calvo. This bed and breakfast is like an art gallery and antique fixtures, such as the claw-foot bathtubs, are reminiscent of Harlem's first renaissance. Calvo serves the home-made breakfast personally.

242 W. 123rd St (near Frederick Douglass Blvd);
Tel 662 06 78.
www.harlemflophouse.com

The Lucerne
This charming and historic hotel was constructed as a dormitory for the university in 1903, but after extensive, multi-million dollar renovations in 1995 it has been turned into a friendly boutique hotel with a European feel. The rooms are extremely good value for a hotel located on the Upper West Side and feature wireless internet access as well as many other extras.
201 W. 79th St
(corner of Amsterdam Ave);
Tel 875 10 00.
www.newyorkhotel.com

Morningside Inn
This spartan mixture of hotel and guest house is somewhat reminiscent of a youth hostel, but the rooms are clean and very good value for money. Unfortunately the bathrooms are shared and there is no air-conditioning, but at least you can prepare your own small meals in the tiny kitchen provided. If you are travelling on a tight budget, this might just be the solution you are looking for.
235 W. 107th St
(near Amsterdam Ave);
Tel 316 00 55.
www.morningsideinn-ny.com

Hotel Newton
Definitely one of the best of the mid-price hotels in Manhattan. For $100 you get a spacious and clean room with an en-suite bathroom. Cable TV and room service are extra, and the service is

extremely friendly. The nearest subway station is located just around the corner.
2528 Broadway
(near 94th St);
Tel 678 65 00.
www.thehotelnewton.com

On the Ave Hotel
Hire a penthouse here and get a private balcony with a magnificent view of Central Park, or you can save some money and use the communal balcony on the 16th floor. All the rooms are elegantly furnished and come with numerous extras; the bathrooms are fitted out in marble. A stay in style!
2178 Broadway
(corner of 77th St);
Tel 362 11 00.
www.ontheave-nyc.com

The Phillips Club
Just the place for someone happy to spend $500 a day on a comfortable and reasonably sized two-room suite: there's even a microwave and dishwasher, and the well-appointed Reebok Sports Club is just round the corner.
155 W. 66th St
(near Broadway);
Tel 835 88 00.
www.phillipsclub.com

36 Riverside Wyman House
This bed and breakfast on Riverside Park is housed in a Victorian house from 1888 and is furnished accordingly. Each of the rooms has a different theme attached – the "Amadeus" recalls historical Vienna, while the "Angelica" is decorated with silk. Every room has a little kitchen area.
36 Riverside Drive
(corner of 76th St);
Tel 799 82 81.
www.wymanhouse.com

Nightlife

Lenox Lounge
The lounge of this legendary Harlem 1940s art deco bar has served as the backdrop for many jazz legends, including Billie Holiday, Miles Davis, and John Coltrane. It still features reasonably well-played jazz. In 1999 it underwent a costly restoration process to bring it back to its original splendor. The atmospheric surroundings are perhaps of a higher standard than the rather average food.
288 Lenox Ave
(near 125th St);
Tel 427 02 53;
12.00–4.00, daily.
www.lenoxlounge.com

Night Café
A comfortable night café with a long bar and a few tables. There are occasional readings and small gigs. The prize-winning owner runs a funny quiz, the winner of which is rewarded with a bottle from behind the bar.
938 Amsterdam Ave
(near 106th St);
Tel 864 88 89;
11.00–4.00; daily.

St Nick's
This is how a bar must have looked in the Golden Twenties: a long counter and a tiny stage in the basement of an apartment building. This jazz bar, located on historic Sugar Hill, has been pulling in the customers for over fifty years. Live jazz seven days a week – the trad jazz is the best.
773 St Nicolas Ave
(near W. 148th St), Harlem;
Tel 283 97 28;
Mon–Thurs 13.00–3.00,
Fri, Sat 16.00–4.00.
www.stnicksjazzpub.net

Museums, music, and drama

Alice Austen House Museum

Known for her scenes from day-to-day New York life, the photographer (1866–1952) spent the greater part of her life in this Victorian cottage.
2 Hylan Blvd, Staten Island;
Tel (516) 816 45 06;
Mar–Dec Thurs to Sun
12.00–17.00, closed
public hols.
www.aliceausten.org

American Guitar Museum

Admire exhibits from 1840 to the present day and instruments once belonging to famous virtuosi. There is also a music store, a music school, and a luthier's workshop.
1810 New Hyde Park Road;
Tel (516) 488 50 00;
Tues, Wed, Fri 10.00–18.00,
Thurs 10.00–22.00, Sat
9.00–17.00, Sun, Mon by
tour only.
www.americanguitarmuseum.com

Bowne House

Built in a Dutch colonial style in stages between 1660 and 1690, the house nonetheless benefited from the latest construction techniques imported from the homeland of its owner, the Englishman John Bowne. Original fixtures and furnishings once belonging to the family give a vivid insight into everyday life in days gone by.
37-01 Bowne St;
Tel (718) 359 05 28;
currently closed for
restoration but group
visits to the grounds and
gardens can be arranged in
advance. Email at:
office@brownhouse.org

Bronx Museum of the Arts

Founded in 1971, the Bronx museum concentrates on the 20th-century and contemporary art.
1040 Grand Concourse;
Tel (718) 681 60 00;
Thurs–Sun 11.00–18.00,
Fri 11.00–20.00, Thanks-
giving, 25 Dec, 1 Jan.
www.bronxmuseum.org

Bronx Zoo (Bronx Park)

The largest and most interesting zoo in New York. Parts of the grounds date back to 1899 and there is also a petting zoo. Don't miss the award-winning lemurs!
2300 Southern Blvd, Bronx;
Tel (718) 220 51 00;
Mon–Fri 10.00–17.00,
Sat, Sun and public hols
10.00–17.00.
www.bronxzoo.com

Brooklyn Botanic Garden

Founded in 1910 and famous for its rose garden, the Japanese gardens, and a garden for the blind, arranged by scent.
900 Washington Ave,
Brooklyn;
Tel (718) 623 72 00; Tues–Fri
8.00–18.00, Sat, Sun and
public hols 10.00–18.00.
www.bbg.org

Brooklyn Children's Museum

The museum was founded in 1899 and is thus one of the oldest children's museums in the world. The emphasis is on close interaction with technology and nature, and the museum is highly recommended for New York visitors with children.
145 Brooklyn Ave;
Tel (718) 735 44 00;
Tues–Thurs 11.00–17.00,
Fri 11.00–19.30, Sat,
Sun 10.00–17.00,

closed public hols.
www.brooklynkids.org

Brooklyn Museum

Founded in 1884, this is one of New York's most important collections. The exhibits are drawn from almost every genre and era of art from around the world: Ancient Egypt, the ancient world, the Near and Far East, art from Africa, Oceania, and America, of course, not to mention European and American art right up to contemporary design and photography.
200 Eastern Parkway;
Tel (718) 638 50 00;
Wed–Fri 10.00–17.00,
Sat 11.00–18.00/23.00,
Sun 11.00–18.00, closed
Thanksgiving, 25 Dec, 1 Jan.
www.brooklynmuseum.org

Edgar Allan Poe Cottage

A farmhouse built in 1812 and the great American poet's last residence. In 1902 it was removed from its original location nearby to the Poe Park and faithfully rebuilt. When Poe penned his works the cottage was in a bucolic setting, and he would have had unobstructed views of the Bronx hills.
2640 Grand Concourse,
Bronx;
Tel (718) 881 89 00;
Mon–Fri 9.00-17.00,
Sat 10.00–16.00, Sun
13.00–17.00, by group tour.
www.bronxhistoricalsociety.
org

Ellis Island National Monument

The museum of immigration's documentation department is housed on the site of the old immigration authority and details the history of immigration to the USA. It opened

on January 1, 1892 and became the nation's premier federal immigration station. It was in operation until 1954 and processed over 12 million immigrant steamship passengers arriving in New York.
Ellis Island;
Tel (212) 363 32 06;
9.30–16.30, daily,
closed 25 Dec.
www.nps.gov/elis/index.htm

Fisher Landau for Art

Emily Fisher Landau's private collection includes prized modern art from 1960 onwards, including works by Robert Rauschenberg, Jasper Johns, Richard Artschwager, Kiki Smith, John Baldessari, and Cy Twombly. It takes 5 to 15 minutes from Manhattan and admission is free.
38–27 30th St;
Long Island City;
Tel (718) 937 07 27;
Thurs–Mon 12.00–17.00,
closed Tues, Wed.
www.flcart.org

Greenwood Cemetery

A romantic park founded in 1838, with a neo-Gothic entrance, many monuments and over 600,000 graves, including those of Mozart's librettist Lorenzo da Ponte, Leonard Bernstein, and Lola Montez, a number of inventors, and several of New York's greatest industrialists. This is an oasis of peace in the heart of Brooklyn.
500 25th St, Brooklyn;
Tel (718) 768 73 00.
www.green-wood.com

Jacques Marchais of Tibetan Art

Founded in 1949, this museum resembles a Himalayan monastery and its exhibits include works of art, musical

Plumbing the depths: a subway in Queens; the gate to Greenwood cemetery; Artfull: the Brooklyn Museum; gateway to the Far East: the entrance of the Jacques Marchais Center of Tibetan Art (from left).

BROOKLYN, QUEENS, THE BRONX, STATEN ISLAND

These pages give additional information for the area of New York described in the "Highlights" section (pp. 180–197). Please note that the area code for New York is **212**.

instruments, and everyday objects. It gives the visitor a fascinating view of Tibetan culture and is a lovely spot to visit. Well worth the trip for those interested in this fascinating and complex country.
338 Lighthouse Ave,
Staten Island;
Tel (718) 987 35 00;
Wed–Sun 13.00–17.00.
www.tibetanmuseum.org

Jamaica Bay Wildlife Refuge Center
The municipal nature reserve, with its variety of natural habitats from salt marshes to forest, is most famous in its role as a bird reserve – guided tours and birdwatching are available – but it is also good just for relaxing in. Come here to chill out after a busy day of shopping!
Broad Channel, Queens;
Tel (718) 318 43 40;
sunrise to sunset, visitors'
information point:
8.30–17.00, daily, closed Thanksgiving, 25 Dec, 1 Jan.

King Manor Museum
The country seat of Rufus King (1755–1827), an important politician who co-wrote the American constitution and opposed slavery. In 1900 it was turned into a museum detailing aspects of the life and works of King and his family. A "Founding Father", King was one of New York's first senators.
15003 Jamaica Ave;
Tel (718) 206 05 45;
Thurs–Fri 12.00–13.30,
Sat, Sun 13.00–16.30, by guided tour only, closed Jan.
www.kingmanor.org

New York Aquarium
An interesting glimpse of the underwater world and its ani-

mal inhabitants, which also examines the ecosystems of various coastal and ocean areas. Animal feeding, dolphin and sea lion displays.
Surf Avenue/W 8th St,
Brooklyn;
Tel (718) 265 34 91;
Mon–Fri 10.00–18.00,
Sat, Sun, and public hols 10.00–19.00.
www.nyaquarium.com

New York Botanical Garden (Bronx Park)
One of America's largest and oldest botanical gardens, based on the Royal Botanical Gardens in London, was founded on this site on the Bronx River in 1891. Admire the orchids, palms, cacti, and tropical plants in the main building and visit the museum and herbarium in the Lorillard Snuff Mill. Other attractions include a rose garden with 2,700 different varieties and a rock garden. The Everett Children's Adventure Garden and the Ruth Rea Howell Family Garden cater for the children.
Southern Blvd/200th St;
Tel (718) 817 87 00;
Tues–Sun 10.00–18.00,
guided tours available,
closed Thanksgiving, 25 Dec.
www.nybg.org

New York Hall of Science
An interactive and hands-on museum of science and technology famed for its provisions for children. If you are visiting with little ones, this will keep them happy for hours. Educational and fun. Just what every parent is looking for.
47-01 111th St;
Tel (718) 699 00 05;
Tues–Thurs 9.30–14.00/
17.00 (Jul, Aug),

Fri 9.30–17.00, Sat,
Sun 10.00–18.00.
www.nyscience.org

New York Transit Museum
A museum dedicated to the development of public transport in New York, with video footage and exhibits illustrating the history, construction methods, and expansion of the first New York subway between 1900 and 1925, road traffic in the city, and guided tours and exhibitions, some of which are held in Grand Central Station.
Boerum Place/Schermerhorn St, Brooklyn;
Tel (718) 694 16 00;
Tues–Fri 10.00–16.00,
Sat, Sun 12.00–17.00,
closed public hols.
www.mta.info

Noguchi Museum
The museum is located in an old studio and is dedicated to the work of the Japanese-American artist Noguchi (1904–1988).
32–37 Vernon Blvd, Long Island City;
Tel (718) 204 7088;
Wed–Fri 10.00–17.00,
Sat, Sun 11.00–18.00, closed Thanksgiving, 25 Dec, 1 Jan.
www.noguchi.org

Queens County Museum
A historic farm has been turned into a working show farm with plenty of activities, which are especially attractive to children. And adults should enjoy it too! It offers a tranquil break from hectic activities without leaving the City. General admission is free, but check the website for exceptions.
73–50 Little Neck Parkway,
Floral Park;
Tel (718) 347 32 76;

Mon–Fri 10.00–17.00 (outdoor areas), Sat, Sun 10.00–17.00 (tours through the farm buildings).
www.queensfarm.org

Queens Museum of Art
Housed in the New York City Building, which was built for the 1939 World's Fair, the museum has a selection of contemporary art and a famous giant New York panorama. From 1946 to 1950 the building was used as the headquarters of the newly formed United Nations, and then was refurbished to become the heart of the World's Fair of 1964–65. It was last refurbished in 2005–2006.
NYC Building, Flushing Meadows Corona Park;
Tel (718) 592 97 00;
Wed–Sun 12.00–18.00,
Fri 12.00–20.00 (summer).
www.queensmuseum.org

Socrates Sculpture Park
Both a public recreation area and an exhibition space for large sculptures, the park was established in 1986 to bring modern art to a broader public. It has some fascinating and unusual pieces.
32–01 Vernon Blvd;
Tel (718) 956 18 19;
10.00–sunset, daily.
www.socratessculpturepark.org,

Sag Harbor Museum
Built in the colonial style in 1845, this country house (with a freemason's lodge on the first floor) houses a museum charting the history of whaling and seafaring. The little port of Sag Harbor was the hub of the whaling industry in the 19th century. Large quantities of liver oil, blubber,

ambergris, and whalebone were used in oil lamps, foodstuffs, and cosmetics, and employed in the manufacture of corsets and explosives. It's a fascinating museum. You will have a whale of a time…
200 Main St, Sag Harbor;
Tel (631) 725 07 70;
Mon–Sat 10.00–17.00,
Sun 13.00–17.00.
www.sagharborwhalingmu-seum.org

Snug Harbor Cultural Center and Botanical Garden

This former retirement home for seamen in wonderful 19th-century premises houses a botanical garden, a theater, a concert hall, the Newhouse Center for Contemporary Art, the Staten Island Museum, and a children's museum, amongst other things. The packed events schedule is augmented with seasonal celebrations and festivities. It is the product of 28 years of restoration and development, and offers a host of things to do and see.
1000 Richmond Terrace,
Staten Island;
Tel (718) 448 25 00;
sunrise–sunset, cultural events Tues–Sun
10.00–16.00.
www.snug-harbor.org

Van Cortlandt Museum

Built in 1748, this Georgian country house has been home to a museum of the 18th century since 1896. Magnificent furniture and household items illustrate life during the period. The museum is a private, non-profit institution, founded in 1896.
W 246th St/Broadway,
Tel (718) 543 33 44;

Tues–Fri 10.00–15.00, Sat, Sun 11.00–16.00.
www.vancortlandthouse.org

Festivals and events

Cherry Blossom Festival

The lovely pink blossom of the cherry trees along the Esplanade beside Brooklyn Botanic Garden is celebrated in this traditional Japanese festival. The emphasis is on Japanese culture in general, with taiko drumming, traditional Japanese music and dance, tea ceremonies, bonsai courses, kimono fashion shows, and various workshops for all the family.
1000 Washington Ave;
Tel (718) 623 72 00;
first weekend in May.
www.bbg.org

Dumbo Art under Bridge

A festival organized by the artists' community DUMBO in the old port area of Brooklyn, with open workshops, galleries, performances, and street art. The name DUMBO stands for "Down under the Manhattan Bridge Overpass".
30 Washington St,
Tel (718) 694 08 31; Sept.
www.dumboartscenter.org

Mermaid Parade

A magnificent parade of mermaids and sea gods in all their glitz and beauty proceeds along the Coney Island Boardwalk, celebrating sand, sea, and the start of summer. A prominent King Neptune or Queen Mermaid, whose task it is to formally open the bathing season, leads the procession. Afterwards there is a massive party with live music, a tombola, comedy, and burlesque shows You won't feel all at sea here!

Tel (718) 372 51 59;
first Sat after 21 Jun.
www.coneyislandusa.com

West Indian American Day Parade and Carnival

With more than three million participants, this Caribbean-inspired festival is one of America's biggest carnivals and almost causes a state of emergency in Brooklyn. The procession, with its fantastic costumes, non-stop percussion rhythms, steel drumming, and other music, lasts all day, and there are tasty Caribbean delicacies. The event takes place every year on Labor Day.
Eastern Parkway;
Tel (718) 467 17 97;
first Mon in Sept.
www.wiadca.org

Sport and leisure

American Football

The Giants and the Jets are the darlings of New York. Both teams play in the NFL (National Football League), the biggest professional league of this all-American sport, and host their sold-out home games at the Giants Stadium in the Meadowlands Sports Complex in New Jersey. The stadium is most easily reached by bus (journey time 20 mins) from the Port Authority Bus Terminal in Manhattan/Midtown.
East Rutherford (NJ);
Aug–Feb
Giants: Tel (201) 935 82 22;
www.giants.com
Jets: Tel (516) 560 82 00;
www.newyorkjets.com

Area Emporium

This spa in the middle of Cobble Hill in Brooklyn comes with a café and a store. The

attached yoga studio is a block away, on Court Street (no. 320) and along with the yoga courses and beauty treatments they sell cosmetics and other products to improve the body and mind.
281 Smith St;
Tel (718) 522 19 06;
10.00–19.00, daily, yoga studio: Mon–Fri 7.00–20.15,
Sat–Sun 10.00–17.00.
www.areabrooklyn.com

Astroland Amusement Park

The Cyclone has been one of the main attractions at this famous funfair on Coney Island since 1927. A frantic trip on this rollercoaster, some of whose drops are almost vertical and which has become a historic New York symbol, is fun for all. You could make it part of a day out on Coney Island.
834 Surf Ave/W. 10th St;
Tel (718) 265 21 00/372 02 75;
mid-Apr–mid-Jun, Sat–Sun 12.00–18.00, mid-Jun–early Sept, 12.00–24.00, daily.
www.coneyislandcyclone. com

Astoria Pool

Opened in Queens in 1936, this art deco pool has a view of the Triborough Bridge. On sunny summer days, New York's oldest and largest public swimming baths can attract more than 1,000 bathers.
Astoria Park;
Tel 626 86 20;
Jun–Aug 11.00–19.00.

Baseball

New York is one of the few places in the USA where baseball is held in higher regard than American football or basketball. The regular season of both major league teams, the New York Mets

BROOKLYN, QUEENS, THE BRONX, STATEN ISLAND

These pages give additional information for the area of New York described in the "Highlights" section (pp. 180–197). Please note that the area code for New York is **212**.

(Metropolitan Baseball Club of New York) and the New York Yankees, starts in spring and runs into the fall (after which the play-offs are held). Ticket prices start at $11 for the Mets' Citi Field Stadium in Queens and at $14 for the Yankee in the Bronx. Well worth trying to get to the game. It will be a once in a lifetime experience for some!
Mets: Tel 507 84 99;
http://newyork.mets.mlb.com
Yankees: Tel (212) 307-1212;
http://newyork.yankees.mlb.com
Apr–Oct.

Belmont Stakes
New York's biggest flat race in Belmont Park in Queens is one of the three most famous horse races in the US, along with the Kentucky Derby and the Preakness Stakes (Baltimore); together they form the so-called Triple Crown. The prize fund is $1 million, and admission is between $2 and $5. In some areas there is seating and even picnic tables.
Belmont Park, 2150 Hempstead Turnpike, Elmont;
Tel (516) 488 60 00;
Start: 9. Jun, course open: end of April–mid-Jun and Sept–Oct.
www.belmontstakes.com

Bike New York
The great 67.5-km (42-mile) "Five Boro Bike Tour" is one of the highlights of the month of May, which is all about cycling. Thousands of participants stamp on their pedals and launch themselves into an exciting race across town. Even more spectators follow the event along the roads and promenades, which are closed to traffic. It's a great spectator

sport for those who don't want to get in the saddle.
Tel (212) 932 24 53; May.
http://bikemonthnyc.org

D'mai Urban Spa
This spa is located in Brooklyn, but at times it feels like Bali. The interior is decorated like an Indonesian healing temple and they play soothing natural sounds to induce an air of calm. You can visit the sauna, get a massage, have a facial or a manicure, and much more, or just seek refuge in the cabana, a tent offering outdoor massages for couples. Take time out to pamper yourself.
157 5th Ave/Park Slope;
Tel (718) 398 21 00;
Mon 11.00–21.00,
Tues–Fri 11.00–19.30,
Sat, Sun 10.00–19.00.
www.dmaiurbanspa.com

Jamaica Bay Refuge
This nature reserve in Queens is also called Birdland, because there is something to see here for ornithologists and birdwatchers throughout the year. Sheltered from the Atlantic Ocean, the bay is a stopping-off point for 350 migratory species, mostly in July and August. The reserve is easily reached by subway from Manhattan and the visitors' information point is a further 20 minutes' walk away.
Cross Bay Blvd/Broad Channel;
Tel (718) 354 354 46 06/ 318 43 40; 8.30–17.00, daily.
www.nps.gov/gate

National Tennis Center
The US Open, one of the four Grand Slam competitions, is held here at the end of August (until mid-September) and you can watch, but not

play. Tickets can generally be bought as early as April (e.g. from Ticketmaster), but tickets for the big matches are usually hard to come by. After the US Open is over, 33 indoor and outdoor courts become available, which can be booked at least two days in advance, as demand is high. Just think how you could tell folks back home that you played at Flushing Meadows!
Flushing Meadows Corona Park, Queens;
Tel (718) 760 62 00.
www.usta.com
www.usopen.org
Ticketmaster:
Tel (212) 307 71 71;
www.ticketmaster.com

New York Aquarium
Young and old alike will be entertained by the many sea creatures, from the exotic to the local, in this aquarium on the Coney Island boardwalk. Shark, otter, and penguins' feeding times are especially popular, as are appearances by the beluga whales (in the winter months only) and the sea lions – the latter because they treat braver members of the audience to free kisses. Have your cameras ready.
Surf Ave/W. 8th St, Brooklyn;
Tel (718) 265 34 74 (or 718 265-FISH);
10.00–17.00, daily,
May–Aug: Mon–Sat 10.00–18.00, Sun 10.00–19.00.

New York City Marathon
Every year, New York's famous marathon attracts tens of thousands of runners, both professional and amateur, from all over the world. It covers 42 km (26 miles 385 yards) across all five bor-

oughs, starting on the Verrazano Narrows Bridge (Staten Island) and finishing at the Tavern on the Green in Central Park. Countless excited spectators cheer on the runners from the kerbside. first Sun in Nov.
www.nycmarathon.org

Shopping

Almondine Bakery
Located not far from Empire Fulton Ferry State Park, this Brooklyn bakery sells fresh croissants and excellent brioche. The master baker, Hervé Poussot, also has a selection of organic bread, baguettes, and tasty cookies.
85 Water St/Main St;
Tel (718) 797 50 26;
Mon–Thurs 7.00–19.00, Fri 7.00–21.00, Sat 7.00–19.00, Sun 10.00–18.00.
www.almondinebakery.com

Burlington Coat Factory
This discount fashion outlet claims to be the cheapest, and sells coats, branded clothes, shoes, and bags. There is a second branch in Manhattan (6th Ave/W. 23rd St). You might find some good bargains to take home here.
625 Atlantic Ave/5th Ave;
Tel 622 40 57; Mon–Sat 10.00–21.00, Sun 11.00–18.00.
www.burlingtoncoatfactory.com

Woodbury Commons
An hour's bus ride north of New York City, this designer outlet mall has good deals on clothes, shoes, accessories, and much more. There are about 220 branded stores, such as Armani, Boss, Hilfiger, and Nike. The discounts are guaranteed to be between 25

and 65 percent. There are several buses (Gray Line, Coach USA) a day to the outlet from the Port Authority Bus Terminal (W. 42nd St/8th Ave). The return journey costs $40.
498 Red Apple Court, Central Valley;
Tel (845) 928 40 00;
10.00–21.00, daily (except Jan–Feb: Mon–Wed 10.00–18.00, Thurs–Sun 10.00–21.00).
www.premiumoutlets.com bus timetable: www.njtransit.com

Eating and drinking

Anthony's
Here you'll find south Italian food "just like mother makes"; the trip is worth it for the crispy and well-topped pizzas alone. All the food is prepared to family recipes and favourites include baked mussels, chicken, veal, and pasta.
426A 7th Ave (near 14th St);
Tel (718) 369 83 15;
Sun–Thurs 12.00–23.00, Fri, Sat 12.00–24.00.

Applewood
A family business in Brooklyn. The owners prefer organic produce, wild fish, and organic beef – without hormones and antibiotics – and conjure up fine dishes such as lobster in butter with fennel and mint.
501 11th St (near 7th Ave);
Tel (718) 788 18 10;
Tues–Fri 17.00–23.00, Sat 10.00–14.00, 17.00–23.00, Sun 10.00–15.00.
www.applewoodny.com

Bacchus
A French bistro with friendly staff and reasonable prices. The house specials include classics such as coq au vin, stews, pies, and cheeses. The

staff are particularly proud of their fine selection of wines.
409 Atlantic Ave (near Bond St);
Tel (718) 852 15 72;
Mon–Fri 17.00–23.00, Sat, Sun 10.30–24.00.
www.bacchusbistro.com

Bamonte's
Banks of chandeliers illuminate the antique-filled dining room of this Italian restaurant, one of Brooklyn's most popular since the 1950s, and the food, such as classic antipasti, cheese ravioli, and lasagne with cheese and spinach, won't be a disappointment.
32 Withers St (near Lorimer St);
Tel (718) 384 88 31;
Mon, Wed, Thurs 12.00–22.30, Fri 12.00–23.00, Sat 13.00–23.00, Sun 13.00–22.00.

Bittersweet
This tiny bar opposite Fort Greene Park in Brooklyn has strong espresso and delicate ice cream in variations such as "Jamaican grape nut" (vanilla with cornflakes). As a contrast, they also have vegetarian sandwiches on the menu.
180 Dekalb Ave (near Carlton Ave);
Tel (718) 852 25 56;
Mon–Fri 7.00–19.00, Sat, Sun 7.30–19.00.

Blackbird Parlour
A friendly, European-style coffee house. The Italian espresso is strong and tasty, and the cappuccino and café latte (naturally) taste better than at Starbuck's. There are also cookies, delivered fresh daily from the famous Artopolis bakery in Astoria.
197 Bedford Ave, Brooklyn (corner of N. 6th St);

Tel (718) 599 27 07;
Mon–Fri 8.00–22.00, Sat, Sun 10.00–3.00.

Bogota Latin Bistro
The walls are resplendent with bright murals of South American themes, and the best and most widely known Central South American food is served up here. All the dishes, especially the steaks and the chicken, are spicy and hot. The tasty specials include roasted calamari and a spicy stew from Costa Rica.
141 5th Ave (near St John's Place);
Tel (718) 230 38 05;
Mon, Wed, Thurs 17.00–23.00, Fri, Sat 17.00–1.00, Sun 12.00–22.00.
www.bogotabistro.com

Café Glechik
Brighton Beach is predominantly inhabited by Russian immigrants and they have spotted a good thing in this Ukrainian café. The first-class dumplings are especially acclaimed, and there are also plentiful soups and stews, e.g. green borscht with eggs and rice. The cabbage roulade is one of the best main courses.
3159 Coney Island Ave (near Brighton Beach Ave);
Tel (718) 616 04 94;
10.00–22.00, daily.

Choice Market
Rather special health food: no shoots and seeds, but instead creative and tasty dishes such as grilled tuna with spicy Amarillo sauce or BLT with rosemary and olive oil.
318 Lafayette Ave (corner of Grand Ave);
Tel (718) 230 52 34,
6.00–21.00; daily.
www.choicemarketbrooklyn.com

Faan
A modern Asiatic restaurant with tasty noodle dishes from Japan, China, Thailand, and Vietnam. The sushi is not quite so good, but amongst the creative dishes on the menu you'll find chicken wontons and beef satay. A very friendly atmosphere.
209 Smith St (corner of Baltic St);
Tel (718) 694 22 77;
11.00–23.00, daily.

Fette Sau
A barbecue restaurant in an old car workshop. Known as "Fat Pig" in German, here you'll find all sorts of meat dishes, including Italian sausage from a butcher friend, chicken, and lamb barbecued for the clientele.
354 Metropolitan Ave;
Tel (718) 963 34 04;
Sun–Thurs 17.00–2.00, Fri, Sat 17.00–4.00.

Five Front
A friendly and atmospheric bistro beneath Brooklyn Bridge. This little bar is famed for its excellent mussels, but also serves fast food, such as chicken fingers and spare ribs. Good wine list.
5 Front St (near Old Fulton St);
Tel (718) 625 55 59;
Mon, Wed, Thurs 17.30–23.00, Fri 17.30–24.00, Sat 11.00–24.00.
www.fivefrontrestaurant.com

Peter Luger Steak House
The best steakhouse in New York, listed in the respected Zagat guide for the last 30 years. It serves only porterhouse steaks for two, three, or four people, and the steaks are served pre-cut on a red-hot plate so they can cook

A wealth of windows: brownstones in the Bronx; Zero Otto Nove – Italian through and through; the Sofia Inn: staying in the Garden Suite; the Enid A. Haupt Conservatory in the New York Botanical Garden (from left).

BROOKLYN, QUEENS, THE BRONX, STATEN ISLAND

These pages give additional information for the area of New York described in the "Highlights" section (pp. 180–197). Please note that the area code for New York is **212**.

further during the meal. The restaurant has been serving fine steaks since 1887 and they are now available to order online. The selection of meat is done only by family members. Steak lovers should make their way here.
178 Broadway (in Brooklyn); Tel (718) 387 74 00; Mon–Thurs 11.45–21.45, Fri, Sat 11.45–22.45, Sun 12.45–21.45.
www.peterluger.com

South Fin Grill
In addition to the magnificent view of the Verrazzano Bridge, the fish dishes have Mediterranean spices and taste fantastic; you'll even find sushi rolls with cooked eel and peach on the menu. Try the cheesecake for dessert.
300 Father Capodanno Blvd (corner of Sand Lane); Tel (718) 447 76 79; Sept–May: Tues–Thurs 11.00–21.30, Fri, Sat 11.00–23.00, Sun 11.00–21.00; Jun–Aug: also Mon 11.00–21.30.

Uncle Peter's Bar and Grill
Uncle Peter is actually an Italian called Ernesto who has spent a graet deal of time in Argentina, and he unites the cooking of his twin homelands in an interesting and tasty fusion. Steaks and ravioli appear on the same plate and later in the evenings you will (of course) be entertained with some Argentinean tango music. The owner is gregarious, the food delicious and the atmosphere infectious.
83–15 Northern Blvd (near 83rd St); Tel (718) 615 86 00; Mon–Fri 12.00–22.00, Sat 16.00–23.00, Sun 13.00–22.00.

Wave Thai
An artistic celebration of Thai cooking in an elegant lounge atmosphere. Fresh fish is spiced up in the wok into a variety of curries, the rice isn't sticky, and the coconut chicken soup is perfection. All the dishes are very hot, so be warned.
21–37 31st St (near Ditmars Road), Astoria; Tel (718) 777 67 89; Mon–Thurs 11.00–23.00, Fri 11.00–24.00, Sat 12.00–24.00, Sun 12.00–23.00.
www.wavethainyc.com

Zero Otto Nove
It certainly seems you can eat well in the Bronx, especially in this atmospheric trattoria, where the pizzas come out of the wood oven topped with the best ingredients. Regulars here highly recommend the margherita and the buffalo mozzarella pizzas.
2357 Arthur Ave (near 186th St), Bronx; Tel (718) 220 10 27; Tues–Thurs 12.00–14.30, 16.30–22.00, Fri, Sat 12.00–14.30, 16.30–23.00, Sun 13.00–21.00.
www.roberto089.com

Accommodation

Baisley House
The interior decorator and architect Harry Paul has installed a friendly bed and breakfast in this romantic brownstone building, owned by a merchant called Charles Baisley in the 19th century. The Victorian décor is reminiscent of America at the time of the Founding Fathers. Very decent prices.
294 Hoyt St (near Sackett St); Tel (718) 935 19 59.

Dekoven Suites
This is actually more of a sublet. The owner has fitted out the cellar of her Victorian house in Brooklyn as a luxury flat with a kitchen and bathroom; tailor-made for a value-for-money family stay.
30 Dekoven Court (near Rugby Road); Tel (718) 421 10 52.
www.bbonline.de

Golden Gate Inn
If Manhattan is too expensive, you may find this simple but clean hotel just right. The rooms cost less than $100, although you will have to take the nearby highway and the less-than-attractive surroundings into account. Coney Island is ten minutes away by car.
3867 Shore Parkway (near Bragg St); Tel (718) 743 40 00.
www.goldengateinnny.com

The New York Marriott Brooklyn Bridge
This large hotel is situated opposite Manhattan at Brooklyn Bridge. Apart from the magnificent views from most of the rooms, the hotel has all the standards you would expect from a luxury chain hotel and extras such as wireless internet access, newspapers, and free coffee.
333 Adams St (near Willoughby St); Tel (718) 246 70 00.
www.brooklynmarriott.com

Sheraton LaGuardia Hotel
Not a typical airport hotel. Although only 5 km (3 miles) away from LaGuardia Airport in Queens, the hotel is best-known for its large collection of Asiatic antiques; even the décor is Asian-influenced. The beds are exceptionally comfortable and the service is generally exemplary.
135—20 39th Ave (near Main St); Tel (718) 460 66 66.
www.starwoodhotels.com

The Sofia Inn
This cheerful bed and breakfast is situated in a brownstone building north of Prospect Park in the heart of Brooklyn. You can choose from a three-room suite with a sitting room, kitchen, and bathroom, or four smaller rooms with bathrooms in the hall. The suite also has the back garden.
288 Park Place (near Vanderbilt Ave); Tel (718) 398 41 85.
www.brooklynbedand-breakfast.net

Nightlife

The Diamond
Something different for Brooklyn: a bar selling only low-alcohol beer. It also has European light beers on the menu, and you can play shuffleboard in the room next door.
43 Franklin St (near Calyer St); Tel (718) 383 50 30; Sun–Wed 17.00–1.00, Thurs–Sat 17.00–2.00.
www.thediamondbrook-lyn.com

Remote Sports Bar
An atmospheric sports bar in Queens – as in every other sports bar they have televisions on the wall with live transmissions of various matches, usually American football, baseball, and basketball. There is also beer and fast food.
2701 23rd Ave (near 27th St); Tel (718) 728 22 58; Mon–Fri 11.00–2.00, Sat, Sun 10.00–2.00.

MAJOR MUSEUMS

If you are interested in modernism, New York is a must. It is a city bursting with new architecture and stunning museums with 20th-century art collections such as the Museum of Modern Art, the Solomon R. Guggenheim Foundation and the Whitney Museum of American Art. Lovers of older art can find treasures too, particularly at the Metropolitan Museum and the Frick Collection, which boast works by the most famous artists in the western world. The museums of natural history, ethnology, and those dealing specifically with the history and culture of the American continent should not be missed either. This is a paradise for those who enjoy nothing more than a day or two (or more!) spent in a museum.

Designed by Calvert Vaux and Jacob Wrey Mould, the museum complex was built between 1877 and 1935 and is entered through John Russell Pope's monumental Theodore Roosevelt Memorial Wing, guarded by James Fraser's 1940 equestrian statue of the president. The latest addition is James Stewart Polshek's Rose Center for Earth and Space, built in 2000.

INFO
American Museum of Natural History; Central Park West/79th St; Tel (212) 769 51 00; www.amnh.org; 10.00–17.45, daily, Fri 10.00–20.45; subway 79th St/81st St.

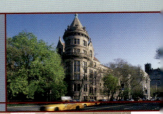

The Dzanga-Sangha rainforest

This diorama of a tropical rainforest in the Central African Republic gives visitors an impression of the natural beauty and impressive variety of the local plants and animals – from insects to reptiles, birds, small mammals, lowland gorillas, to forest elephants – in their natural environment. In reality, the actual area of rainforest was highly endangered by forest-clearing and mining

A rainforest flower.

rights concessions which had fallen into foreign hands. In an exemplary case of successful conservation of diversity and a natural way of life, the Central African Republican government initiative saw the area declared the Dzang-Ndoki National Park, a fully protected conservation area completely given over to the indigenous people for their use.

The Museum

This museum of natural science and ethnology was founded as early as 1869, and is thus the oldest in the city. Comprising 20 buildings, some of which are five floors high, spread over four blocks, this giant museum has something for every adult and child – one day is simply not enough to see everything! The permanent display is complemented with long-running special exhibitions, and an internationally recognized research department with its own laboratories assists the museum's curators. If you have time to visit it twice, it is well worth it.

The collections

The Museum of Natural History is principally famous for its habitat dioramas illustrating the development of life on our planet – preserved animals are shown in their natural environment – and for its numerous departments which use the most up-to-date scientific techniques to research the development of life and civilization on earth. It is also known for its conservation work. The collection's most important sections, whose informative displays are often distributed across several exhibition halls, are listed below.

Fossils

The giant skeletons and models on display in the dinosaur hall are a particular draw for young and old alike, and this spectacular fossil collection is the largest in the world, offering an impressive overview of

The imposing world of the dinosaurs: an Allosaurus skeleton.

The displays on biodiversity can be enthralling.

vertebrate development. Evolutionary connections and relationships between individual species are presented using modern technology. It brings the past alive in a fascinating way.

Mammals

You can increase your knowledge of the animal kingdom here by studying the appearance, behavior, and native habitat of a variety of living and sometimes extinct mammals from around the globe. The focus of the collection is on animals from the continents of Asia, Africa, and North America.

Birds

The museum boasts a comprehensive collection of specimens from New York and North America, as well as a variety of bird species from around the world. A real must for bird enthusiasts.

Anthropology department

The museum's research work in the field of anthropology has involved numerous famous scientists, including Margaret Mead and Franz Boas, and offers an insight into the cultures of Africa, North, Middle, and South

AMERICAN MUSEUM OF NATURAL HISTORY

The setting for the comedy film *Night at the Museum*, this museum has one of the greatest natural history collections in the world; with over 30 million specimens it is also larger than any other by some margin. Try to put this high on your list of must-see venues.

The Hayden Planetarium in the Rose Center for Earth and Space.

America, and the Pacific Basin. Special reference is made to various Native American tribes because the museum's principal focus is on the anthropology of the American continent.

Other halls

In addition to the sections mentioned above, there are also separate halls dedicated to reptiles and primates; the "Ocean Life Hall" has a life-size replica of a blue whale. Man's evolution is dealt with in a further hall, and the Arthur Ross Hall of Meteorites boasts Ahnighito, a piece of one of the largest meteorites ever to strike the earth, which was discovered in 1897. The Hall of Minerals and Gems features such jewels as the "Star of India" – at 563 carats, the world's largest cut diamond; a 100-carat

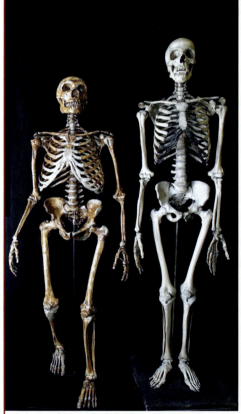

Skeletons of a Neanderthal and a modern *Homo sapiens*.

Our ancestors: the development of the human skull.

Hall of Biodiversity

More than 30 m (100 feet) long, the "Spectrum of Life" installation illustrates the evolution of micro-organisms into mammals. A stroll through the life-size Dzanga-Sangha Rainforest, complete with sounds and smells, is intended to give visitors an idea both of its biodiversity and of the dangers facing this delicate ecosystem. Human intervention and the destruction of natural habitats are also explored, as are the various approaches to conservation and to the ecological crisis we now face.

ruby; and the "Brazilian Princess", a 21,237-carat topaz thought to be the world's largest cut gemstone.

Rose Center of Earth and Space

Affiliated to the museum, this research and exhibition complex houses the Hayden Planetarium and exhibitions dealing with astronomy and space. The museum's IMAX cinema shows nature films and multimedia presentations on a giant screen, including the new show *Journey to the Stars*.

Fascinating specimens in the mineral and gem collection.

INFO
*Guggenheim Museum,
1071 Fifth Ave;
Tel (212) 423 35 00;
www.guggenheim.org;
Sun–Wed, Fri
10.00–17.45, Sat
10.00–19.45, closed
Thurs; subway 86th St.*

Looking like a sculpture, the world-renowned inverted spiral of this distinctive building is the work of Frank Lloyd Wright (1867–1959), the greatest 20th-century American architect. This spectacular setting has been used as a set and location for films such as *Men in Black* and *The International*.

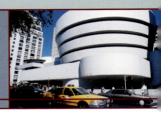

Franz Marc:
The Yellow Cow

A typical work by Franz Marc, a member of the Munich "Blue Rider" group of artists, showing a leaping yellow cow with blue spots on its hide (1911). For Marc, the cheerful yellow represented femininity and gentleness, and yet the orange-red tones of the landscape render it rather unreal. Marc often

Franz Marc:
The Yellow Cow, 1911.

retained recognizable objects in his pictures, with a particular predilection for animals, whose essence he considered innocent and natural, and yet "natural" animals and landscapes were compromised as two-dimensional forms with unnatural hues. Franz Marc thus succeeded in drawing the attention of the observer away from mere recognition of externalities toward a more profound form of engagement with nature, essence, and the spiritual aspects of a motif. He used color especially as a means to convey spiritual elements.

The founder, Solomon R. Guggenheim

An industrialist, mine-owner, and copper magnate from a German-Swiss family of Jewish émigrés, Solomon Robert Guggenheim (1861–1949) was the son of Meyer Guggenheim, a co-owner of the firm Guggenheim Brothers, a passionate art collector, and one of America's richest men. Initially he collected Old Masters, which

Frank Lloyd Wright, 1957.

Visitors on the spiral inner ramp of the museum.

were auctioned off by his heirs in 1961. However, influenced by Baroness Hilla Rebay von Ehrenwiesen, a German painter, Guggenheim turned his attention to the modernist movement, which was gaining momentum in Europe in the late 1920s, and he went on to support numerous avant-garde artists through the purchase of their works. He thus laid the foundations for the gigantic art empire that was to become the Solomon R. Guggenheim Foundation, endowed in 1937. The collection was made accessible to the public in a museum

opened in 1939, and in 1943 Guggenheim commissioned architect Frank Lloyd Wright to design a new, dedicated museum building in the heart of New York.

The museum building itself

Wright's building, a 20th-century architectural icon, was first planned in 1943. However, construction did not begin until 1956, due to the death of Guggenheim

and the financial and planning difficulties that had first to be overcome. The architect himself died six months before the museum's completion in 1959.
Wright's individual approach and spare formal architectural vocabulary, dispensing with ornamentation, made him one of the greatest architects of the 20th century. Today the distinctive, helical museum building is considered the masterpiece of his late work. It has attracted much criticism since its creation: principally that the architecture detracted from the works of art and that the

hanging conditions for the paintings were not the best. On reaching the top by elevator, visitors walk down a curved ramp beneath a glass dome, admiring the artwork displayed on the walls and in little alcoves. In 1992, the museum was extended with a building designed by Gwathmey Siegel. This has provided more room for the permanent exhibition, an auditorium, and office space. It is a thoroughly impressive construction.

The Collection

The focus of the original collection was abstract masterpieces, with important works by Wassily Kandinsky, Piet Mondrian, Fernand Léger, and Robert Delaunay, amongst others. In 1948 the museum's holdings were augmented with a bequest from the New York art dealer Karl Nierendorf, which included works by Paul Klee, Lyonel Feininger, Joan Miró, and Marc Chagall, as well as further pieces by Kandinsky. These extended the collection with important expressionist and surrealist works.

THE GUGGENHEIM MUSEUM

The Solomon R. Guggenheim Foundation owns one of the world's greatest collections of modern art, with branches in Las Vegas (the Guggenheim Hermitage), Venice (the Peggy Guggenheim Collection), Bilbao (Museo Guggenheim), and Berlin (Deutsche Guggenheim), which all complement its base in Manhattan. There was also a branch in the New York district of SoHo between 1992 and 2002.

In 1963 the museum acquired the Justin K. Thannhauser Collection, which was once the property of the Munich gallery owner Heinrich Thannhauser and his son, so increasing the collection with impressionist and Post-Impressionist works, as well as some early modernist pieces and several Picassos. There were also some small sculptures by Edgar Degas and Aristide Maillol. The museum now owns one of the world's

tin Brancusi, Alexander Archipenko, and Alexander Calder, to mention just some of the important acquisitions and bequests in the years since the founder's death.
Along with the artists mentioned above, the Guggenheim Museum has works by Edouard Manet, Vincent van Gogh, Paul Cézanne, Amedeo Modigliani, Georges Braque, Oscar Kokoschka, Kurt Schwitters, Alberto Giacometti, Jackson Pollock, Mark Rothko, and Robert

Amedeo Modigliani (1884–1920), *Nude with Necklace*, 1917.

A view of the glass skylight that tops the interior.

largest public collections of Picasso's works, including *Woman with Yellow Hair* and *Le Moulin de la Galette*.
Acquisition of the Count Panza di Biumo's Collection brought the museum more modern works by American artists of the 1960s and 1970s, minimalist pieces, conceptual artworks, and environments by Donald Judd and Dan Flavin, amongst others. The Robert Mapplethorpe Foundation and the Bohen Foundation donated photos, films, and video installations. Katherine S. Dreier also bequeathed important pieces by Constan-

Rauschenberg, as well as Andy Warhol, Claes Oldenburg, Walter De Maria, John Baldessari, Joseph Beuys, Mario Merz, and Rebecca Horn. The museum therefore provides a good overview of art from the middle of the 19th century to the 20th century.
The museum's comprehensive holdings allow several special exhibitions a year to run concurrently with the permanent exhibition, and thanks to a successful three-year plan of restoration, the Frank Lloyd Wright–designed building is even more breathtaking than ever.

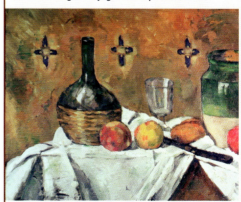

Paul Cézanne, *Flask, Glass, and Fruit*, 1877

This museum of superlatives is located in a complex of build-ings constructed between 1879 and 1913, and was extended several times between 1965 and 1991. Although it has more than 300 galleries and halls, it is far too small for its collection of 3.3 million art objects, with the result that only a fraction of the holdings can be exhibited.

INFO
1000 Fifth Ave/82nd St;
Tel (212) 535 77 10;
www.metmuseum.org;
Tues–Thurs, Sun 9.30–
17.30, Fri, Sat 9.30–
21.00, closed Mon
(except Holiday Mon-
days); subway 86th St.

Rembrandt: *Aristotle Contemplating a Bust of Homer*

Painted in 1653 for the Sicilian nobleman Don Antonio Ruffo, this pic-ture by Rembrandt (1606–1669) shows the great ancient philosopher Aristotle (384–322 BC) as a successful older man with a broad, black hat. He is wearing a white

Rembrandt Harmenszoon van Rijn: *Aristotle Contemplating a Bust of Homer*, oil on canvas, 1653.

coat with wide sleeves, a dark jacket, and a golden chain bearing a likeness of Alexander the Great (356–323 BC), his great-est pupil and admirer. Aristotle's right hand is contemplatively laid on the bust of the old, blind poet and mythmaker, Homer; this emotional connection transcends externalities, showing his real, inner greatness.

The history of the museum

In 1869, a circle of wealthy New Yorkers led by John Jay founded an art collection for the education of the city's citizens. Three years later it was recognized as an official public museum, and in 1881

Sahura, 5th-century pharaoh of Egypt's Old Kingdom.

was able to move into its own premises on Central Park. Countless acquisitions and donations, some of which remained separate entities, such as the Robert Lehman Collection, soon allowed the museum to grow to an impressive size. Addi-tional areas of interest to those already mentioned include Islamic, old Oriental, Pacific, African, and pre-Columbian American art, the Far East, medieval, and 20th-century art, weapons and armor, drawings and prints, photographs, and musical

instruments. Below are some of the highlights.

Egyptian Art

The exhibits range from the Old Kingdom to the Christian era, including tombs such as the Mastaba Tomb of Perneb, the statues of Demedji and

Grave stele of a girl, Greece, 5th century BC.

Hennutsen from 2450 BC, statues of Hatshepsut, gold jewellery, glass, and the Tem-ple of Dendur.

Greek and Roman Antiquities

Starting with Cycladic idols (c. 5000 to 1600 BC), this department has ancient stat-ues, grave stele, the "Calyx-krater with a scene from a phlyax play", and the famous grave relief "girl with two doves" from the Classical period, as well as Roman copies of Greek masterpieces

such as Praxiteles' *Aphrodite*, the so-called "Badminton sar-cophagus", Roman wall art, an Etruscan triumphal char-iot, and much more European sculpture and painting.

European Sculpture and Art

One of the museum's high-lights is, of course, the collec-tion of European painting, sculpture, and handicrafts. Almost all the great names from the 13th to the 19th cen-turies are represented, includ-ing works by Giotto, Duccio, Jan van Eyck, Botticelli, Raphael, Bellini, Dürer, Titian, Bronzino, Brueghel, El Greco, Caravaggio, Rubens, Rem-brandt, Hals, Vermeer, Ruys-dael, Poussin, Georges de La Tour, Velazquez, Chardin, Boucher, David, Goya, Turner, Manet, Vincent van Gogh, 37 canvases by Monet, 21 by Cézanne, and about 100 works by Degas. There are also small-scale Renaissance sculptures and whole room interiors from various periods, brought over from Europe, to illustrate trends in western art and lifestyle.

American art(s) and crafts

The art and culture of mod-ern America, as instanced by authentically decorated rooms, architectural features, and utensils from the 17th to the 19th centuries, including pieces by Tiffany, and paint-ings and sculptures by Amer-ican artists such as J.S. Copley, B. West, T. Cole, a member of the Hudson River School, E. Hicks, J.A. Whistler, J. Singer Sargent, M. Cassatt, and W. Homer.

METROPOLITAN MUSEUM OF ART

With 20 curatorial departments that are probably unique in the world, this museum offers a journey through the history of art and culture from the Stone Age to the present day. The complex also houses the largest art library in America, a provenance research department because the museum is regularly accused of possessing stolen art, and the Cloisters annex for medieval art in the north of Manhattan.

Magnolias and Irises, a window by master glass-maker Louis C. Tiffany.

20th-century painting

American realism is represented by Edward Hopper's work, for example, and American abstract impressionism, including works by Jackson Pollock, Mark Rothko, Willem de Kooning, and Barnett Newman. There are also pieces by European artists, including Joan Miró, Pablo Picasso, Max Beckmann, Paul Klee, Amedeo Modigliani, and Henri Matisse.

East Asia

The artworks in this department date from the second millennium BC to the early 20th century; of special interest are a reconstruction of a garden courtyard from ancient China, the so-called Astor Court, Chinese furniture from the Ming period, Buddhist sculpture, Japanese lacquerwork, jade objects, and pieces of Korean and Indian art.

Fabrics and fashion

A collection of more than 45,000 specimens of textiles, giving an overview of changing fashions from the last seven centuries. Male and female styles, children's clothes, traditional clothing, modern haute couture, and accessories illustrate how people have chosen to present themselves. Fashion students and followers of fashion should head to this collection for inspiration and education.

The Cloisters

This branch of the museum located in Fort Tryon Park in northern Manhattan is of even greater importance than the medieval department in the main building. The complex, acquired through a donation by John D. Rockefeller Jr to house the George Grey Barnard collection of medieval art and objects from his own collection, was assembled from fragments of European monasteries, with a few modern additions. Romanesque and Gothic sculptures, frescos, stained-glass windows, Gobelin's *Hunt of the Unicorn*, a book of hours that once belonged to the Duc de Berry, carvings by Tilman Riemenschneider, and Robert Campin's *Mérode* Triptych are all highlights of the exhibition.

Edouard Manet, *Boating*, oil on canvas, 1874.

Ceremonial robes of Chinese empress Cixi, late 19th century.

Winslow Homer, *Snap the Whip*, oil on canvas, 1872.

The main building is in the International Style, a term used in a 1932 exhibition at MoMA to describe the new formal vocabulary of architecture. Philip Johnson provided side extensions and the sculpture garden in 1951 and 1964, and Cesar Pelli added the tower in 1982. The museum continues to grow: a new extension was added and the museum renovated between 2002 and 2004.

INFO
11 West 53rd St; Tel (212) 708 94 00; www.moma. org; Wed–Mon 10.30– 17.30, Fri till 20.00, closed Tues, Thanksgiving and Christmas; subway 49th St, Fifth Ave, Rockefeller Center.

Impressionism

The stylistic and thematic innovations of impressionism represent perhaps the first attempts at modernist painting. Claude Monet (1840–1926), born in Paris, is the prime exponent of the style. Although he remained loyal to objective painting for much of his life, even in his paintings the dissolution of

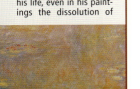

Claude Monet, *Reflections of Clouds on the Water-Lily Pond*, 1920.

the recognizable subject in color and light, its increasingly two-dimensional representation, its every day nature, and the omission of the horizon – a kind of immersion in the picture – all add up to a radical departure from the work of earlier artists. Impressionism was typified by sketchy, stippled brush strokes, and the best-known exponents of the style worked in France: Claude Monet, Auguste Renoir, Edgar Degas, Edouard Manet, Camille Pissarro, and Alfred Sisley. Nonetheless, some artists from the United States were influenced by impressionism, including Mary Cassatt and Childe Hassam, amongst others.

The history of the collection

The museum was founded by Abby Aldrich Rockefeller, Lillie P. Bliss, and Mary Quinn Sullivan, three rich New York society ladies, and it took on the task not only of collecting and curating exclusively modern art, but also of disseminating modern trends in art and bringing them to public attention. Extensive, spectacular exhibitions held

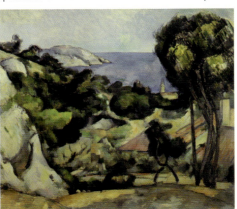

Paul Cezanne, *L' Estaque*, 1882–83.

in the MoMA thus became the starting-point that established many modern movements in architecture, design, and art. The institution still regards the promotion of the understanding of modern art as one of its principal tasks. After temporary accommodation in an office building and the Rockefeller's townhouse, the museum moved in 1939 to its own premises, designed by the architects Philip Goodwin and Edward Durell

Stone. The most recent extension and renovation was conducted by the famous Japanese architect, Yoshio Taniguchi.

The focus of the collection

Complemented by its famous special exhibitions, the museum's permanent collection gives a comprehensive overview of developments in art since 1880. Important Impressionist works are represented, as well as works from artists anticipating fauvism, expressionism, and modernism, including Vincent van Gogh's *Starry Night* from 1889, and works by Seurat, Toulouse-Lautrec, Degas, Gauguin, Cézanne, the scurrilous James Ensor, Modigliani, and Monet's *Waterlilies* from around 1920. MoMA also has the world's largest collection of works by Matisse. There are a number of German expres-

sionist pieces by Ernst Ludwig Kirchner and examples of cubism, whose beginnings are perhaps suggested by Picasso's 1907 canvas, *Les Demoiselles d'Avignon*, and whose highpoint is represented by further masterpieces by Picasso, Georges Braque, and Juan Gris. Visitors to MoMA are also confronted with the first movements towards abstraction, dadaism, and surrealism in works by Paul Klee, Kurt Schwitters, Joan Miró, Max Ernst, René Magritte, and Salvador Dalí.

The first half of the 20th century is rounded off with a collection of Italian futurist works, Giorgio de Chirico's *pittura metafisica*, Russian constructivism, and American realism. Post-World War II abstract impressionism is represented with action paintings by Jackson Pollock, color field paintings by Mark Rothko and Barnett Newman, as well as Willem de Kooning's aggressive brushwork.

The drift of the 20th-century art scene from Europe, most especially Paris, toward New York is also depicted: pop art, minimalism, and conceptual art constituted the next big breakthrough and these are represented with works by Robert Rauschenberg, Andy Warhol, Jasper Johns, Jim Dine, Roy Lichtenstein, and Claes Oldenburg. The best-represented American minimalist and conceptual artists are Donald Judd and Dan Flavin.

MoMA has also found room for installations, video art, and other trends from the last few decades, including works by Joseph Beuys,

THE MUSEUM OF MODERN ART

The Museum of Modern Art, or MoMA for short, boasts the world's greatest collection of modern and contemporary art. Located in Midtown, the museum has painting, sculpture, graphic design, book illustration, architectural plans, film, photography, electronic media, and design, including many design classics. The spectacular special exhibitions have only increased the museum's international fame. A must-see on any trip to New York.

Vincent van Gogh, *Starry Night*, 1889.

Chuck Close, Cy Twombly, and Gerhard Richter.

minimalist pieces by Claes Oldenburg, Ellsworth Kelly, and Donald Judd.

Film and photography

The museum's international film collection is the largest in the United States and includes early works such as Louis Lumière's *Sortie d'usine* from 1895 and Edwin S. Porter's *The Life of an American Fireman* from 1903. The photographic collection

Henri de Toulouse-Lautrec, *Miss Eglantine's Troupe*, 1896.

The Abby Aldrich Rockefeller Sculpture Garden

Sculpture is one of the undisputed highlights of the museum, with a collection of classical modernist masterpieces from the likes of such famous names as Auguste Rodin, Aristide Maillol, Pablo Picasso, Jacques Lipchitz, Joan Miró, Alberto Giacometti, Alexander Calder, and Henry Moore. There are also examples of pop art and

dates back to the beginning of the medium, around 1839, and includes work by leading contemporary artists from the most recent past. There are moving pictures and stills old and new here, in a collection first established by the renowned Luxembourg-born photographer Edward Steichen (1879–1973), who organized the famous *Family of Man* photograhic exhibition here in 1955 and became the collection's first curator.

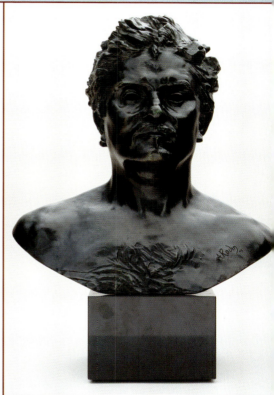

Auguste Rodin, *Bust of the Young Balzac*, bronze, 1891.

Edward Steichen, *Moonrise, Mamaroneck*, photograph, 1904.

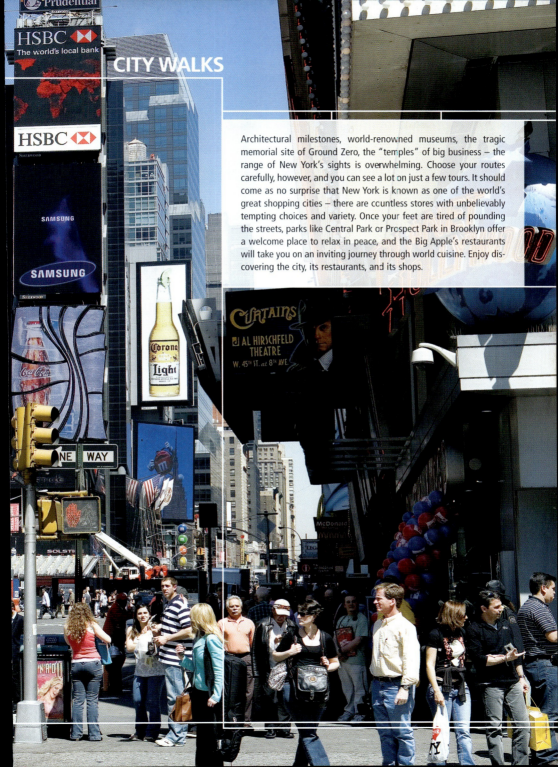

CITY WALKS

Architectural milestones, world-renowned museums, the tragic memorial site of Ground Zero, the "temples" of big business – the range of New York's sights is overwhelming. Choose your routes carefully, however, and you can see a lot on just a few tours. It should come as no surprise that New York is known as one of the world's great shopping cities – there are countless stores with unbelievably tempting choices and variety. Once your feet are tired of pounding the streets, parks like Central Park or Prospect Park in Brooklyn offer a welcome place to relax in peace, and the Big Apple's restaurants will take you on an inviting journey through world cuisine. Enjoy discovering the city, its restaurants, and its shops.

Sights

❶ Tweed Courthouse

New York's oldest county courthouse is located behind City Hall on Chambers Street. A charming classical building with a brightly decorated design, it was named after William M. Tweed, who unfortunately misappropriated large sums of money during its construction.

❷ Park Row

This legendary street is in the Financial District. Its nickname, "Newspaper Row", can be traced back to the vicious circulation battle fought by several newspapers based here in the 19th century; it was originally called Chatham Street. The *New York World*, the *New York Tribune*, and the *New York Times* are just some of the 15 papers that were printed here due to the street's proximity to City Hall in the Financial District.

❸ City Hall

City Hall is the oldest council building in the United States still to house an administration. It was built in a French classical style between 1803 and 1812 by Joseph F. Mangin and John McComb and has an Alabama sandstone façade. In the 19th century, the state governor, whose official residence was in Albany, stayed in the Governor's Room on the first floor during visits to the city.

❹ Woolworth Building

The Woolworth Building, built between 1910 and 1913 to a height of 241 m (790 feet), was celebrated upon its completion as the eighth wonder of the world. Franklin Winfield Woolworth paid the $13.5 million building costs in cash and the design was undertaken by Cass Gilbert, the renowned architect; at Woolworth's request he incorporated numerous Gothic elements into the building.

❺ St Paul's Chapel

St Paul's Chapel was completed in 1766 in a Georgian style, and George Washington worshiped here after being sworn in as the first president. An oil painting of the United States coat of arms now hangs over the pew where he sat. An oak statue inside the church commemorates St Paul, the saint after whom the church is named.

❻ Ground Zero

On 11 September 2001, as part of a concerted attack on both the economic and political centers of the United States, members of the terrorist organization Al-Qaeda steered two fully laden passenger jets into the Twin Towers of the World Trade Center. At 08.46, American Airlines Flight 11 hit the north tower of the World Trade Center and then at 09.03 a second jet (United Airlines Flight 175) crashed into the south tower. At 09.59 the south tower collapsed into rubble, burying not only those trapped inside but also many firefighters. The collapse of the north tower followed at 10.28. More than 2,700 people died in New York alone. A "Wall of Heroes" in Church Street commemorates the victims of the terrorist attack. A futuristic design by the architect Daniel Libeskind was chosen for the construction of a new World Trade Center.

❼ Trinity Church

The church was built of brown sandstone in the Gothic revival style in 1846. In the 19th century it was the tallest building in New York, although since then it has been almost swallowed up by the skyscrapers in the Financial District. The bright stained-glass windows illuminate the high altar and the bronze doors are decorated with Biblical scenes.

❽ New York Stock Exchange

Founded in 1792 by several stockbrokers meeting under a plane tree on Wall Street to deal in state securities arising from the War of Independence, the NYSE is the largest stock exchange in the world. Its current home, a building in the neo-classical style, was constructed in 1903. Chaos still seems to reign on its legendary trading floor beneath a vast skylight. The brass bells that signal the opening and closing of daily trading replaced the Chinese gong that was originally used.

❾ Canyon of Heroes

The "Canyon of Heroes" is a stretch of Broadway in south Manhattan between Bowling Green and City Hall Park along which national heroes, such as astronauts and war veterans, are acclaimed with ticker-tape parades. The parades celebrating the end of World War II saw more than five thousand tons of paper rain down on the heads of the heroes.

Shopping

❶ Babesta

Rock'n'roll parents (and their kids) are well looked-after at Jennifer Cattaui's store, which sells mini T-shirts with cool slogans or portraits of Mao and Kennedy. There are even CDs of rock songs re-recorded as lullabies. It's a trendy cornucopia and a great place to buy gifts to take home.
66 West Broadway (near Warren St); Tel 608 45 22;

From left: St Paul's Chapel is Manhattan's oldest church; old gravestones located in the cemetery of Trinity Church; Babesta sells trendy clothes and accessories for cool kids.

DOWNTOWN MANHATTAN

South Manhattan includes Greenwich Village's maze of streets, exotic Chinatown, trendy areas like SoHo, TriBeCa, and Chelsea, and the Financial District with Wall Street and Ground Zero, the site of the former World Trade Center. Please note that the area code for New York is **212**.

Mon–Fri 11.00–19.00, Sat, Sun 1200–18.00; www.babesta.com

② Brooks Brothers
A respected source of classic gent's fashion wear for over a century. Even presidents have shopped here. The designer, Thom Brown, also caters for modern tastes with a slightly more forward-looking range. 1 Liberty Plaza; Tel 267 24 00; Mon–Wed 8.00–19.00, Thurs 8.30–20.00, Fri 8.30–19.00, Sat 11.00–19.00, Sun 12.00–18.00; www.brooksbrothers.com

③ Denim & Knits
An insider tip for jeans fans since 2007, stocking designer jeans and other denim products at absolutely giveaway prices. 2 Cortlandt St (2nd floor); Tel 571 26 00; Mon–Sat 10.00–20.00, Sun 11.00–18.00; www.denimandknits.com

④ J&R Music and Computer World
A collection of stores with a wide selection of computers, cameras, stereos, and cell phones, but a word of caution for shoppers from abroad – North America runs on 120v current, so check the device you want will work at home before you buy it. 23 Park Row; Tel 23 80 00; Mon–Sat 9.00–19.30, Sun 10.30–18.30; www.jr.com

Eating Out

① Alan's Falafel
Alan's snack bar has long been an insider tip among the lunch crowd in New York's Financial District. His falafel are a welcome alternative to hot dogs. Good value with a smile and a piece of pita. Cedar Street (corner of Broadway); Tel (646) 301 23 16; Mon–Fri 7.00–16.00.

② The Bigger Place
Known as the "Little Place" before 9/11 and now reborn under its new name. Tex-Mex food like tacos and burritos, lovingly prepared. The signature dish is blini (or Russian pancakes). You can order online too (see website). 61 Warren Street (on West Broadway); Tel 528 31 75; Mon–Fri 9.30–22.00, Sat, Sun 9.00–16.00. www.order thebiggerplace.com

③ Mardigras Pizza
The name says it all: the bright interior makes you dream of carnival in New Orleans, and the spicy sauces and crayfish toppings on the pizzas make you think of Cajun cooking. Maiden Lane (near Nassau Street); Tel 233 60 66; Mon–Fri 10.30–21.00.

④ O'Hara's Restaurant
An Irish pub, just a block from Ground Zero. The chicken fingers with honey mustard dip and the steak sandwiches are particularly tasty – as is the Guinness of course. A little bit of Ireland in New York… 120 Cedar Street (near Greenwich Street); Tel 267 30 32; Mon–Thurs 11.00–2.00, Fri, Sat 11.00–4.00, Sun 12.00–23.30.

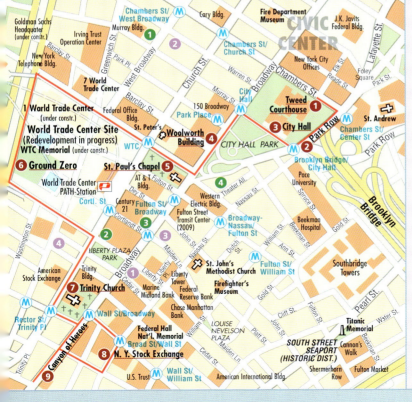

Sights

❶ Empire State Building

After the destruction of the Twin Towers, the Empire State is once again the city's tallest building, at 381 m (1,250 feet) or 449 m (1,473 feet) including the radio mast. It has always been one of the most beautiful buildings in New York: the marble-clad shopping mall is bathed in art deco nostalgia and the viewing platform has an astonishing view: the skyscraper rises in the middle of the city, elevating you high over Midtown. Building work began on 17 March 1930 and was completed by 3,400 construction workers, including dauntless Mohawk Native North Americans, in the record time of a little over a year. President Herbert Hoover opened the building on 1 May 1931. The 102nd floor was originally intended as a mooring-place for airships, but after several trials the scheme was abandoned due to the dangerous updrafts. The skyscraper has played a leading role in many films, including *King Kong* (1933). Every New York photo album or slide show must include a picture of this building!

❷ New York Public Library

A magnificent building, flanked by columns and housing some 18 million books. In good weather, the entrance steps between the stone lions are popular with office folk as a place for lunch.

❸ Grand Central Terminal

The main station, renovated in a Beaux Arts style with baroque and Renaissance elements, was opened in 1913 after several years of construction work. The magnificent main hall is roofed over with an artificial sky of some 2,500 stars and the staircase is a copy of one in the Paris Opera House.

❹ Times Square

The heart of the city is at the intersection of Broadway and Seventh Avenue between 42nd and 47th Streets; the area has been pedestrianized since 2009. The old city fleshpots have now become a consumer arena with mighty shopping complexes and themed restaurants such as the Official All Star Café, run by the American sporting elite, setting the tone in a place that once had a seamy side: the pickpockets, drug dealers, and prostitutes have moved on and the XXX-rated posters, porn stores, and peepshows are all but forgotten. In 1900 when the square was still rural it was called Longacre Square, and was home to stables and barns for carriages. Its name changed to Times Square in 1904, a tribute to the long-respected *New York Times*, which was constructing a giant office building there, the Times Tower. Events from all over the world have flashed across the famous newscrawler on the façade since 1928; nowadays the display is edited from Eighth Avenue.

❺ St Patrick's Cathedral

Built in a neo-Gothic style between 1858 and 1879, the church is the see of the Archbishop of New York and has shades of Cologne Cathedral, although it seems almost lost amongst the mighty skyscrapers of Fifth Avenue.

❻ Rockefeller Center

Originally built in the 1930s at the behest of the oil magnate John D. Rockefeller Jr, the complex is now composed of 21 interlinked skyscrapers housing offices, television studios, restaurants, stores, and an ice rink. A highlight is the Radio City Music Hall, once a cinema, in which concerts and other events are now held.

❼ Lever House

Designed by the architect Gordon Bunshaft, this office block on Park Avenue is a perfect example of 1950s International Style architecture and has been listed as a national monument since October 1983. Its name is a legacy from the British pharmaceutical manufacturer Lever Brothers, who once had their headquarters here. Bunshaft studied architecture at the MIT School of Architecture and won the Pritzker prize in 1988. He is known for his minimalist approach.

❽ Trump Tower

This exclusive apartment block has a spectacular atrium and a mall two floors high with many boutiques. There is a waterfall that flows down seven floors and the façade of this impressive building is clad in bronze glass sheets. It is certainly worth a look.

❾ Plaza Hotel

Designed by Henry J. Hardenbergh, this legendary New York luxury hotel on Central Park was opened on 1 October 1907, and even then belonged with the best hotels in the world. Ernest Hemingway was a regular guest.

Shopping

❶ Tiffany & Co.

This smart shop will always be linked with the film *Breakfast at Tiffany's*, in which Audrey Hepburn admired the company's fine jewellery. More reasonable knick-knacks are available (the Tiffany logo is included in the price).
727 Fifth Ave (near 57th St); Tel 755 80 00; Mon– Sat 10.00–19.00, Sun 12.00–18.00; www.tiffany.com

❷ FAO Schwarz

A toy shop with a huge stock of toys and hand-made collector's pieces. The Christmas window displays are worth seeing. Great for a family outing, particularly in December.
767 Fifth Ave (near 58th St); Tel 644 94 00; Mon–Thurs 10.00–19.00, Fri, Sat 10.00–20.00, Sun 11.00–18.00; www.fao.com

❸ Niketown

Enjoy exploring the five floors of trendy Nike products. Sportswear from tracksuits to sweatbands and trainers with a built-in iPod await your discovery. Perfect for those who like sport, fashion, and logos.
6 E 57th St (near Fifth Ave); Tel 891 64 53; Mon–Sat 10.00–20.00, Sun 11.00–19.00; www.nike.com

❹ Saks Fifth Avenue

One of Manhattan's best-known department stores since 1924. For many well-off New Yorkers, this ten-floor iconic temple to consumerism is still the first place to shop.
611 Fifth Ave (near 50th St); Tel 753 40 00; Mon–Fri 10.00–20.00, Sat 10.00–19.00, Sun 12.00–19.00; www.saksfifthavenue.com

From left: Grand Central Terminal; St Patrick's Cathedral; Times Square; the Lever Building, a curtain wall skyscraper, with sealed windows and heat-resistant glass.

MIDTOWN MANHATTAN

The heart of the metropolis, with the Empire State Building and other impressive buildings such as Grand Central Terminal, the New York Public Library, and St Patrick's Cathedral, as well as Times Square, Broadway, and the smart shops of Fifth Avenue. Please note that the area code for New York is **212**.

Eating Out

❶ Daniel
An excellent restaurant, which mixes home cooking with gourmet fare and is famed for its innovative "French country cuisine". The opulent décor takes a bit of getting used to.
60 E 65th St (near Fifth Ave); Tel 288 00 33; Mon–Thurs 17.45–23.00, Fri, Sat 17.30–23.00; www.danielnyc.com

❷ Hatsuhana
The delicate raw fish, served on Hawaiian *ti* leaves, really melts in the mouth. It's probably best to try the sushi chef's recommendations.
237 Park Ave (near 46th St); Tel 661 34 00; Mon–Fri 11.45–14.45, 17.30–22.00; www.hatsuhana.com

❸ Grand Central Oyster Bar
The oyster bar located in the basement of Grand Central Terminal has long been a New York fixture. The oysters, the clam chowder, and the other fish dishes are delicious. An iconic spot for oyster fans.
89 E 42nd St; Tel 490 66 50; Mon–Fri 11.30–21.30, Sat 12.00–21.30; www.oysterbarny.com

❹ Brasserie
An American atmosphere with large video screens and the finest French bistro cuisine. The onion soup tastes authentic and the delicious chocolate beignets were once voted the best dessert in New York.
100 E 53rd St (near Park Ave); Tel 751 48 40; Sun–Thurs 11.00–24.00, Fri, Sat 11.00–1.00.

Sights

❶ Vanderbilt House

A gigantic brick and limestone townhouse with red tiles located on the southeast corner of Fifth Avenue and 86th Street, built in 1914 and bought in 1944 for the wife of millionaire Cornelius Vanderbilt IV. Generations of Vanderbilts lived off the enormous fortune amassed, not always entirely legally, by Cornelius, the "railroad king", in the 19th century.

❷ Jackie Onassis's Home

Jacqueline "Jackie" Bouvier Kennedy Onassis lived on the 15th floor of the building at 1040 Fifth Avenue on the Upper East Side. She bought the penthouse after the death of her husband, the American president John F. Kennedy, and lived there from 1964 until her own death in 1994. She enjoyed jogging in the area of Central Park close to her home, especially around the reservoir that now bears her name. Widowed a second time in 1975, she worked in publishing in the city.

❸ Benjamin Duke's Home

The former residence of Benjamin Duke is located on the corner of Fifth Avenue and 82nd Street. Duke and his younger brother James originally came from North Carolina and founded the American Tobacco Company. They endowed a small college which was later to be expanded into Duke University. Their house was built in 1901 by an investor. Members of the Duke family and their relatives, the Biddles, lived in the house until recently.

❹ NYU Graduate School of Art History

A magnificent building located on the corner of Fifth Avenue and 78th Street, based on a chateau in Bordeaux, France, and praised by several critics as one of the most beautiful mansions in New York. Benjamin Duke's widow and daughter lived here into the 1950s, leaving the house to New York University; it now houses the NYU Graduate School of Art History.

❺ Pulitzer House

A magnificent building on East 73rd Street between Fifth and Madison Avenue, and once the home of Joseph Pulitzer (1847–1911). A Hungarian who immigrated to the United States in his youth, he joined the Unionist army and fought in the Civil War. After the war he became one of the most successful publishers in the United States and the Pulitzer Prize is named after him. Nowadays 13 proprietors share the living space behind the decorative columns of his house. Pulitzer, who was extremely sensitive to noise, actually spent very little time in the house, despite having a soundproof room built.

❻ Frick Collection

Henry Clay Frick's mansion takes up a whole block between 70th and 71st Streets. A millionaire several times over who had made his fortune in steel, his art collection concentrated on Italian Renaissance painting. Thomas Hastings, his architect, who had also designed the New York Public Library, was charged from the outset to design the house as a museum and gallery. Frick bequeathed his art treasures to a trust, which converted the private apartments into a museum after his death and that of his wife, opening them to the public in 1935. The Frick Collection holds works of art dating from the 12th to the late 19th century, including important canvases from the Italian Renaissance, France, 18th-century England, and 17th-century Holland. The Frick Collection is one of the most important art collections in the city of New York.

❼ Roosevelt Twin Town House

The two houses at 47–49 East 65th Street had only one door to the street and belonged to Franklin D. Roosevelt, who was first elected American president in 1932 and then went on to become the only president to be re-elected three times. The house was lived in by the president and his mother, and now belongs to Hunter College.

❽ Home of Ulysses S. Grant

Ulysses S. Grant lived in this building at 3 East 66th Street opposite Central Park between 1881 and 1885. The legendary Civil War general held office as president of the United States between 1869 and 1877, but was less successful as a politician, his period of office being overshadowed by several corruption scandals. Suffering from terminal cancer, the ex-president wrote his memoirs, which were to enjoy great success, in his house at Central Park.

Shopping

❶ Barneys New York

This temple to designer fashion is located in one of the most expensive areas of the East Side and stints neither on its exclusive offers nor its prices. Exceptional cosmetics department. Essential for any shopaholics visiting New York. *660 Madison Ave; Tel 826 89 00; Mon–Fri 10.00–20.00, Sat 10.00–19.00, Sun 11.00– 18.00; www.barneys.com*

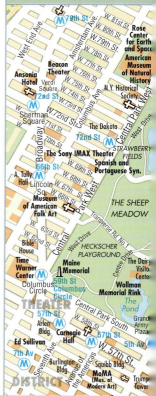

From left: The Frick Collection: once a millionaire's mansion, now a museum and art gallery; the neo-Classical style Vanderbilt House; Best Cellars: good and reasonably priced wine.

CENTRAL PARK AND UPPER EAST SIDE

A green oasis in north Manhattan and on Fifth Avenue at the eastern edge of the Park, with the old townhouses of the super-rich. Just round the corner there are the city's most famous museums and exquisite specialist stores and bistros. This is a great place to spend the day. Please note that the area code for New York is **212**.

❷ La Maison du Chocolat

Who says there's no good chocolate in America? This is first-class quality from Paris, served in a branch of a French chocolatier. Excellent pralines – home-made of course – imaginative creations, and gift ideas. Resist temptation if you can…
1018 Madison Ave; Tel 744 71 17; Mon–Sat 10.00–19.00, Sun 12.00–18.00; www.lamaisonduchocolat. com

❸ Artbag

Artbag's wide selection of imaginative purses, handbags, and other leather goods has been serving up surprises to New Yorkers for more than 60 years. They have everything here, from a humble coin purse to a sturdy rucksack. Bags of choice, quite literally!
1130 Madison Ave; Tel 744 27 20; Mon–Fri 9.30–17.00, Sat 10.00–16.00; www.artbag.com

❹ Best Cellars

This cellar is well-named – the wines on its wooden shelves are first-class and good value into the bargain, with no bottle costing more than $15. The bottles are divided into such categories as "soft" and "juicy".
1291 Lexington Ave (near 86th St); Tel 426 42 00; Mon–Thurs 9.30–21.00, Fri, Sat 9.30–22.00, Sun 12.00–20.00; www.bestcellars.com

Eating Out

❶ Cafe Boulud

Pepped-up home-made food at affordable prices. Four menus offer French country cuisine, vegetarian food, and seasonal dishes. The fish dishes are very tasty.
20 E 76th St; Tel 772 26 00; 17.45–23.00, daily, Tues–Sat 12.00–14.30; www.danielnyc.com

❷ Nick's Family-Style Restaurant and Pizzeria

Since 2003, Nick Angelis has been serving up his popular dishes on the Upper East Side. Fresh tomato sauce, home-made mozzarella, and fine vegetables make for an extraordinarily pleasant dining experience and the pizzas are just great.
1814 Second Ave; Tel 987 57 00; 11.30–22.00, daily.

❸ Paola's

The charming Paola has been a reassuring presence here for 12 years, serving classic Italian dishes and first-class wines. Worth a visit.
245 E 84th St; Tel 794 18 90; Sun–Fri 13.00–16.00, Sun–Wed 17.00–22.00, Thurs–Sat 17.00–23.00; www.paolasrestaurant.com

❹ Park Avenue Summer

This innovative restaurant reinvents itself every year. The dishes are consistently high in quality and contain surprisingly few calories.
100 E 63rd St (corner of Park Ave); Tel 644 19 00; Mon–Fri 11.30–15.00, Sat, Sun 11.00–15.00, Mon–Thurs 17.30–23.00, Fri, Sat 17.30–23.30, Sun 17.30–22.00; www.parkavenyc.com

Sights

❶ The Children's Museum of Manhattan

An exemplary "hands-on" museum where children can learn the secrets of the earth and everyday life through interactive exhibits and play. Changing displays show how amusement park rollercoasters and roundabouts work, and smaller visitors can play at being police officers and firefighters in toy towns. Birthday parties can also be booked here. If you are visiting New York *en famille*, spend some time here. The kids will have a great time.

❷ Ansonia Hotel

Financed by William Earle Dodge Stokes, a rich mine owner, the Ansonia Hotel, located at the intersection of Broadway and Amsterdam Avenue, was built between 1899 and 1904 as one of the Upper West Side's first luxury hotels. It was also one of the first to feature the luxury of air-conditioning. The singer Enrico Caruso and the baseball star Babe Ruth both spent long periods staying at the hotel.

❸ Beresford Building

This monumental *palazzo* is one of Manhattan's smartest addresses. Designed by the master architect Emery Roth, the three towers on the roof have become the building's trademark. Various façades and decorations help to mask the building's rather solid appearance. The Beresford replaced the six-floor Hotel Beresford, which was built in 1889 by Alva Walker. Several millionaires live in the luxurious apartments.

❹ Rose Center for Earth and Space

The American Museum of Natural History houses a four-floor planetarium. Narrated by the Hollywood star Harrison Ford, the space show "Are We Alone?" uses sensational special effects in an unusual way to demonstrate the view that we cannot be the only living beings in the universe. The "Cosmic Pathway" illustrates some 15 billion years of space history.

❺ American Museum of Natural History

Covering four city blocks, the largest natural history museum in the world is located on the corner of Central Park and 79th Street; its 46 exhibition halls house more than 35 million exhibits. The building was constructed between 1874 and 1899 to a design by Calvert Vaux and Jacob Wrey Mould and is reminiscent of ancient Roman triumphal buildings. The collection of dinosaur skeletons is one of the main attractions for young and old alike and includes *Barosaurus lentus*, one of the world's largest dinosaurs. The Hall of Ocean Life has an impressive 30-m (100-foot) long skeleton of a blue whale and the Hall of Minerals and Gems boasts the Star of India, the world's largest sapphire. Try to fit a visit to this museum into your itinerary.

❻ New York Historical Society

The society was founded in 1804 and has set itself the task of conserving the history of the city by placing it in context to the present. There is a library and an archive with many newspapers, manuscripts, and other documents available for research purposes, and the history of New York comes to life in the museum next door.

❼ Dakota Building

The Dakota is one of the smartest apartment buildings in New York. It was built in a German Renaissance style between 1880 and 1884 by Henry J. Hardenbergh, and has often been compared to a Hanseatic town hall. One legend has it that Edward Clark, the boss of the Singer Sewing Machine Company who commissioned the building, named it after the American states North and South Dakota, as the Upper West Side was still outside the city at the time and almost as far away from Manhattan as the Dakotas. The suites have been home to such celebrities as Judy Garland, Leonard Bernstein, and John Lennon, who was shot dead by a crazed fan outside the building on 8 December 1980.

❽ Strawberry Fields

Strawberry Fields in Central Park is a memorial to John Lennon and his song of that name. The area was officially listed as "Strawberry Fields" on 26 March 1981 and Lennon's widow, Yoko Ono, donated $1 million to the Central Park Conservancy for the creation and upkeep of the site. Lennon's song refers to an orphanage of the same name in Liverpool. The focus of the memorial site is a mosaic, made by Italian craftsmen from Naples – in the center is the word "Imagine" from one of Lennon's most famous songs.

Shopping

❶ Barnes & Noble Superstore

The biggest chain of bookstores in the US, a "book supermarket" that offers more than just the titles in the bestseller list. There are attractive price reductions on older books, sometimes just a few weeks after publication. *1972 Broadway; Tel 595 68 59; 9.00–12.00, daily; www.barnesandnoble.com*

From left: Home to some legendary personalities, the Dakota Building is a legend in itself; Ansonia Hotel: a jewel in the Beaux-Arts style; a Mecca for bookworms: Westsider Rare & Used Books.

UPPER WEST SIDE AND HARLEM

The Upper West Side is home to the American Museum of Natural History and famous buildings like the Dakota Building, in front of which John Lennon was shot. Harlem lies to the north and has recently been enjoying its second period of renaissance. Please note that the area code for New York is **212**.

❷ Westsider Rare & Used Books

This shop is famed for its wide range of second-hand books, current novels, and reference works, often at half price. The valuable and expensive first editions are on the first floor. A great place in which to rummage for that book you haven't been able to find...
2246 Broadway; Tel 362 07 06; 10.00–12.00, daily; www.westsiderbooks.com

❸ Crocs

A shop devoted to Crocs? Only in the Big Apple. But once you've entered the shop and seen the almost inexhaustible range and variety of these plastic clogs you'll realize just how much is included under the name Crocs. Okay – they've got flip-flops as well.
270 Columbus Ave; Tel 362 16 55; Mon–Sat 10.00–20.00, Sun 10.00–19.00; www.crocs.com

❹ Maxilla & Mandible

This natural history knick-knack shop has unusual stones and shells from all over the world, butterflies in little wooden boxes, fossils, and toys for the little ones. If you're looking for a unique gift, this is the place to go. You won't see a place like this on every corner!
451 Columbus Ave; Tel 724 61 73; Mon–Sat 11.00–19.00, Sun 11.00–17.00; www.maxillaandmandible.com

Eating Out

❶ Zabar's

The enormous selection of deli and generously filled sandwiches will satisfy even the most demanding palate. This gourmet paradise has been voted the best deli in the city on several occasions.
2245 Broadway (corner of 80th St); Tel 787 20 00; Mon–Fri 8.00–19.30, Sat 8.00–20.00, Sun 19.00–18.00; www.zabars.com

❷ Josie's West

Healthy food doesn't have to be boring, as Louis Lanza, the head chef of this first-class health food restaurant has proven. Delicious and good for you. Perfect combo!
300 Amsterdam Ave; Tel 769 12 12; Mon–Thurs 12.00–23.00, Fri 12.00–24.00, Sat 11.00–24.00, Sun 10.30–22.30; www.josiesnyc.com

❸ H & H

This bagel bakery is a New York institution. The bagels, especially good with cream cheese and smoked salmon, arrive fresh and warm from the oven every few minutes.
2239 Broadway; Tel 595 80 03; 24 hours, daily; www.hhbagels.net

❹ Fairway Market

Fresh meat, seafood, appetizers, sandwiches, and tempting biscuits are just some of the highlights at this gourmet market. The café and steakhouse are an insider tip. A fascinating spot for those who like to check out unusual and tasty produce!
2127 Broadway (corner of 74th St); Tel 595 18 88; 6.00–1.00, daily; www.fairwaymarket.com

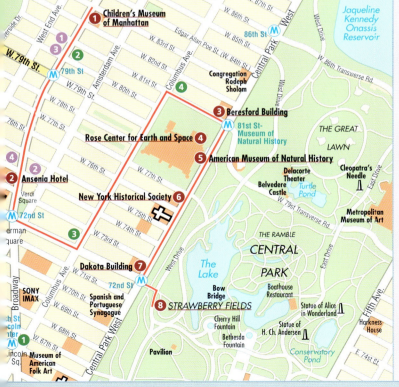

Sights

❶ Prospect Park
This park in the heart of Brooklyn was designed by Frederick Law Olmsted and Calvert Vaux, who were also responsible for Central Park, and it has been a popular destination for excursions since 1866. There are extensive meadows and paths through this green oasis, you can go skating at the Kate Wollman Rink, and Grand Army Plaza has the Soldiers' and Sailors' Monument for the fallen of the Civil War.

❷ Flatbush Avenue
Brooklyn's main artery runs between Manhattan Bridge and Jamaica Bay, following an old Native North American path. Long Island University, Fulton Mall, the Brooklyn Academy of Music, the Brooklyn Public Library, Brooklyn Botanic Garden, and Prospect Park are all to be found along this road, which has four lanes for much of its length. Immortalized in many songs, Flatbush Avenue is also one of New York's busiest roads.

❸ New York City Transit Museum
This little museum, located in an old subway station, has historic trains that would have rattled through New York at the turn of the 20th century, as well as photos, tickets, old subway maps, and other exhibits illustrating the history of the world's largest underground network.

❹ Brooklyn Historical Society
Located at 128 Pierrepont Street, The Museum of the Brooklyn Historical Society is an informative recapitulation of the history of Brooklyn, bringing the narrative of this area to life with historic film, photos, and other documents; changing special exhibitions concentrate on various topics. The four-floor building was designed by the architect George B. Post and built in Queen Anne style in 1881; the façade has impressively ornate terracotta reliefs. It was listed in 1991.

❺ Willow Street
The three brownstone houses at 155 to 157 Willow Street are amongst the most beautiful and interesting buildings from the so-called Federal period, which lasted from the War of Independence to the 1830s. During this time architects restricted themselves to simple façades with little decoration. Since the course of the street has been altered, the houses no longer run parallel to it. A tunnel runs from the cellar of one of the houses to what used to be a stable but is now a house. Truman Capote once lived at 70 Willow Street.

❻ Fulton Ferry Landing
Before the construction of the Brooklyn Bridge in 1883 and the Manhattan Bridge in 1909, ferries used to travel between the independent City of Brooklyn and Manhattan, known then as the City of New York. Fulton Ferry, the ferry stop on the Brooklyn side, was named after Robert Fulton, who built the first steamship and ran the ferry service; the last ferry ran in 1924 and now only water taxis stop here. The streets on both sides of East River lead-ing to the ferry stops are called Fulton Street.

❼ Brooklyn Heights Promenade
This romantic district with lots of historic brownstones and townhouses lies at the mouth of the East River and was a stopping point for the ferry to Manhattan in the 19th century. Sunset over New York is at its most beautiful seen from Fulton Landing. Truman Capote and Arthur Miller both lived on Willow Street and bustling Atlantic Avenue, known as "Little Arabia", is famous for its spice stores. The views of the Manhattan skyline from Brooklyn Promenade on the shores of the East River are considered the very best.

❽ The Brooklyn Bridge
The bridge which spans the East River, connecting Manhattan and Brooklyn, was opened in 1883. Not counting the approach roads, the bridge is 1,052 m (3,451 feet) long, and more than 150,000 people crossed it the day it opened. The initial designs for the bridge were undertaken by the German architect John August Roebling, although he died in an accident shortly after construction had begun. The Brooklyn Bridge was the first suspension bridge to use steel wire; in all some 24,000 km (15,000 miles) of wire were incorporated. The total length of the bridge is 1,825 m (5,987 feet). It celebrated its 125th anniversary in 2008 with five days of festivities, including a live performance by the Brooklyn Philharmonic, special walking tours, music, dance, and a superb firework display.

Shopping

❶ Heights Books
An antiquarian bookstore with an exquisite stock of science books and reference works, and especially popular with professors and students. Art lovers will also find a good selection of art books. This is one of the city's leading used bookstores.
120 Smith St, Boerum Hill; Tel (718) 624 48 76; Mon–Thurs 11.00–21.00, Fri, Sat 11.00–22.00, Sun 12.00–21.00; www.heightsbooks.com

❷ Tango
One of the few boutiques still in family ownership. Businesswomen buy designer suits, dresses, and fine quality leisure wear here. This is the place to come If you are looking for a suit for a new job.
145 Montague St; Tel (718) 625 75 18; Mon–Fri 10.30–19.30, Sat 10.30–18.30, Sun 12.30–18.00.

❸ Overtures
The store is best-known for its excellent paper; there is writing paper of every quality and shade here, and you can have it headed, of course. Lovers of stationery will be in heaven.
216 Hicks St; Tel (718) 643 93 45; Mon–Fri 10.30–19.00, Sat, Sun 11.00–18.30.

❹ St Mark's Comics
Comic collectors from all over the world come here to shop. An almost inexhaustible selection of comics to suit the tastes of every comic fan.
148 Montague St; Tel (718) 935 09 11; Mon, Tues 10.00–23.00, Wed–Sat 10.00–21.00, Sun 11.00–19.00; www.stmarkscomics.com

From left: In the shadow of the Brooklyn Bridge: Fulton Ferry Landing; Flatbush Avenue is Brooklyn's main traffic artery; the NYC Transit Museum has real trains as well as models.

BROOKLYN

The Brooklyn Heights promenade has the best view of Manhattan, and the streets are lined with 19th-century houses. The end of Fulton Street, where the Brooklyn Bridge crosses the East River, is where George Washington hid from the British. Please note that the area code for Brooklyn is **718**.

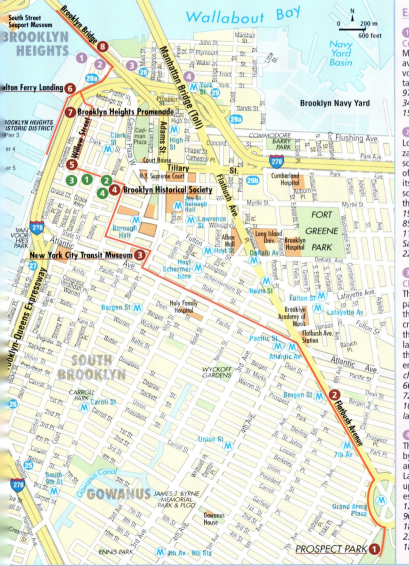

Eating Out

● The Brooklyn Ice Cream Factory
Mark Thompson's ice cream, available in eight classic flavors, is famed for its pure taste and creamy consistency. *97 Commercial St; Tel (718) 349 25 06; Thurs–Sun 15.00–21.00.*

● Grimaldi's Pizzeria
Loud and hectic, but the pizzas from the wood oven taste so good that it won't put you off. Even Italians have sung its praises. It has become something of an institution in the world of pizza. *19 Old Fulton St; Tel (718) 858 43 00; Mon–Thurs 11.30–22.45, Fri 11.30–22.45, Sat 12.00–23.45, Sun 12.00–22.45; www.grimaldis.com*

● Jacques Torres Chocolate
This little chocolatier's is a paradise for chocolate fans the world over. Torres' wild creations lay to rest the tale that there is no decent chocolate in America. Sit at one of the three small tables and enjoy a freshly baked *pain au chocolat*. Heaven… *66 Water St; Tel (718) 875 97 72; Mon–Sat 9.00–19.00, Sun 10.00–18.00; www.mrchoco-late.com*

● Superfine Restaurant
The atmosphere, with works by local artists on the walls and a lively bar in the cellar. Laura Taylor, the chef, serves up Mediterranean cuisine, especially excellent fish. *126 Front St; Tel (718) 243 90 05; Tues–Fri 11.30–15.00, 18.00–23.00, Sat 15.00–23.00, Sun 11.00–15.00, 18.00–22.00.*

Underground movement: New York can offer this in all senses of the expression – art, politics, music, and, more prosaically, transport! Millions of people use the subway to get around the city each week. It's a scene all of its own.

KEY

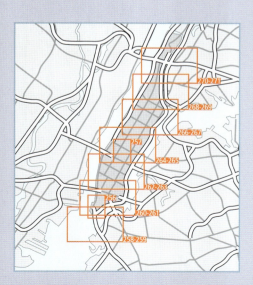

	Freeway/Expressway
	Highway
	Major road
	Local road
	Footpath
	Tunnel (vehicles)
	Railroad
	Industrial railroad
	Railroad tunnel
	Subway
	Passenger ferry

CITY ATLAS

The maps in the City Atlas section give detailed practical information to help make your stay more enjoyable. Clear symbols indicate the position of buildings and monuments of note, facilities and services, public buildings, the transport network, and built-up areas and green spaces (see the key to the maps below).

	Densely built-up area; Thinly built-up area
	Public building
	Building of note; High-rise building; Industrial building
	Green space; Cemetery
	Pedestrian zone
	Main railroad station
	Regional/PATH station
City Hall Ⓜ	Subway/MTA station
	Bus station
	Cablecar

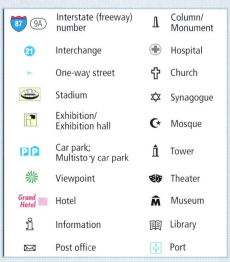

87 9A	Interstate (freeway) number		Column/Monument
21	Interchange		Hospital
	One-way street		Church
	Stadium		Synagogue
	Exhibition/Exhibition hall		Mosque
P P	Car park; Multistory car park		Tower
	Viewpoint		Theater
Grand Hotel	Hotel		Museum
	Information		Library
	Post office		Port

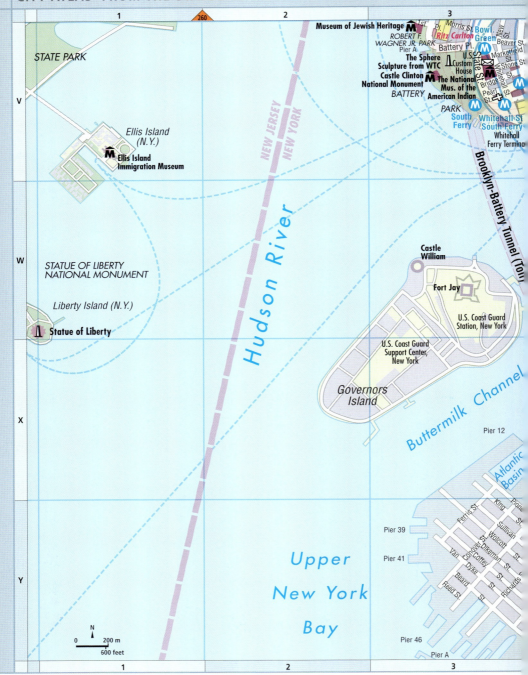

STATE PARK

Ellis Island (N.Y.)

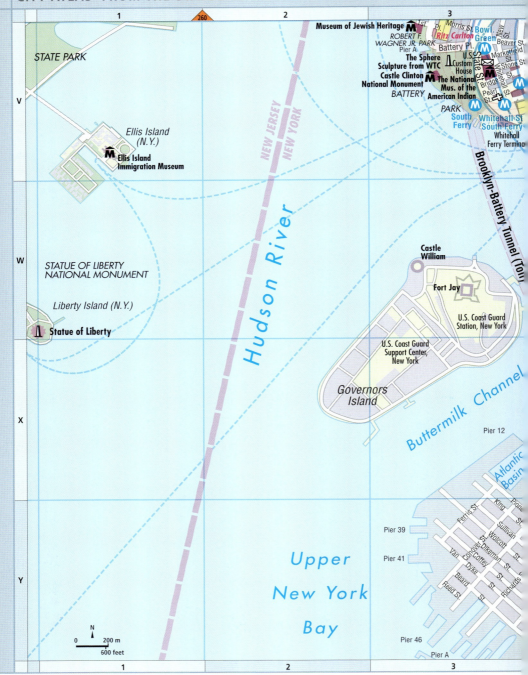
Ellis Island Immigration Museum

STATUE OF LIBERTY NATIONAL MONUMENT

Liberty Island (N.Y.)

Statue of Liberty

NEW JERSEY
NEW YORK

Hudson River

Museum of Jewish Heritage
ROBERT F. WAGNER JR. PARK
Pier A
The Sphere
Sculpture from WTC
Castle Clinton
National Monument
BATTERY

Ritz Carlton
Battery Pl.
Custom House
The National
Mus. of the
American Indian

1st Pl.
Morris St.
Bowl.
Green
Beaver St.
U.S.
State St.
Marketfield
Stone St.
Bridge St.
Pearl St.
Whitehall St.

PARK
South Ferry
Whitehall St.
South Ferry
Whitehall
Ferry Termina

Brooklyn-Battery Tunnel (Tou

Castle William

Fort Jay

U.S. Coast Guard
Station, New York

U.S. Coast Guard
Support Center,
New York

Governors Island

Buttermilk Channel

Pier 12

Atlantic Basin

Pier 39

Pier 41

Ferris St.
King St.
Sullivan St.
Wolcott St.
Dikeman St.
Coffey St.
Van Dyke St.
Beard St.
Read St.
Richards St.
Pione

Upper

New York

Bay

Pier 46

Pier A

N
0   200 m
600 feet

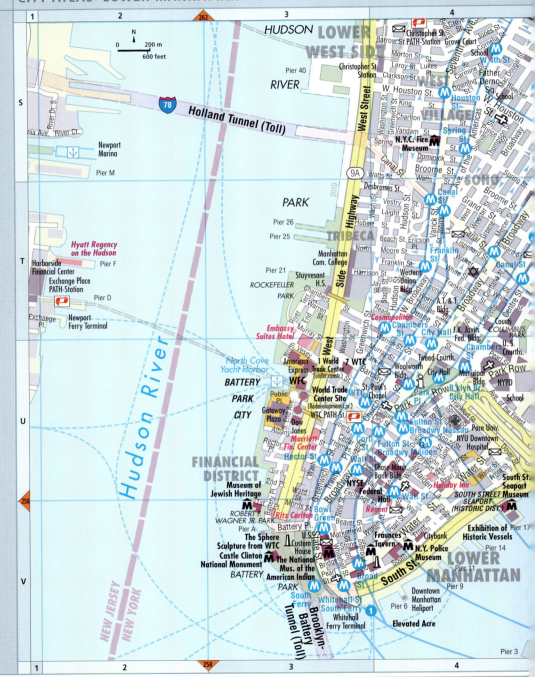

Lincoln Harbor

Penn-Central Tunnels

264

Jacob K. Javits Convention Center

Twelfth Avenue

W. 40th St.
W. 39th St.
W. 38th St.
W. 37th St.
W. 36th St.
W. 35th St.
W. 34th St.
W. 33rd St.

W. 42nd St.
Holy Cross
St. Raphael
42nd St
Port Authority
Bus Terminal

Madame Tussauds Mus.
New Amsterdam

GARMENT DISTRICT

Trans-Hudson Express Tunnel
(under constr. 2009 – 2017)

Heliport

Pier 72

W. 30th
W. 29th St.
W. 28th St.
W. 27th St.
W. 26th St.
W. 25th St.

W. 34th St
34th St
Penn St

Navarre Bldg.
407
B'way

Nelson Tower

Hoboken North
Ferry Terminal

Pier 67

Pier 66a

Twelfth Avenue

Selton Coll. &
St. Michael's H.S.

Moynihan Station
(planned)

34th St
1 Penn
Plaza

34th St
Macy's

Pier 64

W. 24th St.

James A. Farley Bldg.
(General Post Office)

Madison
Square
Garden

Pennsylvania St.
Amtrak &
Long Island R.R.

9A

Dia Center
for the Arts

CHELSEA
PARK

Chelsea
Houses

Penn Station
South Houses

Penn Station

St. John

W. 31st St

W. 30th St

28th St

Pier 62

HIGH LINE PARK (under constr.)

W. 23rd St.

Chelsea
Antiques
Building

Castle Point

Pier 61

Pier 60

Chelsea
Piers

General Theological
Seminary

School

W. 22nd St.

23rd St
CHELSEA

23rd St

26th St

Eleventh Avenue

Pier 59

W. 21st St.
W. 20th St.
W. 19th St.

W. 23rd

23rd St

23rd St
PATH-Station

MADISON
SQUARE
PARK

Pier 57

Joyce
Theater

Chelsea
Hotel

W. 22nd St.

Flatiron Bldg.

Pier 54

School

W. 18th St.
W. 17th St.
W. 16th St.
W. 15th St.

Maritime

School

MANHATTAN

W. 20th St.
W. 19th St.

23rd St.

E. 21st
St.

Pier 53

Fire Boat
Station

W. 14th St.
W. 13th St.
Little W. 12th St.

Hotel
Gansevoort

Rubin Museum
of Art

W. 16th St.

14th St
8th Av

14th St

Xavier H.S.
14th St.
PATH-Station

Th. Roosevelt
Birthplace

Pier 51

Gansevoort

Horatio
Jane

Gansevoort
Jackson
Sq.

St. Vincent's
Hospital

14th

UNION
SQ.
PK.

GREENWICH

West Street

W. 12th

Bank

Abingdon
Sq.

W. 12th St.

Forbes
Magazine
Galleries

14th St.
Union Sq.

HUDSON

W. 11th St.

Bethune

Perry

W. 11th St.

Jefferson
Market Courthouse

14th St
Union Sq.

LOWER

Charles

9th St.
PATH-Station

Grace
Church

Pier 46

Christopher St

Sheridan Sq

Renwick
Triangle

WEST

Pier 45

Christopher
Sheridan Sq

Grove Court

VILLAGE

8th St

Fourth Ave.

SIDE

Christopher St.
PATH-Station

Barrow St

WASH. SQ. PK.

Astor

Stuyvesant

Pier 40

Morton St.

Leroy St.

Clarkson St.

St. Lukes

School

Cornelia St.

Wash.
Sq.

WASH. SQ.
PARK

Astor
Place Th.

Cooper Union
Found. Bldg.
St. George

RIVER

Christopher St.
Station

Father
Demo
Sq.

N.Y.
University
WASH. SQ.
VILLAGE

Astor
Pl

Cooper
Square

Academy

Holland Tunnel (Toll)

78

W. Houston St.

Judson
Mem. Ch.

SOHO

Ukrainian
Museum

Russian
Orthodox Cath.

N
200 m
600 feet

N.Y.C. Fire
Museum

Spring
St.

Spring

University
Plaza

Broadway
Lafayette

Bleecker St

Prince St.

9A

Watts St.

Canal St.

Broome St.

SOHO

E. Houston St.

Hudson River

NEW JERSEY
NEW YORK

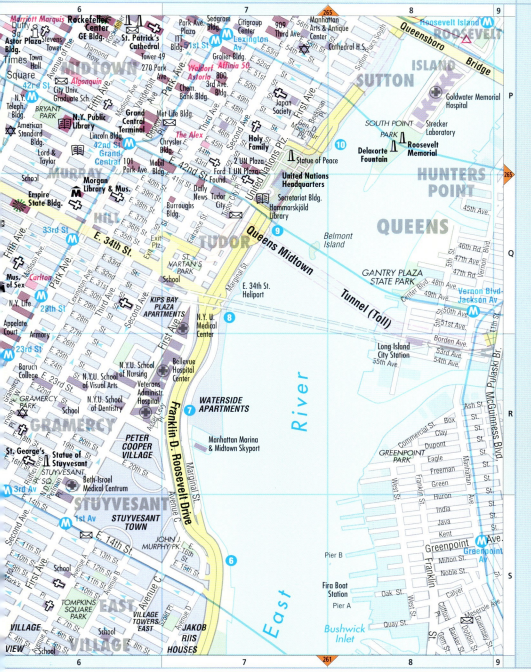

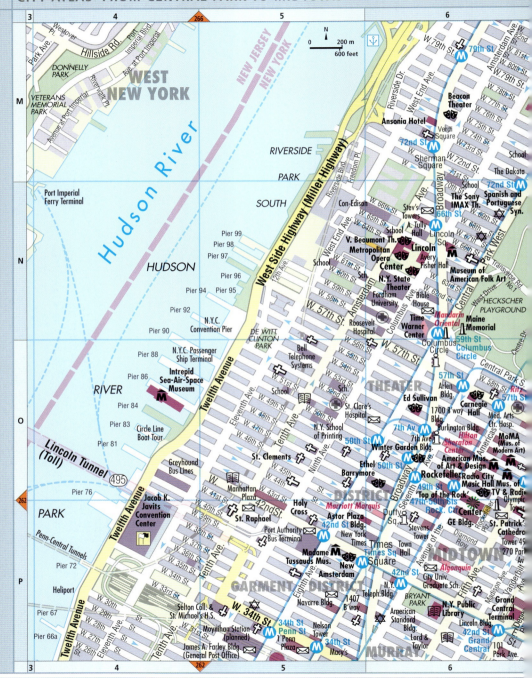

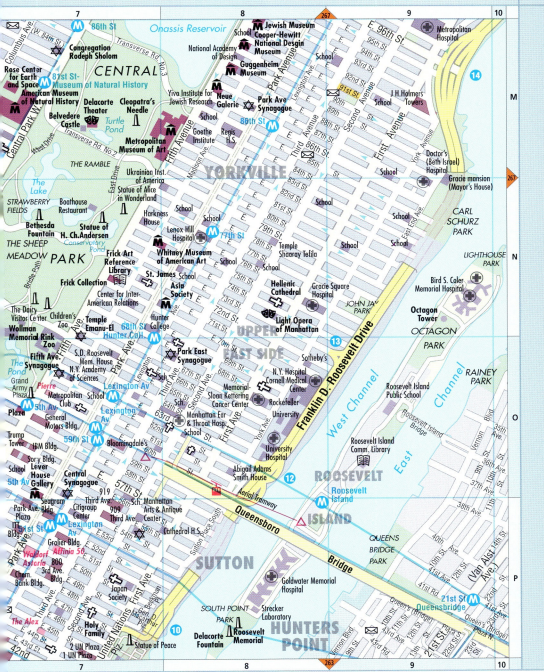

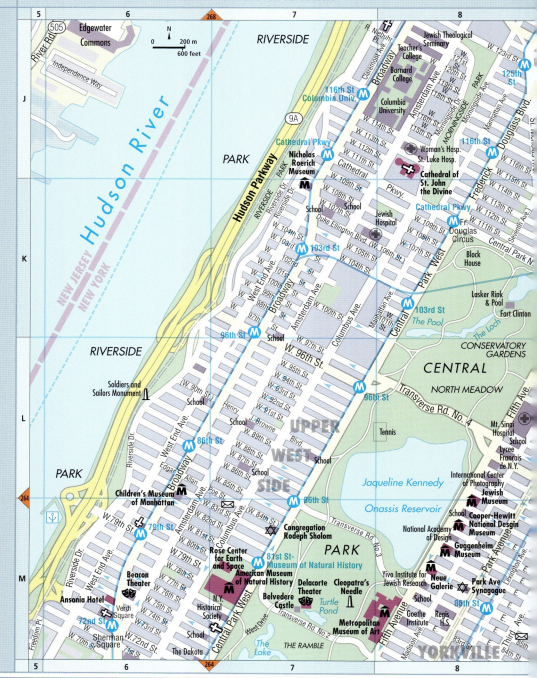

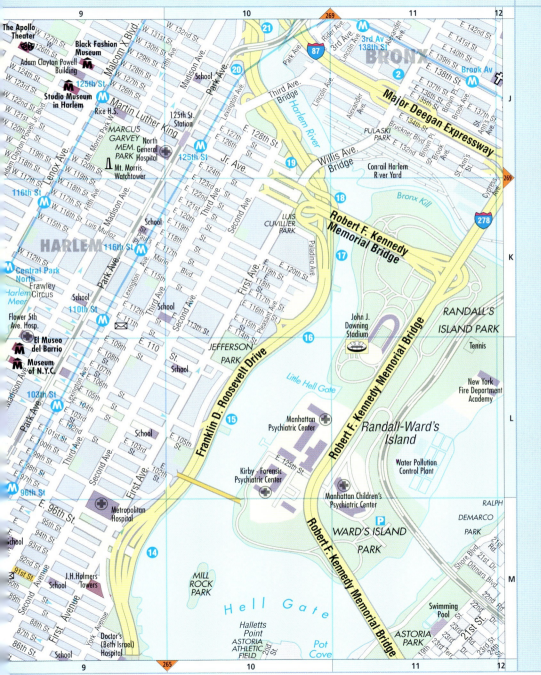

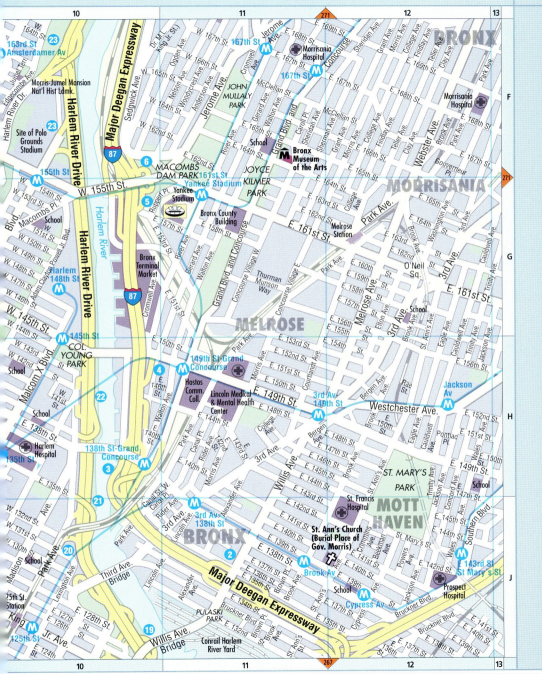

Street	Page	Grid	Street	Page	Grid	Street	Page	Grid
75th Street, East	265	N8	112th Street, West	267	K9	150th Street, West	268	F9
75th Street, West	264	M6	112th Street, West	266	J7	151st Street, East	269	G11
76th Street, East	265	N8	113th Street, East	267	K10	151st Street, West	268	F9
76th Street, West	264	M6	113th Street, West	266	J7	152nd Street, East	269	H11
77th Street, East	265	N8	114th Street, East	267	K10	152nd Street, West	268	F9
77th Street, West	264	M6	114th Street, West	266	J8	153rd Street, East	269	G11
78th Street, East	265	N8	115th Street, East	267	K10	153rd Street, West	268	F9
78th Street, West	264	M6	115th Street, West	266	K8	154th Street, East	269	H12
79th Street, East	265	N8	116th Street, West	266	J8	154th Street, West	269	G10
79th Street, West	264	M6	117th Street, East	267	K10	155th Street, East	269	G12
80th Street, East	265	N8	117th Street, West	266	J8	155th Street, West	268	F9
80th Street, West	264	M6	118th Street, East	267	K10	156th Street, East	269	G12
81st Street, East	265	N8	118th Street, West	266	J8	156th Street, West	268	F9
81st Street, West	264	M6	119th Street, East	267	K10	157th Street, East	269	G11
82nd Street, East	265	N8	119th Street, West	266	J8	157th Street, West	268	F9
82nd Street, West	264	M7	120th Street, East	267	K10	158th Street, East	269	G11
83rd Street, East	265	N8	120th Street, West	266	J8	158th Street, West	268	F9
83rd Street, West	265	M7	121st Street, East	267	K10	159th Street, East	269	G12
84th Street, East	265	M8	121st Street, West	266	J8	159th Street, West	268	F9
85th Street, East	265	M8	122nd Street, East	267	K10	160th Street, East	269	G12
85th Street, West	266	L7	122nd Street, West	267	J9	160th Street, West	268	F9
86th Street, East	265	M8	123rd Street, East	267	K10	161st Street, East	269	G11
86th Street, West	266	L7	123rd Street, West	266	J8	161st Street, West	268	F9
87th Street, East	265	M8	124th Street, East	267	J10	162nd Street, East	269	F11
87th Street, West	266	L7	124th Street, West	267	J9	162nd Street, West	268	F9
88th Street, East	265	M8	125th Street, East	267	L10	163rd Street, East	269	G12
88th Street, West	266	L7	126th Street, East	267	J10	163rd Street, West	269	F10
89th Street, East	265	M8	126th Street, West	267	J9	164th Street, East	269	F11
89th Street, West	266	L7	127th Street, East	267	J10	164th Street, West	269	F10
90th Street, East	265	M9	127th Street, West	268	H8	165th Street, East	269	F11
91st Street, East	265	M9	128th Street, East	267	J10	165th Street, West	270	E9
91st Street, West	266	L7	128th Street, West	268	H8	166th Street, East	269	F12
92nd Street, East	265	M9	129th Street, West	268	H8	166th Street, West	270	E10
92nd Street, West	266	L7	130th Street, West	268	H8	167th Street, East	269	F11
93rd Street, East	265	M9	131st Street, West	268	H8	167th Street, West	270	E10
93rd Street, West	266	L7	132nd Street, East	267	J11	168th Street, East	269	F11
94th Street, East	265	M9	132nd Street, West	268	H8	168th Street, West	270	E10
94th Street, West	266	L7	133rd Street, West	268	H8	169th Street, East	269	F12
95th Street, East	265	M9	134th Street, East	267	J11	169th Street, West	270	E10
95th Street, West	266	L7	134th Street, West	268	H8	170th Street, East	271	E12
96th Street, East	265	M9	135th Street, East	267	J11	170th Street, West	270	E10
96th Street, West	266	L7	135th Street, West	268	H8	171st Street, East	271	E12
97th Street, East	267	L9	136th Street, East	267	J11	171st Street, West	270	E10
97th Street, West	266	K7	136th Street, West	268	H8	172nd Street, East	271	E12
98th Street, East	267	L9	137th Street, East	267	J11	172nd Street, West	270	E10
98th Street, West	266	K7	137th Street, West	268	G8	173rd Street, East	271	E12
99th Street, East	267	L9	138th Street, East	269	H10	173rd Street, West	270	E10
99th Street, West	266	K7	138th Street, West	268	G8	174th Street, West	271	E12
100th Street, East	267	L9	139th Street, East	267	J11	174th Street, West	271	D11
100th Street, West	266	K7	139th Street, West	268	G8	175th Street, East	271	D13
101st Street, East	267	L9	140th Street, East	267	J11	175th Street, West	271	D12
101st Street, West	266	K7	140th Street, West	268	G8	176th Street, East	271	D12
102nd Street, East	267	L9	141st Street, East	267	J11	176th Street, West	271	D11
102nd Street, West	266	K7	141st Street, West	268	G9	177th Street, West	271	D12
103rd Street, East	267	L9	142nd Street, East	269	H11	177th Street, West	270	E10
103rd Street, West	266	K7	142nd Street, West	268	G9	178th Street, East	271	D13
104th Street, East	267	L9	143rd Street, East	269	H11	178th Street, West	270	D10
104th Street, West	266	K7	143rd Street, West	268	G9	179th Street, East	271	D12
105th Street, East	267	L9	144th Street, East	269	H11	179th Street, West	271	C12
105th Street, West	266	K7	144th Street, West	268	G9	180th Street, West	271	D13
106th Street, East	267	L9	145th Street, East	269	H11	180th Street, West	271	C12
107th Street, East	267	L9	145th Street, West	268	G9	181st Street, East	271	D13
107th Street, West	266	K7	146th Street, East	269	H10	181st Street, West	271	C12
108th Street, East	267	L9	146th Street, West	268	G9	182nd Street, East	271	C13
108th Street, West	266	K7	147th Street, East	269	H12	182nd Street, West	271	C12
109th Street, East	267	L9	147th Street, West	268	G9	183rd Street, East	271	C13
109th Street, West	266	K7	148th Street, East	269	H11	183rd Street, West	271	C12
110th Street, East	267	L9	148th Street, West	268	G9	184th Street, East	271	C13
111th Street, East	267	K9	149th Street, East	269	H11	184th Street, West	271	C13
111th Street, West	266	J7	149th Street, West	268	G9	185th Street, West	270	D10
112th Street, East	267	K9	150th Street, East	269	H11	186th Street, West	270	D10

Important addresses and contact details

Emergency numbers and contact details:
Country dialling code USA: +1

New York Borough area codes:
Manhattan: 212
Bronx, Brooklyn, Queens and Staten Island: 718

Emergency number:
Tel 911 (Police, Fire, Ambulance)

Medical Emergency:
Tel 511

AAA-breakdown number:
Tel (1-800) AAA-HELP, i.e. Tel (1-800) 222 43 57

Operator:
Tel 0 (help with all enquiries, including emergencies)

New York on the Internet:
www.nycgo.com
www.nyc.gov

NYC & Company
(official New York tourist office)

Official NYC Information Centers
810 Seventh Ave (between 52nd and 53rd St, north of Times Square), Tel (212) 484 12 00
Times Square, 1560 Broadway (between 46th and 47th St), Tel (212) 484 12 22
Harlem, The Studio Museum in Harlem, 144 West 125th St (between Adam Clayton Powell Jr Blvd and Malcolm X Blvd), Tel (212) 222 10 14
City Hall, Park Row (at southern end of City Hall Park), Tel (212) 484 12 22
Chinatown, at the intersection of Canal, Walker and Baxter St, Tel (212) 484 12 22
Federal Hall, 26 Wall St (between William and Nassau St), Tel (212) 484 12 22

NYC Directory Assistance
(Latest tourist information service): Tel 311
from outside NYC: Tel (212) 639 96 75

Train stations
Grand Central Station, 42nd St/Park Ave (East Side, between Lexington and Vanderbilt Ave), Tel (212) 532 49 00
Penn Station, 31st–33rd St (West Side, between 7th and 8th Ave), Tel (212) 630 64 01

Bus stations
Port Authority Bus Terminal (P.A.B.T.), 625 8th Avenue (near Times Square), Tel (212) 564 84 84
George Washington Bridge Bus Station (GWBBS), 4221 Broadway (between 178th and 179th St), Tel (800) 221 99 03

Ferry service
South Ferry Terminal – Staten Island Ferry, near Battery Park (on the southern tip of Manhattan), Tel (718) 815-BOAT/(718) 815 26 28

Airports
John F. Kennedy International Airport (JFK), JFK Expy/Cargo Road, Jamaica, Queens (24 km/15 mi south-east of NYC), Tel (718) 244 44 44, www.jfkiat.com, www.jfk-airport.net
LaGuardia Airport (LGA), Flushing Bay/Bowery Bay, Queens (9 km/5 mi north-east of NYC), Tel (1-800) 247 74 33, www.panynj.gov/CommutingTravel/airports/html/laguardia.html
Newark Liberty Airport (EWR), Essex County and Union County, New Jersey (26 km/16 mi south-west of NYC), Tel (973) 961 60 00, www.panynj.gov/CommutingTravel/airports/html/newarkliberty.html

Airport transfers
JFK AirTrain, Tel (212) 435 70 00
Newark AirTrain, Tel (888) EWR-INFO/(888) 397 46 36
New York Air Shuttle (JFK, LaGuardia, Newark), Tel (718) 875 82 00
Olympia Trails (Newark), Tel (908) 354 33 30
Port Authority Information (JFK, LaGuardia, Newark), Tel (800) AIR-RIDE/(800) 247 7433

Mail
Main Post Office, 421 8th Ave/33rd St (open 24/7)

Embassies and Consulates

Australian Consulate-General
150 East 42nd Street, 34th Floor
New York
Tel (212) 351 6500
Fax (212) 351 6501

British Consulate-General
845 Third Avenue
New York, NY 10022
Tel (212) 745 0200
Fax (212) 754 3062

Consulate General of Ireland
345 Park Avenue
17th Floor
New York, NY 10154-0037
Tel (212) 319 2555
Fax (212) 980 9475

New Zealand Consulate-General
222 East 41st Street
New York, NY 10017
Tel (212) 832 4038

South African Consulate General
333 East 38th Street, 9th Floor,
New York, NY 10016
Tel (212) 213 4880
Fax (212) 213 0102

Canadian Consulate General - New York City
1251 Avenue of the Americas
Concourse Level
New York, NY 10020
Tel (212) 596 1628

MONACO BOOKS is an imprint of Verlag Wolfgang Kunth

© Verlag Wolfgang Kunth GmbH & Co.KG, Munich, 2009/2010
Concept: Wolfgang Kunth
Editing and design: Verlag Wolfgang Kunth GmbH&Co.KG
English translation: JMS Books LLP (translation Malcolm Gerrard,
editor Emma Shackleton, design cbdesign)

For distribution please contact:

Monaco Books
c/o Verlag Wolfgang Kunth, Königinstr.11
80539 München, Germany
Tel: +49 / 89/45 80 20 23
Fax: +49 / 89/ 45 80 20 21
info@kunth-verlag.de

www.monacobooks.com
www.kunth-verlag.de

ISBN 978-3-89944-530-5

Printed in Slovakia

All facts have been researched with the greatest possible care to the best of
our knowledge and belief. However, the editors and publishers can accept no
responsibility for any inaccuracies or incompleteness of the details provided.
The publishers are pleased to receive any information or suggestions for
improvement.

NEW YORK
Major subways